Waiting for the Messiah

IRVING LAYTON

Waiting for the Messiah

A Memoir

with David O'Rourke

McClelland and Stewart

The Canadian Publishers
McClelland and Stewart Limited
25 Hollinger Road, Toronto M4B 3G2

Canadian Cataloguing in Publication Data

Layton, Irving, 1912–
  Waiting for the Messiah

ISBN 0-7710-4919-6

1. Layton, Irving, 1912–   2. Poets, Canadian
(English) – Biography. *I. O'Rourke, David.
II. Title.

PS8523.A98Z53 1985   C811'.54   C85-099156-0
PR9199.3.L39Z477 1985

Design by: Linda Gustafson

Printed and Bound in Canada by T.H. Best

"They dance best who dance with desire,
Who lifting feet of fire from fire
Weave before they lie down
A red carpet for the sun."

ONE

1912. The poet to be was born with the smell of baked *challa* in his nostrils. Other smells have come and gone, that smell has remained, dictating rage and tenderness, a metaphysics individual as himself and tougher than nose-hairs. For I was born into a world of fable, a world of stories charged with significant meanings, the world of the Jews, a people like no other on this planet. The stories I heard from my mother, and repeated by my older sisters, made me feel there was something mysterious and awesome about my life.

More than any other fact that sociologists and psychologists may unearth about me, it accounts for the glories and disasters I have known, my almost daily commuting between heaven and hell. For the feeling of strangeness became stronger as I grew older, and was reinforced by my readings about heroes and saviours – Moses, Buddha, Alexander the Great – and the unusual circumstances that always attended their birth. Didn't the story of my own birth fall neatly into this packet of legends, myths, or miracles? Conceit, or perhaps an imagination hungering for the extraordinary, enticed me to believe that I, Israel Lazarovitch, was also marked for something special. My life had been set on rails of a different gauge.

I must have been about six or seven when my mother told me that I had been born circumcised: the messianic sign. Rabbis, she said, had come from many hamlets, some had journeyed to our Roumanian village from as far as Poland and Russia to see for themselves my miraculously foreshortened member and, afterwards, their reverent gaze still fixed on it, to break into psalm-singing and prayer. Jews have always been on the lookout for a messiah. Picture a history of ghettos, discrimination, the nightmare of pogroms; is it that unnatural for them to engender out of their misery a messiah to lead them to the Promised Land or, at least, out of their unending tribulations? Moses had been the only Jew before me born circumcised and that was because the cruel Pharoah had ordered all Hebrew boys to be killed at birth. Because Yahweh had some mission for Moses, and because under the circumstances it was impossible to perform the rite of circumcision, it was by divine will that the child was born without a foreskin. He was born circumcised and destined to create a people.

It is not hard to understand how this would take a tremendous hold on the imagination of a child who, because he is Jewish, has been studying the Talmud in Hebrew, which he takes to be the original language of his forbears. Of Moses himself. The identification with the great Jewish leader was swift and unopposed. Despite my impoverished home, I was one of the favoured. Like Moses, in my eyes, I had a mission to perform. Great things were in store for me. My mind parts the bath water in the tiny washbasin as if it were the Red Sea. I throw my stick on the floor; it turns into a hissing viper.

Of course I continued to lead the normal vigorous life of a Jewish kid on St. Elizabeth Street, to play baseball, to wrestle and fight bare-fisted anyone who threatened to take away the title of Jack Dempsey from me. But the intelligence that I had been favoured with the messianic sign stayed in my mind and sometimes, suddenly, in the midst of the roughest and most boisterous game, I would find myself standing quite apart, a solitary brooding figure surrounded by shouting companions, their gestures theatrical as in a slowed-down film.

The second circumstance connected with my birth had no less of a powerful effect. When my mother was carrying me in her womb, she became dangerously ill with double pneumonia. The doctor who was called in despaired for her life. There was no way, no way, that she would recover. The doctor had told my grandmother, "When hair will grow on my palm, that's when your daughter will recover from this illness." I remember my mother telling me this when I was seven or eight. I can still see the scene. We are in the kitchen, beside the stove. It's winter, it's bitter cold outside, the snow is piled up against the windows, the stove giving off the only heat in the house, and my mother is holding out her hairless, deeply furrowed palm to me.

What happened was, my grandmother, sturdy as a peasant, and blessed with perfect health, went into the sick-room where my mother was lying on her bed. She stretched out on top of my mother's fevered body and spoke these words: "Whatever death is intended for you, may it come to me. Because you are filled with fruit and I am barren. Not even by a miracle can I give birth to another child. Let your death come upon me." One week later, my grandmother, who had never even complained of a headache, took sick and died. My mother recovered and gave birth to me.

My earliest memories of my father: black beard, dark eyes, a body frail and unexercised, more silent than a shadow, shutting himself off in the small undecorated bedroom, his tabernacle and sanctuary where he entertained God's messengers. This was very real to me. I was quite sure, when my father closed the bedroom door behind him, that he was about to communicate with God himself, or to receive a message from Him through His angels.

It now seems to me that I always had the feeling I was living in two worlds: the world of St. Elizabeth Street where there were French-Canadian anti-Semites, where I played ball with my streetmates or swung from the boughs of the few remaining trees. That was the actual world of rough-and-tumble encounters, rivalrous brawls, of quiet Sunday mornings and the sound of distant church bells. But inside the domicile inhabited by my parents, siblings, and the stray cat I was determined to keep despite my mother's protesting curses, was the world of fabulous people and events. Of heroic suffering in the face of persecution, where saviours and messiahs were not an impossibility. And, my destiny-laden member pointing to a unique future, mortised comfortably into my mother's blessing of the Sabbath candles each Friday night, her hands together in prayer next to the Quebec stove, the candles themselves sending a warm glow through our small kitchen. I can still see them flickering. Later, I went on to describe them in one of my poems as joyful old men dancing in ecstasy, throwing their shadows on the white tablecloth, and it always impressed me that the shadows could come together in a wonderful dark unity.

Behind my mother was the sink, a cockroach roaming leisurely from one end of the wallpaper to another, and the toilet, painted an ugly verminous green. It was a narrow cabinet that reached from the floor to the ceiling. I remember thinking how odd, what a contradiction the toilet was to the candles and the spotless tablecloth. The one dark green like grave-covering grass, the other white like fresh snow. But there they were, side by side, the sacred and the profane, their propinquity forever fixed in my mind and indisseverable, so fused that neither priest nor rabbi, theologian nor philosopher, would ever be able to split them asunder or for long keep them apart.

Then my mother would remove the prayer shawl from her head and reveal her serene face, the benediction over, her amber beads and small, light-brown eyes shining as brightly as the Sabbath candles flickering above the tablecloth.

It begins with sensations. A smear of red paint on your left thumb. The white vapour from the kettle disintegrating before your eyes. The cold wetness of pee in your underpants on a frosty morning. Later on there are feelings. Much, much later comes thought.

I must have been four years old. The house was illuminated by oil lamps. We didn't have electricity. We were too poor. It was summer. My mother was entertaining guests in the bedroom; it would have been too cold for her to play hostess there in the winter as the kitchen was the only room in the house warmed by a stove.

I remember I had to go to the toilet. I was wearing a nightgown and found a lighted candle. It couldn't have been a Friday night because I wouldn't have been allowed to touch a Sabbath candle, and yet I think it was and I did. I went to the toilet, candle in my fist and, as I was seating myself, out of pure curiosity tipped the flame towards my nightgown just to see what would happen. Before long, of course, I became a sheet of fire. I remember seeing the flames rising higher and higher and hearing shouts of alarm, screams, then somebody banging on the latched door. My mother and her guests were hysterical, but they pried the door open and took me out covered in flames. I had by then lost consciousness.

The doctor thought it looked very bleak for me, but he went ahead with the prescribed brutal treatment of the time. For months the blackened skin was ripped off my neck and chest. First, Dr. Budyck swathed me in Vaselined cloths and then the torture of the skin being torn off would begin. My sisters tell me that I lived through this very painful period – I still bear the scars – only because of my superlative constitution. I was also very lucky that Dr. Budyck was both patient and conscientious. That is my earliest memory, so traumatic that it has blocked out all others anterior to it.

I am now six. I have fully recovered and it is time for the spring cleaning. Every year just before Passover began, my family waged war against the cockroaches that proliferated during the year. It is a vivid memory. Huge pails of water, four or five of them, were set on the kitchen stove for scalding. They would then be taken down, and my mother, my sister Dora, Cousin Fanny, who lived with us for a number of years, my brother Hyman, and myself got ready for the great attack.

The kitchen wallpaper was ripped from the walls, exposing millions of the vermin. The heaving mass, almost like a small tidal wave, was a reddish-brown agitated movement: it was as if the wall itself were beginning to move. As a child, I was filled more with fascination and curiosity than revulsion at seeing this syrupy mass of brown, yellow, black, short, long, fat, thin cockroaches racing with comic dignity along the wall, foolishly exposed and vulnerable now that their cover was gone. Then my mother, Dora, Fanny, and Hyman would fling the scalding water, pailful after pailful, against the walls. The insects would fall to the floor in violent little struggles, moving around with decreasing conviction and fervour because they were badly scalded, their senses benumbed by the relentless downpour of hot water over their paper-thin bodies. But some of them still displayed remarkable vitality, and I remember thinking, my God, what strength, *where did they get it from*? There they were: the lowest form of life protesting their extinction, demanding their rights, saying we too have our place in the cosmos and you have destroyed us.

My job was to kill them as they tried to flee into some corner, floor-crack, or under the linoleum. I could use a book or folded newspaper, but my heels were always the fastest and most effective. I recall the pop and crunch they made under my heel and the smell of formic acid, and then the smear: what all life reduces itself to ultimately. Before long, I would find myself standing triumphant over hundreds of their squashed and mutilated bodies. I remember the expansive feeling of power that swept through me when I looked down on the now silent battlefield with its armies of slain cockroaches. Napoleon could not have felt more elated after one of his military victories than I did in my kitchen surveying the vermin

I had murdered. Those that had survived the scalding water and my stamping feet by clinging to the walls were finished off with kerosene. The walls would reek of it for many days afterwards.

Of course I had read nothing about Napoleon or any other successful mass killer in history, but I was studying Exodus in Hebrew. On the one hand, I was just a slayer of cockroaches. I felt no spasms of guilt or shame. I regarded them as mortal enemies, vermin; they had to be exterminated. But on the other hand, it was for me a very thrilling way to bring in the Passover, a marvellous prelude to my favourite holiday. In my mind these were Egyptians whom I had slain, tyrannical slave-owners. They were an army to be destroyed by the righteous Israelites, to be swallowed up forever – or at least for a year – by the Red Sea. It was God's will. And I, yes, I was Moses.

It's now the Day of Atonement, Yom Kippur, the holiest day in the Jewish calendar. My parents are in the synagogue. As a young boy I didn't have to be there all day. I'd be in and out, that was expected. My parents had to remain until the service was completed, until late afternoon or twilight.

Around noon, I decided to leave the synagogue and return to the house. It is early September, and there is a feeling of quiet autumnal mellowness when I open the door at the end of the passageway and enter. I go to the bedroom and there is Cousin Fanny. She has been to the synagogue but is not expected, a mere female, to spend the whole day there. She is standing beside the window. The linen curtains are yellow with sunlight. Parted, they let me see the tree in our neighbour's yard towering dark and rabbinical above the fence separating the two dwellings. It is a very narrow room, oblong-shaped, with three plain beds with immaculate white coverlets and white cushions at the heads. My father had his own bed and on the other side of the dresser, my sister Dora and Cousin Fanny shared one. As the youngest child, I slept in my mother's bed. There is also a chair, a calendar tacked to the wallpaper, and a picture of my mother's father, whose squinting eyes seemed to follow me wherever I went. There are no other pictures on the wall. Immigrant Jewish families didn't indulge in that kind of decoration, at least my family didn't.

Cousin Fanny, attractive with her mass of luxuriant black hair and crimsoned lips, was eighteen, living in an orthodox Jewish home, and suffering from sexual repression. She was too ignorant or too timid to do anything sensible about it. Barely eight, I was certainly too young to provide her with what she needed most. But she embraced me and before I understood what she was doing, she took my hand, put it under her skirt, and squeezed it convulsively against her exposed pudenda. At least I think it was her pud, for I'd never seen one and didn't know what it was supposed to feel like. I quivered with surprised delight, a thrill running through my whole body. The warm wetness made my palm tingle as if a ruler had been brought down sharply on it. The exquisite sensation made me feel tremendously alive. I sensed we were doing something unhallowed and forbidden; that if my mother or father ever came in on us we would both be killed on the spot. Disgraced in our own eyes, and everyone else's, we'd be flung into outer darkness. In this instance, intuition raced ahead of experience and its deposit of guilt only increased the rapture I felt at that moment.

And then something wonderful happened, amazing me by its unexpectedness. With my hand on her naked vulva, a stillness in the room that was almost audible, very gently Cousin Fanny began to pee in my hand. I could feel it on my skin as if it were a garment made from the lightest gauze and the yellow sunshine that the windowpanes splattered on the linoleum seemed to glow with an uncanny vividness. I didn't want to take my hand away because the sensation was so pleasurable. I wanted to leave it there forever and feel the warm, moist

14

hairs in my palm. The pee rolled off my hand onto the linoleum floor; the dripping sound excited and fascinated me as I watched the glistening beads arranging themselves in broken strings of rosary. I had never before seen a woman urinate, having been brainwashed by the piety and puritanism that prevailed in our home not to imagine that females had physiological needs that were no different from those of males.

While I was savouring all these exquisitely unfamiliar sensations, there were my grandfather's eyes squinting down at me. He did not seem amused. We were doing something that would have been forbidden at any time, but this was Yom Kippur, the most awesome day of the year. For a fleeting moment I remember thinking: now I have Cousin Fanny in my power. Being older than I, surely her sin must be greater. If I were to tell my mother what we had done, certainly Fanny would be thrown out of the house. However, these thoughts didn't last more than a few seconds for my senses were overwhelmed by a less abstract joy, one more immediate and closer to hand.

A horse-drawn wagon, the horses clomping down the street. The iceman cometh, or it could be the fruit vendor or baker. If it's summer, the boys are out on the street playing baseball or tippie, a game that consisted of hitting as hard as you could with a wooden stick, a short piece of wood, pointed at both ends. The further you sent the wood flying through the air, the more likely you were to end up the winner. In winter we iced a part of the lane that ran between St. Elizabeth and Sanguinet and played a rough-and-ready version of hockey till it grew dark.

Our neighbourhood was mainly made up of Jews, French Canadians, and Italians. Most of the Italians inhabited the houses and stores along De Montigny Street. No more than five or six French-Canadian families lived on our street, side by side

15

with the Jews though they might just as well have been living in Mozambique for all the intercourse Jews had with them. Most francophones lived in the area that stretched east of St. Denis. To the Jewish boys on our street, that was dangerous territory. I never found myself in it without feeling menaced. The anglophones inhabited houses west of Bleury. Sandwiched tightly between the French and the English was the Jewish ghetto, composed of Yiddish-speaking immigrants recently arrived from Russia, Poland, Roumania, and a leavening of other minorities including Slovaks and Chinese.

On Saturdays, the Jewish kids who could wheedle the necessary dime out of their parents went to the Midway, the movie house on the corner of Main and St. Catherine. I was nine when I went to see my first film, though I have no specific recollection of the experience. Years later, I remember playing truant as often as I could, so great was the enchantment movies held for me. They enthralled me and gave me an entirely new world of sights and sensations. Once inside the movie house, I forgot who I was or where I came from. I forgot my teachers, my failure to do my homework, my laziness, my jealousies, grudges, and hopes. I always came home yearning to emulate the derring-do of Tom Mix or Buck Jones. Those movies gave me my sense of morality. There were always goodies and baddies, heroes and villains. Naturally you sided with Tom Mix and Buck Jones against the crafty horse-thief or the shifty-eyed slicker trying to bamboozle the widow out of her farm. Right and wrong were as far apart as heaven and earth, as the Jews and French Canadians living next door to each other. The morality was not too dissimilar from that which my parents, my rebbes, the Talmud itself, enjoined upon me – but how much more inspiring, making the pulse race and the eyes glisten with virtuous fervour. No doubt about it: Tom Mix spoke more loudly to me than Yahweh.

In the afternoon, after day school, the Jewish kids in the

neighbourhood attended the *cheder*, where they were given instruction in Hebrew and in the pieties of their faith. The rebbe would sit at the head of the long wooden table; the boys and girls, his pupils, on the long bench between table and wall. Each one moved up towards the head of the table to take his turn beside the rebbe. The lesson is recited, a passage from Exodus or Genesis, and the Hebrew translated into Yiddish. Some routine questions are put and answered and the pupil vacates his place for the next one. The rebbe has a *conchik*, a little stick, and since he's ill-paid, hen-pecked, and morose, he exercises his power at the slightest excuse, and, sometimes without any excuse at all, just flicks the *conchik* very sharply across the fingers of some innocent child. That was the only fun he got out of life. The toothless grin he couldn't quite hide may have helped to turn me away from the faith of my forbears.

I remember a little girl about my age. Only a boy of eight could have hoped to get away with what I did. My recitation done, I was supposed to let her take her turn next to the rebbe. Out of sheer perversity, I took it into my head not to let her do so. I stretched myself out full length on the bench to prevent her from taking her place. The rebbe protested and brought his *conchik* down on my exposed wrists.

The little girl started to shout and whimper but, stubborn as a young mule, I refused to budge. Finally, sensing that a devil had gotten into me, he said wearily to the girl, "Well, sit on his face." So she sat down on my face and she wasn't wearing panties. How unforgettably delicious was that first contact between her warm, naked skin and my cheek. The sharp, unexpected pleasure was so intense I think I could still graph its course through my body. A thirsty man's first swallow of water in a desert could not be more rapturous than the sensation that flew from face to chest and stiffening limbs. I made no movement because I didn't want her to move. She was reading from the Holy Book, reading about how Moses had led the Israelites out of Egypt and slavery, and there I was helplessly pinned down on the wooden bench with her soft naked ass on my face.

Next day, in the lane beside our house, I noticed a huge dead rat, a familiar enough sight in our neighbourhood. It was after school and I was on my way to the rebbe's house for my Hebrew lessons. Swallowing my disgust, I picked up the dead rat, ran with it a distance, and hurled it into the rebbe's kitchen. His wife came rushing out screaming hysterically, shaking her upraised arms at me. I felt the woman's anger but her cries and gestures seemed to me theatrical and unconvincing. I had learned to distance myself from whatever tumult my mischief caused. The louder people shouted, the more frantic and outraged they appeared, the more deaf I became, the uncomprehending grin on my face adding to their outrage. Only my own strong emotions, my own passions, convinced me. Those of other people never did. Perhaps it was because my mother was always shouting and swearing. Her curses were so horrendous ("You should have run out of my womb before you were born. Your father should have been paralyzed before he impregnated me"), that I couldn't believe she meant them. She *must* be playacting, I concluded. But she wasn't, and the injury done to a tender and sensitive soul, gave it a sinister twist and made it grow lopsidedly like certain trees lightning has seared.

In the Jewish faith you're not allowed to touch anything that is dead. If you do, you must wash your hands immediately afterwards. So I knew when I threw the dead rat into the rebbe's kitchen that I was doing something impiously foul and nasty. But *why* had I done this? I had nothing against the rebbe and certainly nothing against his wife. I wasn't doing it for revenge, but as mischief, out of a wish to create turmoil, an excitement, to see people running and shouting, opening and shutting their mouths as in a silent Tom Mix film, the piano player banging away, guns blazing, and the smoke from their barrels floating in small lazy clouds above them. The woman's angry shouting finally roused me from the stupor into which I had fallen. Very contritely I walked into her kitchen and picked up the dead rat by its limp, leathery tail. Running out with it, I dumped it in the first empty crate I saw.

The punishment for my misdeed came soon, for that night a live rat bit my ear when I was sleeping. I woke everyone up with my yell of pain and fright, certain that it was the dead rat which had come alive and bitten me.

Another day, I was going for my Hebrew lesson when I heard loud wails coming from a house only a few doors away from my rebbe's. I had never before heard such cries and was curious to know what caused them. I walked slowly up the flight of stairs, my heart beating faster and faster with every step for the sounds of moaning have grown louder and more distinct. The door is slightly ajar: I can hear the wails with a sharp clarity that seems to etch them into my consciousness and to drive everything else out. The heart-rending wails are coming from a woman. I push the door open a bit wider. A small passageway gives onto an unfurnished room. In the centre of the room a body is lying flat on its back, at its feet a candelabra. At its head, candlesticks are glowing. Bending over the dead body, a woman is weeping. Every few seconds she puts her hands to her shawled head and emits a loud moan, almost a shriek. I intuit they are mother and son. There is no one else in the room. Since the room is small, the single window curtained, there is not much light.

A sensation of illusion and terror gripped and held me, I had experienced something like it in the Midway where I had seen a mystery film not long before. It alerted my senses and kept me rooted to the spot. I didn't want to run. I wanted to see and hear more. I wanted to stand near the body and stare at the grey, waxen face. Above all, I remember those candles: how they sparkled and cast their flitting dark shadows

19

on the corpse's head and feet. It struck me as incongruous that the shadows seemed to be dancing. So insistently did they move it was as if they were almost inviting the lifeless corpse to get up from the floor and join them in their dance. The mother went on rocking her body and crying. When her sobbing had almost ceased, I finally turned away and walked out of the room. The bereaved woman paid no more attention to my leaving than she had to my entrance.

Above our flat was a semi-brothel. The lady of the house, with her husband's connivance, played fast and loose with her morals. It was one way of supplementing their meagre income. Every Saturday night we knew there would be a party going on upstairs. Wild drinking, shouted obscenities, the clatter of an overturned table, of falling chairs, a whole orchestra under the baton of a demented conductor, made it impossible to get any sleep. My poor parents would groan aloud but my father was too timorous to do anything about it. Even my mother, usually intrepid and vociferous, was cowed. Since I was the youngest, already a dreamy rhymer, it fell to me to leave the snug warmth of my mother's bed, find the broomstick, and pound the ceiling. Silence seemed to flow from the broom's handle; but it didn't last long. Ten minutes later, bedlam was again loosed over our heads.

We thought of calling the police, but they weren't very friendly, not to immigrant Jews anyway. They were mostly French Canadians, part of the hostile world that surrounded us. They were there to harry street-walkers or to see that my mother kept her small grocery store closed on Sundays. The sense of being picked on, of injustice, the sense that a Jew cannot expect protection or human decency, was very strong. It was as though Jews and their gentile neighbours lived in different worlds. We could do nothing but stand our ground and suffer. And call Pharoah's ten plagues down on the brutes.

I was probably five or six when I began to notice the difference. The close-knit family life, the intimacy and warmth (despite my mother's explosive cursing) and then slowly the feeling of apartness, my first awareness that somehow *we were different*. And I remember not being able to understand exactly what the difference was; just that we were not accepted, that we were hated. It was that strange spiky flower which holds in its cup the venom of anti-Semitism. But a child lives almost entirely in the world of his sensations. He hasn't developed the capacity to reason in the abstract, to conceptualize. Sex, death, anti-Semitism: they're all concepts. If someone had said the words anti-Semitism to me I would not have understood. But it was in the streets and alleyways. It blanketed us like a fog. *Maudits Juifs!*

It's winter. I see my father walking towards the house. He is coming back from the synagogue. I'm watching through the window the way only a child can watch, waiting for his father to come home. A gang appears as if from nowhere and someone throws a snowball. It hits my father's fur hat squarely and knocks it to the ground. I see my father bend down to pick it up. The hat is made of black fur and on the snow it looks like a stunned animal. My father has straightened himself up, his dignity restored. On his face there is pain and contempt. Cold contempt. But also something like serene indifference. The badge of suffering borne with pride.

He would wear the same look when the French-Canadian kids followed him down the street mimicking his gait and launching into what they thought was Yiddish, jabbering, laughing out loud. My father, like others of his generation, would not retaliate. It would lead to further trouble. The Holocaust and the Israeli air force have changed all that.

Every Easter, young barbarians descended on our street armed with bricks, bottles, stones, and knives. We had spies stationed to give early warning. The alarm given, the older Jewish boys came running out of their houses prepared to give battle. Soon the street was covered with groups of adolescents clawing and tearing at one another. The snarls and screams were terrifying. Everyone fought with a savagery an Iroquois might envy. You could lose an eye, have a leg broken, or get your face badly cut up. If you were unlucky you might even get killed.

The older boys fought like Maccabeans. Gallant and tough, heroes every one of them. My sixteen-year-old brother Joshua was in the fray. So was Cross-eyed George, a heavy, clumsy but enormously powerful fellow. And Hymie Lindover, Max Cherry, and Benny the Beanpole. Everyone was on the street taking or giving blows. I remember Hymie Lindover getting a stone thrown at him. It hit his forehead, barely missing his eye. I can still hear the yell of pain, and see the blood running down his nose.

There wouldn't be any French-Canadian kids our age to fight with, so our job, the job of the younger Jewish kids, was to act as auxiliaries. We'd grab cans, bottles, and stones for the older boys to hurl. As a rule, we beat back our adversaries because we had to. If they really got you down, you could get worse than a beating, your bones might be broken. After all, we were Christ-killers. We had killed their God. The only way they could avenge this terrible deed was to beat the daylights out of his kin. George was eventually blinded in one eye. They took their religion seriously. To them, we were evil incarnate. So we knew we had to win. If we did, it would postpone their coming back until Jesus was resurrected again the following year.

The first break in the anti-Semitism which surrounded us came when one of our neighbours died, one month after my own father died. The Labelles lived two or three doors away. The two sons, Henri and Gaston, were an especially nasty pair. The eldest, Henri, was the same age as my brother Hyman. Gaston was slightly older than myself. They were always throwing snowballs at my mother and father and took a special delight in picking up horse-buns – frosted and hard in winter; moist, round, and soft in the summer – and throwing them into the passageway when my mother was serving a customer. My mother would run to scoop the mess up but half an hour later they'd be back with more horse-buns. The supply seemed endless. I wondered whether they were foraging for them in streets other than St. Elizabeth.

Shortly after M. Labelle's funeral, his widow came into my mother's grocery, something she had never done before. I remember my mother's excitement as she came running into the kitchen, crying: "It's a miracle! God be thanked! God be praised!"

From that day on, all show of dislike or hostility stopped. The two boys who had been so vicious, the same Henri and Gaston whom my family would have joyously torn limb from limb and cursed to end their lives as lepers, now displayed a real friendliness. They no longer called me a dirty Jew, they no longer hurled horse-buns into the passageway. They always waved at me and my brothers whenever we passed them on the street.

That episode gave me a feeling about death that persists until today, and has inspired several poems of mine. In them I hail death as the great reconciler, as mankind's greatest benefactor, as the Messiah.

> *Death washes the face of the world*
> *as the light-filled water*
> *purling over the beachstones at my feet.*

TWO

I don't think my father ever spoke to me at any length more than five or six times. Nevertheless, though silent and remote, he influenced the tenor of my life more than any other individual. It was my father who made me feel there was another world quite different from the solid, vexatious one into which I had been dropped or flung.

It would never have occurred to me at the time to wonder whether he was handsome or not. In a household such as ours, one did not think in terms of physical attractiveness. And these thoughts would not have arisen in a child's consciousness. But, in retrospect, I would say my father had a handsome face. Certainly with his black beard always neatly trimmed, the firm red lips showing, and his dark eyes, he possessed an attractive countenance. My brothers were all considered to be good-looking. Hyman, who strongly resembled our father, also had his dark complexion and build. Taller than myself, in his youth Hyman was called Gable. People nicknamed my brother Joshua, Ronald Coleman. My oldest brother Harry was also favoured with good looks, though I'm not sure the neighbourhood accorded him movie-star status.

I can't remember ever having had a meal with my father. I don't recall his ever doing any of the ordinary things a household required. He was a dark presence that floated around and over me, coming to rest where I could see him only when he had some order or admonition for me.

He always wore dark clothes made of the very best cloth. He was immaculate, a virtue that has always eluded me. A single spot on his shirt was cause for him to take it off. The smallest stain on his trousers or his jacket would upset him almost as much as the discovery of an unpaid bill. He wore only black shoes which he polished every day. He'd wake up at six a.m., while the rest of the family was still fast asleep, to do his morning devotions. These consisted of long prayers to God, after he'd accoutred himself in the proper regalia for the occasion. The black phylactery cubes ritually worn on his forehead and bicep gleamed as brightly as his polished shoes on the one occasion that I saw him at his morning devotions.

After his prayers he would lift heavy cans of milk onto the Quebec stove, and curdle it into cheese for the handful of steady customers he had for it. The small sums he earned enabled him to be independent of my mother's charity or goodwill, for it was she who was the breadwinner in the family. It gave him enough money to purchase his cigarette makings and the modest bottle of whiskey he'd bring to the synagogue for the confection after the Sabbath's last service. Praise the Lord and pass the small tumbler around. Let the whiskey warm the insides of the hard-pressed Jews who had to meet as best they could the unsympathetic world waiting for them outside.

After the cheese-making, we'd be together in the bedroom, my father's sanctuary, where he'd read from his holy books, undisturbed by wife or children. I inhaled the hushed piety that filled the room. I remember the stillness that enveloped me, my father poring over the battered tomes, grey and green with age, books that had been handed down for generations from father to son. Memory still images for me the crumbling leaves and how tenderly, turning the pages, he handled them. To see that kind of reverence for a book, to hear his murmured humility before the Lord he worshipped, put an indelible stamp on my soul. At those moments of prayer he asked for nothing more from life than for continuing years to praise the Lord with the same serene assurance that transfigured his countenance. He'd pray and study and pray some more, while I rolled his cigarettes for him. After he'd counted out the completed one hundred, he'd silently take out a penny from his pocket and give it to me without a word of thanks or affection. That was the extent of our father-son relationship.

My father was always received in the synagogue with great respect for his piety and scholarship. Had he wished it, he might have been a rabbi. However, he could never bring himself to accept money for any virtuous or pious thing he did, and certainly not for any instruction in the hallowed law. No payment must be taken for anything that glorified the name of Israel. On seeing him enter, the other worshippers would rise from their benches and seats to offer him a place. The middle-class philistine Jew of Old Forest Hill or Westmount today has little of this awe for scholarship or virtue. But the Jews of my father's generation offered the highest esteem to a sage or someone noted for his learning, not to the man who could accumulate money or apartment buildings. In those days, the best thing a rich Jew could achieve with his money was to marry his daughter to someone like my father.

So on the rare occasion when I accompanied my father to the synagogue, and saw the respect accorded him, I sensed there were values beyond this world: values that this world could never challenge or violate. All you needed was the kind of gentleness and integrity my father had. If you possessed these qualities you were one of the elect, you need not bow or scrape before anyone. You were close to God and only He and His sky were above you. You were close when you read the Bible in Hebrew and you were close to Him when you said your prayers. You were also near Him when you blessed the bread you ate and saw a rainbow arcing in the heavens, or washed your hands after you'd relieved yourself. There was divinity in everything you did.

The synagogue was a dilapidated, airless house on Cadieux Street, two or three blocks away, which later had to have its name changed to De Bullion because of the malodorous reputation it had acquired. Put in benches and chairs, put in a cabinet to house the scrolls of the Torah, and this rundown slum domicile was transformed into a House of the Lord. The impact was enormous on the mind of a sensitive young dreamer whose everyday world of maternal reproofs, menacing anti-Semites, bullying superiors, and tedious schoolwork lacked the slightest presence of beauty and magic. I wondered how it was possible for God to reveal Himself in all His majesty in a shabby, ill-painted house, a dwelling that could just as well have been used as a whorehouse. Coming out of the synagogue on the Sabbath, the Jews looked outlandish in their shiny gabardines, their corkscrew forelocks seeming to both invite and defy the smiles of the blowzy whores sitting on their doorsteps, for this was Cadieux Street.

Although poorly lit, the synagogue did not strike me as gloomy because I felt there was a kind of illumination when my father and his grim-visaged cronies were present. And, of course, there was always that nice custom after the Sabbath had been sung and prayered out, of decorating the white tablecloth of the small ante-room table with plates of herring, cakes, and tumblers for whiskey. The synagogue orisons, as I remember them, were very noisy: not like the decorous mutterings heard in a Protestant church. These earnest Jews wished to make known their devotions and anxieties. Convinced that they worshipped a God who stuffed his ears with clouds to deafen Himself to their entreaties, they raised their voices as if to hurl their complaints and demands at the blank, wooden-faced cabinet that contained the holy scrolls. They wanted to let the Almighty know they were in trouble, that their wives were ill, that they couldn't pay the rent, that things simply were not going as prosperously for them as they should. Listen O Lord, to what we have to tell You! The gentiles mock us at every turn, our piety is rewarded by blows and insults, our cupboards are bare, and the Messiah still delays His coming!

There was one strange prayer where a devotional Jew rose, and since he thought himself surrounded by invisible devils – how else could his strange behaviour be explained? – he would expel large gobs of spit from his mouth. He'd spit to the front, he'd spit to the rear, and to make certain he got the devils on either side of him he'd spit to the right and left. I'd be sitting next to a Jew with a long white flowing beard and suddenly I'd get a gob of spit right smack in my eye intended as a dismantling blow to the devil on his right.

In the evening my father again retired to his sanctuary, there to read the holy books and then lie down to sleep because there was nothing else for him to do. Sometimes he returned to the synagogue to discuss interpretations of the *Chumash* with like-minded Jews with a craving for theological dialectics. There is a Hebrew word for such activity: *pilpul*. *Pilpul* is an excellent training for the mind, very rigorous in its emphasis on logic, and perhaps one of the reasons many Jews have done so brilliantly in mathematics and physics. However, it starves the imagination and nourishes a disdain for intuition and feelings.

Oddly enough my first terrible sin, or so I felt it to be at the time, was the theft of two dollars from my father's wallet. I did that shortly after my ninth birthday. I went through his jacket, which I found hanging on its wooden peg in his sanctuary, extracted a two-dollar bill from his brown wallet and, feverishly stuffing it into my pocket, ran out of the house. The big question that loomed up in my mind was, "What can I buy with it?" Guilt scratched my insides like the heated point of a needle, but I also had a feeling of release and elation. Once again I was doing something forbidden. Theft in the sanctuary! I'd let myself in for God knows what heavenly punishment, never mind the earthly punishment I knew would be swift to follow. And yet I felt somehow stronger, taller. I felt I had come out from under a covering shadow, that I was doing something glorious; something as fraught with consequence and terror as Jacob stealing his brother's birthright. I was asserting my mundane self against all the sanctity that had been thrust on my defenceless young ego. I was saying, "Here I am, Lord, You must take me as I am."

With the two dollars burning a hole in my pocket and soul I remembered that on St. Dominique Street, where my rebbe lived, I'd once caught sight of his neighbour, a thin, angular gentile, probably a Slovak or a Pole. He had been swinging a sword over his head as if leading a cavalry charge. Because it was an absurd spectacle it stuck in my memory. Now the feeling suddenly gripped me to possess that sword. Why, I don't know. There was nothing martial about me, though the kids on my block had nicknamed me "The General." I was too much imbued with Jewish passivity and pacifism to think that the Messiah, when he came galloping down the street on his white horse, would be brandishing a sword. The only foreign-sounding name I knew was Ivan, so I gratuitously conferred that name upon the man who owned the sword. That day, I saw him bending over the chicken whose head he was about to hack off with a sharpened axe, and called out to him in a tremulous voice, "I-van." He turned his face to me and the chicken gave a grateful flutter of its wings for having been momentarily spared. He waved me into the yard while still holding the chicken down on the block with his other hand, and asked me what I wanted.

I pulled out the crumpled two-dollar bill from my pocket. When I told him I wanted his sword he gave me what I took to be a friendly grin, showing the few discoloured teeth that were still in his head. Without saying a word, he went into the house, and a few moments later returned with the sword.

It was almost as big as I was, and when I stood it against my shoulder, I felt myself as tall as Joshua or the imagined, prayed-for Messiah.

My mother was the first to see me with the rusted, unsheathed blade and at once asked me sharply where I had gotten the thing. Emulating in ignorance the great English queen who had observed that a lie was an intellectual way out of a difficulty, I told her that I'd picked it up in the lane where I'd found it under a pile of discarded rubbish. Under my mother's gaze, which was filled with suspicion and anger, I changed my story several times. The denouement came swiftly.

My father had returned and discovered that two dollars were missing from his wallet. Two dollars was a small fortune at that time. My father saw the brutal sword which my mother had snatched out of my hand and flung against the fence that separated our yard from that of our neighbour. After a few Yiddish sentences heavily interlarded with my mother's curses, my father looked at me sorrowfully, the disappointment showing in his eyes. But he didn't raise a hand to beat me. He didn't even reproach me. He just looked at me with utter disdain and contempt. A thief and a liar! What a fine product to issue from his loins. In a while, he turned silently and walked back to his sanctuary, no doubt to console himself by turning some of the yellowing pages of one of his well-thumbed books.

After another avalanche of curses had descended on my head, I found myself going with my mother to the man who had sold me the sword. She quickly convinced him to return the two dollars and take back the blade that he had sold to her thoughtless son who was forever inventing troublesome incidents like this for her. My young heart did not know to whom the laurels should go: to my mother for being so persuasive, or to "Ivan" for allowing himself to be persuaded and trying to assuage my childish discomfort by grinning and winking at me. Given my experience of gentiles, my feeling that they liked nothing better than to insult and torment Jews, I felt a wonderful sensation of relief. Without knowing it, I had learned a great lesson. Revelations could take place in a yard cluttered with egg crates and mouldering planks just as well as they could on Mt. Sinai. Such epiphanies prefigured the certain coming of the Messiah.

The tragedy of my father was the tragedy of many Jewish males of his generation. Respected for their learning and piety in the East European cities, towns, and villages they had come from, their reception in North America was frighteningly cool or hostile. It was as if, after they had removed their *yarmulkas*, someone from above splashed jugfuls of water over their exposed heads. They shivered in the drench, and raised beseeching orbs to the unanswering skies. In Montreal they were exiled princes, magicians, whose incantations no longer worked. Conscious that the power had gone out of them, that the formulas unheeded by the Almighty no longer even impressed their wives and children, they compensated by reciting them in ever shriller tones.

In the New World, roles became reversed. And if one seeks for the origin of the Jewish mother in North American literature, it should be sought for in that fact. It was my mother who wore the pants, so to speak, and provided for the family. My father felt his humiliation very deeply but was powerless to do anything about it. He became increasingly silent and reclusive and shuttled disconsolately between his sanctuary and the synagogue, finding in both places the solace denied to him by his wife and a progeny growing more and more estranged from him by the practical demands of their new lives.

There is a vengeful streak in most human beings and my mother was by no means free of it. She enjoyed the gratifying rush of adrenalin which the seen or felt weakness in another individual unfailingly manufactures in human glands. My father's helplessness afforded her a constant supply of this energizing secretion which gave a pronounced firmness to her voice and carriage, an alert brightness to her small brown eyes. At every opportunity she'd throw up in my father's face that it was she who put the Sabbath chicken on the table and kept a roof over our heads. Deprived of the veneration she had once had for him, he felt himself becoming a useless parasite dependent on his wife's goodwill and favour, with only his cheese-making forestalling complete defeat and surrender. My father saw his world crumbling and felt himself incapable of doing anything about it. How else can I explain what happened one day?

My father's nature was gentle and uncomplaining. Circumstances had tamed him to make few demands. Whatever expectations he might have had from life, piety had turned submissiveness into a virtue. He bore his trials with patience. But his anger on a never-to-be-forgotten afternoon, when my ear almost came off in his hand, startled me by its unexpected ferocity. I had been playing pitch-and-catch on the street. It was after school and I should have been at *cheder* for instruction in Hebrew and *Chumash*. My back was turned to the house and I did not see my father coming towards me, arms raised and fists clenched. My rebbe had informed him that I'd not been to *cheder* for several days and the money spent for my instruction was being wasted. This was open defiance by his youngest child, another sign that he was losing his authority. Another sign that the secular, money-oriented world he despised was taking over, leaving him as an open-mouthed, frustrated nobody in his own household.

My father seized my ear, it seemed to me, with superhuman strength. Had I resisted, I think he would have pulled it away from my skull. Hymie Lindover, the streetmate I was playing with, became frightened and started to run. Our French-Canadian neighbours laughed and jeered. It was a measure of my father's rage that he was oblivious to the spectacle he was creating. Not for a second did he release my ear, but kept pulling at it all the way down the street until we rounded the corner. Even then he did not let go: all along De Montigny Street, past the solitary Chinese laundry, and the synagogue, past the store run by the man I called "Patch-in-Tuchus" after he had administered a spanking to one of my streetmates.

The door of the *cheder* was ajar and my father, red-faced from the exertion, pushed me over the threshold. He was about to stomp on me when the rebbe's wife appeared, wiping her hands on her apron. Without a word, my father turned around and left. And, since Dora also found it difficult to keep her hand away from my ear, I prudently decided that enough was enough. Never again did I play truant. And though the painful episode did nothing to increase my religious fervour, it substantially raised my respect for my father.

With the passage of time, my father came to feel himself hemmed in by mercenary oafs and boors. Though in the House of the Lord their frenzied outpourings for His attention momentarily conferred a kind of sanctity on their inescapable materialistic pursuits, very few remained untouched by the fever to succeed in this golden land of opportunity and build businesses they could hand on to their children. Not many of them could lay claim to my father's friendship. In the Old Country not one of them would have presumed to address a word to him, so vast was the difference between him and them, so huge the disdain they knew he felt for them. But here, everything was changed. The ground on which they stood, rearranged as if by a geological upheaval, had flung my father onto a lower shelf. Here, the silent, ungodly reproach was formulated: "So you have learning, virtue, and piety, but are they bringing you any *parnoosa*?" – livelihood.

Was it this unheard taunt that kept ringing in my father's ears, the need to gain some measure of respect in his wife's eyes, or was it a bitter, contemptuous capitulation to a world he had begun to fear that made my father announce he'd rented a small, empty store on St. Dominique Street? Having saved two hundred dollars through his cheese-making efforts, he was going to use that sum to stock his convenience store with cigarettes, gum, soap, tinned food, milk, and other sundries. He said he hoped to obtain a licence to sell beer. Relying on the saying, *"A goy a shikker,"* my father was going to make his fortune. Instead of averting his face from the drunk lying sprawled out on the sidewalk, he would now regard him with affectionate concern. My mother promptly punctured that balloon for him. So did his daughters. My brother-in-law Strul Goldberg, when he heard about it, laughed in my father's face, his gold fillings flashing under the kitchen bulb. My father said nothing but stubbornly went on with his plan.

His utter impracticality was soon evident. By temperament and training my father was as far removed from being a merchant as he was from being a money-lender or a marine. It would have been hard to imagine him trying to cajole a customer into buying an additional pack of cigarettes, or even smiling at him with forced affability. Daily conversations with his God had rendered him awkward in the presence even of those he knew. The easy courtesies expected from a shopkeeper were quite beyond him.

It wasn't long before he asked my older brothers Joshua and Hyman to look after the store in the evenings. Young and inexperienced, they gave credit to anyone who asked for it. In less than two weeks, my father's small stock was almost depleted, and the shelves that had displayed it were left bare. Perhaps at first when he saw how quickly his goods were moving, he may have deceived himself about the true state of his venture. Almost as if to ensure its failure, my father decided to sell ice cream, and one of the dairy companies installed a freezer with gallon containers. Since my father seldom came to the store after dark, my brothers helped themselves to as many scoops as it took to relieve their boredom or their appetite. Hyman, but not Joshua, invited friends and streetmates to admire the generosity with which he handed them cone after heaped cone. There probably wasn't a pimp or a prostitute in the neighbourhood who didn't savour my father's free ice cream that torrid July. Luckily, my mother's prediction turned out to be accurate, and the application for a beer licence was turned down. Otherwise, the number of drunks seen reeling on the sidewalk would have doubled or tripled.

The end to this farce came abruptly. One evening, my father showed up unexpectedly to find neither Hyman nor Joshua minding the store. He went to look for them but they were nowhere in sight. This was a sad, bitter blow. I can picture him standing in the doorway, undecided what to do next. Then he saw his two sons turning the corner. They were in a cart and being pulled along the street by a big black dog whose tail Hyman was clutching while Joshua yelled, "Giddyap, giddyap!" My father shouted a Yiddish imprecation at them as they passed him. Then he went into the store, turned out the lights, locked up, and went home. After that, the doleful, trapped look in my poor father's eyes deepened.

My father has to be seen in relation to my mother's god, Strul Goldberg. Strul was married to my oldest sister Gertie whom the rest of the family had dubbed "The Princess." Strul was the successful, enterprising Jew: loud-mouthed, vulgar, and so avaricious he might have served as a model for Balzac's M. Grandet. He could never talk without shouting, and though my mother adored him, or rather his money-making abilities, she would often remark that his booming voice frightened the cockroaches off the kitchen walls. My father used to say, "If you spit on his face, he'd say it was raining."

Because Gertie was delicate and pretty and flattered Strul's vanity by seeming to walk fearfully in his presence, he valued and even loved her as one might love an ornamental vase. However, his real love was money and he determined, with every fibre of his being, to make as much of it as he could.

Too stingy to pay a stenographer wages or hire a shipper and order-taker, he conducted a one-man business, selling his imported religious articles to convents, monasteries, and seminaries in the province. His loudest boast was that he was better-known in Quebec than Jesus Christ himself. Once when he'd had a glass of wine too many, he stood up and, slapping his thick rump, chortled loudly, "Here is where your doctors, lawyers, and accountants can kiss me! When they need money, who do they come running to? To me, to the *meshuggenah* Strul Goldberg, and where do they kiss me? Right here...." and he pointed to his fat butt, which seemed about to burst out of the shiny skin of pants cloth.

But to help explain Strul's worship of money, I must tell the story of his arrival from Roumania. He landed in Montreal and at once went to see his father's older brother. Instead of inviting him to stay for supper, his nearest blood relative tossed him a quarter and told him to go find himself a meal at a nearby restaurant.

His own honesty and fair-dealing, as well as the maniacal devotion he put into building a successful business single-handedly, made him feel entitled to sneer at the merchants and peddlars with whom he dealt. Truthful and scrupulous himself, he suspected everyone else of cheating and lying. Though he ardently worshipped money, he was totally free of cant or cynicism. His drive to amass wealth gave him a serene purity that only an Aristotle or a Shelley could rival.

Yes, Strul was himself the Golden Calf gleefully kicking up his heels in my mother's kitchen. Bull-necked, red-faced, loud-voiced, how sad his end was when, stricken with throat cancer and thin as a wisp of straw, he was heard to whisper from his hopsital bed, "I lived like a fool, I am dying like a fool."

Life has always presented me with many disturbing pairs of antinomies. Without doubt the most seminal pair of opposites was that of Strul Goldberg and my father, of whom many years later I wrote the following poem:

MY FATHER

His voice is low. He leaves behind
The cold, the dross, the hates of men.
He will extol the ways of God
And grow disdainful of the blind.

Of Israel's breed he hums and sings.
He slowly stirs his jaundiced tea
And sighs for lemon...ach. His room
Is empty and he talks with kings.

I was nine years old when my father died. It was a cold day in December, and for many days afterwards I could see his black-bearded face propped up by small hillocks of snow; in the yard, in the lanes, against sheds and houses. When I wished to frighten myself I imagined his lifeless black eyes staring at my back as I ran down the whitened lanes and streets. I could not make this eerie contrast of black and white leave my head.

My father died of a cerebral haemorrhage, probably caused by lifting heavy cans of milk onto the stove. Taken to the Montreal General Hospital, he died two days later and the manner of his death was like the life he had lived for fifty-four years: dignified and gentle and unimportant.

The hospital sent a policeman around to inform the family. We were still in bed when he knocked at the door. It was a frosty morning, and snow was falling spectrally between the houses of the empty street. My mother threw her woollen shawl over her shoulders and ran into the kitchen where she was joined by my brothers, greatly alarmed by the loud knocking. Dora went to the door. When she came back she was in tears. "Papa is dead!" she cried. "Papa is dead." Hyman put his head upon his arms and cried into them. My mother, after the first outcries of grief, began to moan softly. She looked dazed. Quite mechanically she sat down on her straight-backed, uncomfortable chair beside the stove. Her nose was blocked with weeping and she eased it with her fingers and flung the slime off with a vigorous shake of her hand. Outside the kitchen window the yard was filling up with snow and the black fence-wall was oily wet. "I'm a widow," she moaned aloud, "a forlorn widow." She rocked herself from side to side, her hands clasped together. Her mane of strong, thick hair rose and fell upon her shoulders and the tears ran freely down her face, which she never relaxed for a moment.

Dora made a fire and filled our mother's glass with hot coffee and I, looking up, saw my mother blowing on it to cool it, each time making a whistling sound before she swallowed. It struck me as absurd that my mother could be at once so careful and so grief-stricken. And when I observed her after every three or four swallows wiping her mouth with the back of her hand, I was easily persuaded that whatever this misfortune was that had come upon us, the heavens would not fall that day; that tomorrow and the day after and forever my mother would go on making the same familiar gesture, leaving a broken rosary of black coffee beads upon the mysterious tufts of hair which sprouted close to her knuckles.

I turned to my brother and said in a whisper: "Hymie, what is death?"

"You stop breathing."

I put my fingers over my nose and squeezed until my face got red. "Like this, you mean?"

"No, you don't have to hold your nose."

"Do all people die?"

"All people die sometime," Hyman said maturely.

I turned to Dora. "Dora, will I die sometime?"

"Not ... not if you're very good."

"I'm never going to die!"

"I hope so, child." Dora said gravely.

The next day when, my father's body was being washed,

I ran into the bedroom, closing the door behind me. I was glad to be there all by myself, away from the mourners with their strained faces and stiff, unnatural movements. I was glad to find the room bright with sunshine and the thought flew into my head: "My father was here a week ago!" and instinctively I glanced at his bed in the corner. It was made, the unwrinkled coverlet white and innocent, as if it had never been slept in.

Hyman came into the room and found me playing with a button and an elastic that I pretended was a miniature accordion as I stretched and released it between my fingers. I was singing softly in accompaniment to the slight whizzing sound I made. When he saw me, he gave me a savage blow on the face and then began to shove me towards the door and out of the room.

The kitchen was filled with old crones and fierce-looking men. Everyone was standing except my mother who sat red-eyed and rocking herself near the stove. Hyman kept on pushing me until we reached the dining room where my father's washed body, robed in its cerements, was laid out in the coffin that rested on the dining-room table. I caught sight of Strul's red, uncomfortable face. His thick hands dived into the cluster of men and, lifting me up, he held me over the coffin. A muffled cry arose from the dark faces. Then there was a long silence.

"Take a last look at your dead father!" he shouted, squeezing me tightly against his chest. "Kiss him, Srulick." And he pushed my head down to make my mouth touch my father's face. I turned my head away. The sombre, bearded men terrified me and I began to kick with my feet to tear myself away. But Strul held onto me firmly and when I jerked forward my hand fell on the cold body of my father. An awful stillness seemed to rise up from the coffin along with a faint smell of gas. I gave a loud scream and pulled back my hand but Strul held me fast for several moments more. Then he put me down roughly and took no further notice of me. I pushed myself to the wall, where I remained raw-nerved and trembling. Sunshine danced on the pine-wood coffin and was carried out with it by the black-suited men. As they filed past me, they looked like a frayed standard that had given its last stiff flutter.

Shaken and bereft, instinctively I felt that now the only force opposing Strul's crass materialism and that of the family which the new land had also infected, though not so virulently, had been taken away. When, later, I put my head inside the cupboard of the sideboard where my mother kept the clean towels, I thought I could smell gas and disinfectant. I uttered a loud cry and pulled back quickly as if I'd found a rat curled up on the white towels. I banged the door shut and threw myself against it, making the sideboard quiver. I stepped back and stared at the door uneasily. Something was tight inside me like a small fist in my throat. For the first time I felt a sense of loss, and sad, shivering with fear, I began to cry.

Years later I wrote this poem:

DEATH OF MOISHE LAZAROVITCH

My father's coffin pointed me to this:
O arrogant with new life, his black beard
Fierce and stiff and partner to the dark wood
Sent me the way to what I most had feared.

Became at the last a ring of bright light,
A well whose wall of mourning faces turned
My sighs to silence to a deep wound
Which stained the outstretched figure as it burned.

I swear it burned! If not, why the bright light
Like a tall post that had caught the sun's ray?
White the figure was and bright O so bright,
I have not seen its equal since that day.

I do not know how they lifted him up
Or held the vessel near their mourning silk,
But their going was like a roar of flames
And Matter sand in my ears like poured milk.

THREE

Very early in life, the children of the poor get the virtue of submissiveness knocked into them. Also unquestioning respect for their superiors, whoever they may be, however nasty and undeserving. Ignorant and defenceless, children of the poor are receptacles for whatever resentments frustrated adults are able to fill their heads with. No wonder the world goes from bad to worse.

My public school, Alexandra, was situated on Sanguinet, one street east of St. Elizabeth and running parallel to it all the way to Craig. Grey and squat, the building could have been taken for a factory (which in a sense it was) or a prison (which in a sense it also was).

I entered in Grade One, having skipped kindergarten since I'd been too old for it. My high spirits got me into trouble with teachers from the start. Most of the day, pupils were made to sit with their hands behind their backs and to remain mute. Relief came when the class was told to do sums or spell words the teacher had assigned the previous day. Once a week we were asked to draw the likeness of an apple or a pumpkin placed on the teacher's desk. Jolly red apple, jolly yellow pumpkin. Prim, bespectacled face floating above both. Prim and grim, and the body untrim. No, that wasn't my first poem, but it could well have been.

My performance in class depended almost entirely upon my feelings about the teacher. I was hungry for praise because my mother never praised me (nor did she praise any of her other children). So if I had a teacher who showed even the slightest sign of interest or affection, I would do everything I could to please her. I once got a report card that put me second in the class, a most unusual distinction for a pupil who was habitually ranked at the bottom. History and English were my favourite subjects. I possessed an excellent memory and assimilated information easily and quickly.

If, however, I didn't like the teacher or felt she didn't like me, my natural laziness took over. Becoming bored and inattentive, I'd go from one mischievous frolic to the next until the exasperated teacher ordered me out of the room to cool my heels in the corridor.

These expulsions had little or no effect. I enjoyed my status as class jester. I enjoyed the sense of power my reputation as trouble-maker and class wit gave me, enjoyed the almost daily dramatic tussle between the teacher and myself. When I became really unmanageable, when the blood rushed to my head so that I didn't know what I was doing or saying, the poor bewildered teacher had no alternative but to send me down with an explanatory note to the principal. ·

Mr. Spinney, a grey-faced, soft-spoken man, hardly the prototype of the stern principal, would study the note and say he'd have to send me home to bring my mother to see him before I could be admitted back to class. This was a more severe punishment than being told to remain in the corridor until the lesson I'd disrupted was over. I hated it even more than being suspended. My mother would have to close the store for several hours and that meant a loss of time and money; a serious thing, really.

Of course she would begin rolling out her curses from the minute I brought her the evil tidings, doubling her volume and vehemency when she closed the door, and she never stopped for a single moment until we reached the school five or six blocks away. When she saw the principal in the office, she composed her face, her voice took on a pleading tone. She promised him that from now on, I'd always behave myself and never trouble the teacher. Mr. Spinney was a kindly man, an English gentleman of the old school, and his courtesy had its effect on my mother, whose painful, foreign-accented English syllables had their effect on him. Their foreheads nearly touching, they struck me as being two blades of grass in a field made to nod to each other conspiratorially by a summer breeze.

In spite of my promises to keep out of mischief, three weeks or a month later I was again up to my old tricks. I'd talk back to the teacher, deliberately make my sneeze sound like an explosion, or put a tack on a pupil's seat. The next thing we might hear was a big scream that frightened teacher and classmates and always delighted me.

My *pièce de résistance* was the time I put a dead rat in the teacher's drawer. There were always dead rats in the unpaved lanes and I used to regard their inert bodies with fascination since rats lead an underground subversive existence. The rats in the lane near Alexandra School were monstrously large; some of them bigger than cats.

The one I found lying in the dust was young, judging from its whiskers, tail, and the comparative smallness of its corpse. I picked it up by its short tail and shoved it into one of my mother's grocery bags, later to deposit it into the teacher's drawer at the first chance her absence offered. Well, that afternoon she opened the drawer, reached for a piece of chalk, and she let out a yell that made the windows rattle. It was undoubtedly one of my most successful pranks and won me the admiration of my classmates for the whole year. I was suspected, but the teacher had no proof. And of course I maintained an air of complete innocence.

I was now in Grade Five and eleven years old. Though nearly all the pupils in the school were Jewish, almost all the teachers were English Canadian. With few exceptions, they were juiceless English spinsters with flat chests and no buttocks. Their animation took the form of anger, their verbal inventiveness came out as sarcasm.

Certainly the teacher who walked into our classroom that September had all these traits. She was tight-lipped, humourless, as full of menace as the pointer she constantly held in her hand. I disliked her from the moment I clapped eyes on her. She handed out punishments left and right, demanded absolute silence from thirty normal children, and even made us sit with our hands behind our backs all through morning and afternoon lessons.

One day I put my hand up and asked to be excused. Number one. Stupid business, but she wouldn't allow me to leave the room. "Well, I think I can put you over a barrel, miss," I thought to myself. The rebel/agitator was there in the making. I opened my fly and relieved myself on the classroom floor. Pure defiance, with the ghost of Byron, whose poems we were being told to memorize, patting me on my shoulder.

The pupils in the next aisle saw the stream of piss coming their way. You can imagine the commotion that caused. They stood up and began to holler with Miss Flatchest demanding to know what the ruckus was about. By then she had approached the aisle, saw the wetness on the floor, and her eyes took on an expression of disgust and horror. I had a ready excuse on the tip of my tongue, and when she looked accusingly at me, I spat it out at her without any embarrassment: "You wouldn't let me go, Miss Rankin." But the truth of the matter, though I alone knew it, was that I could have contained myself until the recess bell had rung. I had done it out of pure spite, from the desire to play my trump card in the knowledge that she had made herself tactically vulnerable. What could she say? If she sent me to the principal, I would answer, "Look, I mean, my bladder was bursting. I was waving my hand for five minutes.

I asked to leave and Miss Rankin wouldn't let me." Self-righteousness, cunning, and the intuitive sense of knowing when to press your advantage are an unbeatable combination. That's how political agitators are made. At any rate, I was the big hero of the day, the triumphant rebel who had put one over on the teacher all the pupils hated, even Louis Greenberg and Harry Cramer, her star pupils.

From that day on, Miss Rankin had it in for me. The piss-wet floor was not only an affront to her genteel sensibility, but I also had indisputably pulled her nose out of joint. For a while she bided her time, secure in the knowledge that my recklessness would give her the opportunity to repay me for my act of defiance. She did not have to wait long. My success made me overbold, and I felt that I could get away with anything in that class. I threw caution to the winds, my clowning grew more and more manic as the days passed. Friends tried to warn me I was going too far but I was so puffed up with a sense of power I paid no heed.

One morning, before Miss Rankin entered the classroom, I tied a string to the vase of flowers on her desk and attached the other end to her chair. When she pulled the chair out to seat herself, the vase crashed to the floor and splintered into many fragments. Though none in the class had seen me setting up this latest act of sabotage, everyone's head instinctively turned in my direction. The guilt must have showed plainly on my face. There was no doubt in her mind as to who was the culprit. After a single meaningful look at me, she began writing a note to the principal. Placing it in an envelope, she told me to take it down to the principal's office. My punishment was a week's suspension from school.

Because Miss Rankin was not well-liked, most of my class-mates thought the punishment was too severe. Sensing that their sympathies were with me, I decided that it was now or never. As they gathered around me in the school basement,

I began to harangue them about going to the principal's office and making a complaint about a teacher who had shown herself to be domineering and unfair.

With an inspired shrewdness that amazed me, I realized that if this demonstration were to succeed, I must not be a part of it. The protest could be effective only if some of the best students gave it their support. The top students were Harry Cramer, Louis Goldberg, Jennie Fleischman, and the solitary token gentile among us, Bogdanowski, all of them, like myself, the children of immigrants. But good students, like the prosperous and well-situated everywhere, have something to protect. Caution is a natural result of their high marks and the high regard in which they are held by teachers and classmates.

So I employed all my oratorical gifts towards firing them up with a spirit of rebellion against Miss Rankin. If I didn't go as far as to call her an anti-Semite, it was because I was sensitive to Bogdanowski's presence in the group. My impassioned speech converted them. As my arguments succeeded in winning them over to my plan, my sense of triumph was mixed with a feeling of contempt for the group's malleability, the same contempt I was to later have for mobs responding like docile sheep to the bark of demagogue or agitator. However, their earnest pleas did convince Mr. Spinney, and the next day was a double triumph for me. Miss Rankin was transferred to another school and I was back in class.

Along the road there were other teachers who tried to break us in to serve the purposes of employers, bureaucrats, politicians, tax-gatherers, admen, conmen, and the fathers of fat, unmarriageable daughters. Miss Hecht: whom we wrongly believed to be a Jewess trying to pass for a German. I thought that was the reason she always appeared so stern; she was obviously trying hard to conceal her warm Jewish heart. Miss McIldouie: horse-faced, hair lifeless like a covering wig, her crossed eyes giving her an unmerited look of severity. A sense of humour moderated her Protestantism, as did her gentleness and her need to be seen exhibiting fairness and benevolence. Though she was the only teacher to flunk me, I fondly recall her loose lips and the discoloured teeth they revealed when she opened her mouth to reprimand me. Miss Franklin: her long bony nose and nervousness told us plainly enough she was Jewish, the only Jewish teacher in the school (besides Miss Benjamin about whom I will say something later). Miss Franklin was the replacement for Miss Rankin. Unlike the uncomfortable Anglo-Saxon teachers before her, she understood the fun-loving, restless chap I was. She saw clearly my mischief derived from a desire to use my imagination, as an outlet for my high spirits, and an attempt to get attention. Understanding the reason for my devilry, she, and later Miss Benjamin, had a measure of tolerance for it. Neither one ever attempted to expel me, however demonic my behaviour was.

Neither home nor school truly provided the soil I needed for my developing self. At home, my imagination was starved, my verbal inventiveness unexercised. Piety and good works may get people into heaven, but these appear to do little to encourage the natural playfulness all animals are born with. I suppose it was the effort to relieve the solemnity that all people intent on saving their souls acquire, which made me engage in constant guerrilla warfare against them. Very early in life, I was unconsciously learning that both school and home were implacable enemies to everything unique and precious in my own makeup; that their chief aim was to obliterate individuality. If they did not succeed in destroying the traits that go with creativity, their survival was not due to resolution on my part but to a visceral defiance. The school's regimental discipline made me a rebel, the piety at home made me a joyous unbeliever.

My daily battles at home and in the classroom strengthened my confidence in what my feelings told me about myself and the world.

Miss Benjamin, ah, Miss Benjamin: young, beautiful, Jewish, an oasis in a desert where there were choking sandstorms, where grace and beauty were not missed simply because they were unknown. But my soul thirsted for them as the waterless plant thirsts for rain. I was twelve when she walked into my class and stopped my breath. Her light-brown hair, her large brown eyes and healthy complexion, her sturdy body, trim in the dress that outlined her flowing curves, almost put me into a trance. She had beautiful teeth, even and white. I was enchanted by her dazzling smile; I loved her coral lips. My awakened sexuality focussed on the tantalizing swell of her breasts under the white blouse she wore that first day.

My personality underwent a total change, as if a lobotomy had been performed on that part of my brain which demanded shouts or frowns from teachers, leaving an obedient pupil whose submissiveness astonished his classmates. One of them was bold enough to call me teacher's pet and the taunt put a flush into my face redder than that on the cheeks of the teacher whom I adored with all my young excited heart. It was that humiliating taunt that made me disrupt the lesson one morning with an episode whose nature I can't, after these many years, recall.

To punish me, Miss Benjamin kept me in after school. I was supposed to do arithmetic sums during the hour's detention. However, instead of adding up the columns of figures she'd assigned, I kept gazing at her sitting at her desk and wrote a poem for her. That was my first real poem. Since the class had also taken some sonnets by Shakespeare, my first poem may have been a sonnet, though more likely it consisted of several quatrains modelled on those of Sir Walter Scott's narrative lyric, "Lochinvar." ("O young Lochinvar is come out of the West,/Through all the wide border his steed was the best.")

I can't remember how my verse went. Undoubtedly it was an erotic poem in which I lavishly praised Miss Benjamin's physical charms. Her eyes, her hair, the red blush that began at her dimpled chin and crept down to her cleavage. Ah, her cleavage. I used to pretend I couldn't do my maths to get her to bend over my desk so that I could see the flush that lost itself between her perfumed breasts.

The hour's detention over, I walked up to Miss Benjamin's desk and, slapping the poem down on it, ran out of the room. She never again kept me in after school. Perhaps, I've been telling myself for the past six decades, because she feared the fierce lust she had generated in her young votarist.

Several years ago, I gave a reading in Vancouver. When someone in the audience asked me how I came to write my first poem, I related the above incident. During the reception held afterwards, a woman came over to me and said quietly, "Miss Benjamin was my mother." My heart turned over. Miss Benjamin had been a goddess and in my mind had lost none of her remembered divinity. Her daughter, though attractive, was but a faded copy. Achingly curious, I listened as she told me what had happened to her mother when she gave up teaching, about her marriage and mothering, and her untimely death. When she paused, I blurted out, "Have you any pictures of your mother?" She told me she had and readily agreed to send me one. I received the photograph some weeks later. My fingers trembling with anticipation, I eagerly unwrapped it and looked at it. Alas, this was a picture of a respectable, middle-aged Jewess, wearing glasses, looking very sober and staid, exhibiting the grooves which repression digs into the forehead and cheeks of all its victims.

I'm reminded of a wonderful story by de Maupassant. The narrator revisits the island where, many years ago, he had met a young native girl. What memories he had carried around in his head of her lithe body, of her dancing on the seashore for him alone, of her fragrant hair and skin. The woman he now beheld was wrinkled and nearly toothless. Under the soiled dress she was wearing, her body was curveless as the trunk of a tree. If I were to write a similar story I would call it "The Picture." It would contain exactly the same emotions as the de Maupassant story, the same hatred for "time's vicious reaping."

I feel the same heavy weight of depression whenever I think of that picture lying unlooked-at on top of the bookshelf where I placed it after that first disillusioning moment.

The boy's magazines, *Gem* and *Magnet*, gave me my first picture of England and the English people. The Misses Cook (whose first names I never was to learn) unknowingly helped to enlarge that picture.

They lived upstairs, having rented the flat which had now become vacant. Though they bore the same name, they were unrelated, which didn't surprise me when I was first told of it since they were as dissimilar in appearance and temperament as any two people could be. It was the thinner, shorter, more flat-chested one that I used to see going up the stairs and wave to over the banister. The other woman was more a name to me than a presence, though from time to time I would see her on one of the visits I began to make with increasing frequency. When the frail-looking Miss Cook introduced me to her, I was astonished to see a tall, broad-shouldered, portly woman who towered above her friend. What flashed irreverently through my mind was the comic strip "Mutt and Jeff," but I kept that observation to myself and, with puppy-dog gladness, smiled happily at both of them.

I shall always think fondly and with gratitude of the thin

Miss Cook from Sussex, England, who fluttered around me. She was goodness itself, never failing to give me cookies and her attention when I went to visit her upstairs. She had a soft, concerned voice; her sincerity when she asked me to relate something about myself could never be questioned. We played dominoes and talked easily, like two old friends, over the glass of milk she handed me to wash down the gingersnaps. To me her kindness was a revelation in terms of its naturalness and the spontaneity with which it was displayed. I shall never forget the gentle look in her small, grey eyes and the slight tremor in her right hand when she offered me a sweet or a cookie. It was to her that I told about my fights at school, my love for Miss Benjamin, my boyhood adventures. Getting her to lose some of her seriousness and making her laugh I began to feel was some repayment for the comforting attentions she gave me. I felt my emotional range widening, since our friendship provided me with feelings and sensations I had never known or experienced.

Early were the two faces of love unveiled to me, Eros and Agapé. While Miss Benjamin had stirred the sexual impulse, Miss Cook awakened in me a spiritual aspiration to be as kind and generous, humble and compassionate as she herself was. She was a gentile and I was Jewish but we never discussed our religious differences because on the level of human kindness, giving and receiving, there were none. Unlike in the French-Canadian homes into which I occasionally found entrance, there were no pictures on her walls, no oleographs of Jesus or bleeding hearts, no wooden cross to frighten or disturb me. My own faith taught unselfishness and compassion, but until then Miss Cook was the only authentic example of these qualities I had ever met.

There were times when I honestly believed the Messiah was in the kitchen, wearing a tasselled apron woven from goat's hair and wild flowers, and offering me a gingersnap in a sweet English voice. The quietude I experienced each time I was with

Miss Cook, the peace that enveloped me in its soft mantle, made a sharp contrast with the noise and hysteria, the constant bickering that went on downstairs like the never-ceasing surface explosions of a sulfurous mud-pool.

When I had a near miss and almost killed myself, to whom did I tell the story? To my mother? To my sister Dora? To Cousin Fanny? That would never have occurred to me. For neither the derring-do nor my miraculous escape from injury or death would have elicited the appropriate response. My mother would only have started to scream and bemoan her misfortune in having me for her child. As for Dora and Fanny, they might have shaken their heads over my tale, nothing more. It was to Miss Cook that I told of my adventure, and it was she who let fall gratifying sounds of concern as I explained how I had piled three rickety crates on a roof across the street, one on top of the other, in order to reach the edge of the one onto which I wanted to climb. Like the reckless fool I was, I had piled the crates near the edge of the roof and had one of them given way, I would have plummeted to the cement sidewalk below. Indeed, just as my fingers touched the roof's lip, I felt the boxes beginning to sway and pushed my hands forward to achieve a firm grip. I heard the crates crash into splinters on the sidewalk and, my heart thumping with fear and thankfulness, I slowly pulled myself up.

Miss Cook was an unmarried woman in her middle thirties whose fiancé had been killed in the first Great War. I learned this when one afternoon, visiting her after school, she took out a picture from a drawer and showed it to me. There was a hole in it and the brown stain of a gunpowder burn. The hole had been made by the bullet that had killed him, for he was carrying it inside her letter in the breast-pocket of his uniform. The picture was of herself and had been taken a week before his regiment crossed the Channel for France. When I handed her back the picture, her lower lip trembled and her small face looked pathetic. She looked at me from the sofa where she was sitting and said, "Do you think Mr. Palmer will propose?" I had met Mr. Palmer several weeks earlier when he had come to pay Miss Cook a visit. Intuition told me she wanted an affirmative answer. It stroked my vanity to know that she had given me the power to make her happy or unhappy with a single word.

Since I had told her that I was reputed to be a fortune-teller, I asked her to bring out her pack of cards. Laying them out on the table I pretended to study them with great concentration. We both remained silent. Then, picking up the jack of diamonds, I stared at it for a time, shuffled some of the other cards on the table, and picked one of them up. It was the nine of clubs. Looking solemnly into Miss Cook's questioning eyes, I said with affected gravity, "Miss Cook, you will be married within nine weeks." She gave a joyful laugh and exclaimed, "I knew it, I knew it!" Then she told me that Mr. Palmer had indeed been courting her for some time but she was delaying her answer to his proposal. Mr. Palmer had been in the trenches with her fiancé.

Then she wanted to know whether she would be happy if she married him. Once again I shuffled the cards and put them face down on the table. I picked up three of them, looked at them for several minutes and slowly put them down. I picked up another three and did the same thing again. Then I turned the other cards up and, since there was a king of hearts and a queen of diamonds among them, I was able to assure Miss Cook, as I held those cards, that her union with Mr. Palmer was going to turn out well. That afternoon she gave me a second glass of milk and an extra gingersnap. Indeed Miss Cook and Mr. Palmer were married before three months had elapsed and they opened up a restaurant on Inspector Street where one sunny Passover afternoon, years later, I went to visit them. I never saw Miss Cook again after that but if there is any kindness rooted in my soul, it was she who planted its seed. I cannot see the word Sussex, or hear it spoken, without seeing her small, intense face and hearing the chimes of a church bell ringing out from an ivy-covered tower.

Was it sleeping in my mother's bed or my awakening sexuality at the sight of Miss Benjamin's cleavage that gave me my early tremendous interest in girls? Or were there nostalgic tremors in my ganglia whenever Yom Kippur came around? Not even Freud would be able to say and even if he did, I wouldn't believe him, so complex and multi-faceted is human motivation. The ocean's depths may be plumbed and measured; the human soul, even that of a twelve-year-old child, is unfathomable.

It was Jennie who made my public school years tolerable. She was my first great love. Enamoured, I thought of little else except how I could win her favour. When she allowed me to carry her books, no knight about to take his part in a tournament could have been prouder or more hopeful when his lady's glance fell on him and his lance. The huskiness of my voice, my shy manner whenever she spoke to me, betrayed my feelings. I would have done anything to earn her good opinion. I used to wait hours outside Jennie's house to catch a glimpse of her when she came out. I even tried to ingratiate myself with her friends so that their good report of me would bring success to my courtship. For court her I did, in and out of the classroom – with scribbled notes, with hot looks and unfeigned tremors. My stammerings told her plainly how much I adored her.

Jennie lived in the top flat of a triplex. Behind it, her father kept some goats in the yard, for their milk or for resale after he had fattened them. One Sunday afternoon, I found myself in the yard, hoping to spot Jennie when she came out or to catch a glimpse of her if she appeared at the window. I saw her all right, her blonde hair and rather pallid face. She waved to me, but not with much enthusiasm, I thought.

Lowering my eyes, I saw round black pellets that looked like stunted olives lying scattered on a brown grocery bag that had been ripped open. Was it curiosity or clowning that made me bend down to pick some of them up? I told myself they were indeed olives and shoved them into my mouth. I remember thinking, when the bitter taste on my tongue informed me that it wasn't olives I was about to swallow, "Jennie must think I'm some kind of fool if I can't tell goat shit from olives." So I smiled deceptively up at the face in the window. Jennie was too far away for me to clearly see her expression. However, I don't think my smile fooled her, for when I saw her in school the following day there was a strange look in her eyes and she gave me a twisted, thin-lipped grin, which not even I, as lovestruck as I was, could interpret as an encouragement to further courting.

The Four Horsemen were myself and three classmates. To them I poured out my longings and griefs. To them I recounted my triumphs and defeats. They cheered me whenever I got into a fistfight in the school basement, grieved with me whenever I told them of my troubles at home or at school. Louis was the brainy one in our gang, David the most reliable, and Mendel, though he was less inventive than I, and also less cocky, assumed leadership because he had the most effective scheme for whatever plan we had in mind. Of course, they unfailingly teased me about my crush on Jennie Segal. Lacking my imagination, they found her ordinary-looking and dull. (Naturally, I never told them about my amorous encounter with goat droppings.)

After graduating from Alexandra School, the only one I ever saw again was David Rubin, who one recent Sunday afternoon spotted me eating a smoked meat sandwich at a deli in Montreal's

Van Horne Mall, and joined me. He was now middle-aged, balding, and spoke with a nervous stammer he tried hard to suppress. I wondered whether the same thought was going through his mind about what time does to bright young boys, their eagerness not yet dimmed by disappointment and their hopes untarnished by failure. We both munched our sandwiches slowly, aware of the different directions our lives had taken and of the unbridgeable gulf the years had put between us. When I asked him whether he had ever married and he replied he hadn't, I reminded him of my prophecy that he would live and die a bachelor. There was a shy, defeated smile on his lips. Where are you now, David Rubin?

Where are you, Mendel Aaron, Louis Binder? Alive and happy, I hope, the after-school years in which we buried our illusions laden with many gifts and blessings.

By the time I was in my final year, I was known to be the best scrapper in the school. I was light on my feet and my feints were swift and clever. In school, I was compared to Benny Leonard, the lightweight champion of the world at that time. Because I had a fight every day and emerged victorious from most of them, an older pupil dubbed me "Napoleon" and the nickname "Nappy" stuck. All the little kids knew that Nappy was their champion. If anyone picked on them they had only to come to me and I would take care of the older boy who had bullied them. I would go over to him and say, "Moishe, if you lay a finger on Sammy, I'll knock your block off." And that meant that Sammy could play with his mates without fear or worry.

Well, one day, a Syrian boy came to Alexandra. He was a solitary figure in a school not known for its Arab population. He had dark skin and black woolly hair. He was lithe and agile, unlike myself who had a stockier build. The kids knew that a fight between us was inevitable because he began to throw his weight around the first day he arrived.

The fight started in the basement, which had grey cement

walls and long benches bolted to the floor for eating on or for bleachers when we had our baseball games indoors. I think he must have pushed me, for I've never started a fight in my life. It was during the midday break, and the fight lasted for the whole hour and a half. We moved back and forth in the basement, from one end to the other, staying clear of the benches. The crowd of kids followed us as if we were competing champion golfers. This way and back again, we pummelled each other with hard, swift blows, the blood flowing from my nose and his cut lip. At the end, through sheer exhaustion, he gave up. He'd given up not because he was beaten but simply because he was tired. I'd rather have died than lost that fight. He was Syrian, I was Jewish. I think he must have felt the same way about the disgrace of losing. Afterwards, the Syrian and I became, not chummy but we treated each other with respect. We never touched each other again, and I don't think we ever spoke to each other again.

I was also the school's best wrestler, which is another reason all the kids came to see me as their protector. However, I remember this one fellow I once wrestled for sheer competitive sport. Well, in one second he had me on my back. He was so powerful I didn't even have time to put my famous armlock on him. His strong arms gripped me, and I'm a feather, his exhalations blow this way and that. I'm a thread he pulls through a needle as if he were a tailor smiling with half-closed eyes. I'm a mop and he's wiping the floor with me. Down, down he forces me and my surprise is greater than my anger. Finally I'm on my back and he sits on me as if I were a stool.

There was no shame in such a defeat. I knew I had been matched unfairly against a supernatural force. I was grateful to the Horsemen. They had watched my disgrace and when they vigorously shook their heads to indicate they understood and were in full agreement with me, I knew I would cherish them until the day I died.

FOUR

Though my mother cursed obsessively and never, or seldom, praised me, I have one or two joyful memories. Every Monday morning during the summer months my mother went down to the Champ-de-Mars where the farmers from outlying villages marketed their produce. She always took me along with her, me and a cart that I'd constructed. Since I was no mechanical genius, it was a very rickety affair. The only thing I can say for sure about it is that the four wheels turned, though not always at the same time. Still, it was stout enough to hold the box of tomatoes, the cabbages, the bag of onions, and the cucumbers and radishes that my mother bought after some haggling with the farmer who'd grown them.

Standing beside her, holding the cart's pullrope, I marvelled at her boldness as she went from one farmer to another, arguing with each one about the high price of their goods. Since she knew no French, her haggling consisted of pointing to the vegetables she wanted and some vigorous sign language to indicate the price she offered. Though unsmiling and business-like during these negotiations, it seemed to me my mother enjoyed herself. She was, I suppose, reminded of the Roumanian peasants she had known in Neamtz. The health, sturdiness, and easy humour of the French-Canadian farmer was not much different from that of his Roumanian counterpart. Besides, my mother liked the hustle and bustle, the noise, colour, and vitality in evidence all about her.

Ah, the delicious smells that wafted to me from the bags of potatoes, from the onion skins, and damp straw scattered underfoot. The dazzling array of colours, the white purity of cauliflower, the glossy robustness of tomatoes. I wanted to reach out and take their shine into my hand and walk off with it. The wonderful matter-of-factness of carrots and turnips, of the farmer's wagon, and patient horse standing in the shafts. And the people all around me, in crowds and bunches, the vigour and animation with which they moved and struck bargains. This, my young mind intuited, was what being alive meant: scramble, confusion, and disorder.

For all that I or anyone can tell, the Dionysian in me was born then and there. Thereafter, at great cost to me, I was to equate chaos with vitality, order and respectability with moribundity and stagnation. My life, no doubt, would have been a great deal easier had disorder not been accompanied by insight and rapture. At the time unaware, I was being given a standard by which to judge my own poetry and that of others. Poems, I have always believed, have to have the vitality and rough vigour of the marketplace. If I despise formalism and academic poetry, it's because I remember onions falling from their burlap sack and comically rolling down the cobbled hill and along the gutter, to be followed by an ambitious potato trying to catch up with it. Who knows what metaphors were spawned in my unconscious from seeing them race one another towards the gutter at the end of the short street?

A poem I wrote many years later tried to capture the memory of my mother and myself in the Champ-de-Mars, when the days were full of sunshine, fresh and crisp as the lettuce she bought.

THE EXECUTION

> *Because the glowing morning*
> *Dropped from the rooster's beak*

The frozen famous statue
Was too amazed to speak

    But watched my mother go and come
Like a fish in an aquarium
    Sinister alone
And me upon my boycart throne.

    Her cheeks were red with bargains
And she moved to the money cries
    Like an enchanted dancer
With wide enchanted eyes.

    The yells, the cries were frenzying;
Her cheeks grew pale with bargains:
    I laid my boyhood head
among the golden onions.

Despite my mother's admiration for her son-in-law, Strul Goldberg, she thought of other things besides amassing lots of money. She was not closed-fisted, gave fair weight, and never overcharged any customer. People came to see her because they thought she was a very clever woman with good advice to offer. Self-assured to the point where she could be perceived as domineering, she always spoke with a tremendous sense of authority. My mother was shrewd but never sly or cunning.

By law, the store had to be closed at six. Of course, if a customer knocked on the door after closing hour, my mother would let her in after a quick look outside to see whether a policeman was on the beat, though he was probably bribed anyway. He would take the bribe out in comestibles, several pounds of potatoes, or onions, a bag of flour or a tin of biscuits. As long as the policeman assigned to the beat could walk away with some merchandise, he didn't interfere with my mother.

This was my first lesson in the nexus between law and money; Marx had nothing to teach me on that score.

One of my mother's favourite topics was the Steinberg family down the street, the founders of the successful supermarket chain in Quebec. Mrs. Steinberg was a widow and, like my mother, she had converted the small front parlour of her house into a grocery store. My mother had five sons and felt that if she had been served by them as Mrs. Steinberg had been served by hers, she too could have acquired wealth and status.

I must have been twelve when I first heard my mother say in a mournful tone, "What a scandal my sons are not like Mrs. Steinberg's." I can't say her tragedy touched me deeply or that it affected my four brothers. None of us was ambitious that way; we were not keen-minded to become affluent grocery retailers. Certainly that was not what I was after, and since I wasn't fired up to sell more bags of potatoes than Mrs. Steinberg's boys did, I was not devastated to be told, from time to time, that I and my brothers were not as smart and ambitious as the Steinberg boys.

I think every male child should have the experience poverty forced upon me. For reasons of economy, I slept in my mother's bed until the age of thirteen, when Dora routed me out and made me sleep on a cot near the kitchen stove. I'd had a ritual about going to bed in wintertime. We couldn't afford to keep even a small stove in the bedroom, and to conserve heat from the stove in the kitchen we kept the bedroom door closed. I recall there actually being ice on the linoleum of the bedroom floor; sometimes a patch of it enabled me to slide from the door right into bed. Since the sheets were ice-cold and clammy, I would put my cat into the bed to warm up a spot for me while I retreated hastily from the bedroom we'd dubbed the North Pole to the kitchen and its gratifying warmth. After about twenty minutes, I'd again slide over to the bed, jump in, and quickly pull the covers over me, thankful for the tiny warm spot the cat had made. I hugged the cat close until my shivering stopped. Having her warm fur against my body was certainly one of my earliest sensual pleasures.

After the cat and I had warmed a larger area of the bed, my mother came to join us. She had that beautiful smell that all healthy bodies give off. I'd snuggle close to her and she'd put her arm over my head and shoulders. I think that's where I got my feeling for a woman's body; I can't think of it other than warm and comforting, and I am still thrilled when a woman puts her arm around my neck to pull me close to her. Were I to compose a novel called *Sons and Lovers*, this is what I'd write about.

The cat, my mother, and I huddled close and took whatever warmth we could from each other. Of course my mother never failed to object to the cat's presence. She'd start off by saying, "Get rid of the cat! Put the cat out!" And I'd respond, "No, no, I want the cat with me!" This could go on for as long as ten or fifteen minutes. I think these protests helped my mother release some of the frustrations she had accumulated during the long day and calmed her for a good night's sleep. After a while her complaints subsided and I'd feel her drifting into relaxed unconsciousness. Several minutes later I'd hear her gentle snoring. Before falling asleep, I think: "When the Messiah comes, how will he increase the pleasure I get from holding the cat to my chest or from feeling the warmth that comes from my mother's body?"

My mother was expected to heal all difficulties, all quarrels and animosities that arose in a family. Such was her reputation as peace-maker, troubled wives and mothers came from the adjacent neighbourhoods to seek her help. When she scratched her nose with her forefinger and screwed up her eyes, no pawnbroker assaying an article for a needed loan could have looked more shrewd. Her small eyes shone with pleasure like brown agates. Then she was indeed in her element, almost audibly purring over the admiration she knew she was extracting from those who sought her help.

The Stauffers who lived down the street had had a falling out. Naturally, my mother was asked to see what she could do about mending the rift between husband and wife. It was a cold day in early December. The snow had not yet fallen, but it looked as if it might powder the streets at any moment. My mother was setting out to make peace. On all such occasions, she could be heard to murmur, "One must think of the children," and her lips would acquire a deeper tinge from the virtue such pious observations always gave her. My mother asked me to come with her to the Stauffers'. She threw a grey woollen mantle over my head and shoulders to keep me warm, pressing me close to her body and holding me there until we reached the neighbours' house. Under the protective shawl we were mother and child against the outside cold. Not only the cold of this wintry day, but the cold of the neighbourhood where hostile anti-Semites lurked in almost every lane and street. In a world that I was beginning to recognize was full of trouble, my mother was on a mission to reconcile an estranged couple and bring peace to a household.

I remember, at the age of fourteen, I developed a swelling in my groin. I had no idea what caused it, for neither cut nor contusion was visible in the area. I only knew that it was getting bigger and becoming very painful. I should have told my mother about this but the puritanism that a stupefying orthodoxy reinforced made unmentionable anything to do with crotch or groin. Finally the pain became unbearable, and one day I blurted out the truth. Well, my dear puritanical mother could think of only one thing: I had contracted a venereal disease. I didn't even know what that could possibly mean, so untouched was I by the ribaldry of the boys with whom I occasionally played street hockey. Nevertheless, I intuited that my mother thought there was something wrong with me because I'd gone to a whorehouse.

It was simply too ridiculous for words, but that's the way my mother's mind worked. She told my older sister Esther about the swelling in my groin and asked her to take me to the doctor's. I had no idea what was wrong with me and Esther certainly didn't know either, but my mother's suspicions had infected her. She kept giving me queer looks all the way to where we were going.

The doctor looked at my groin and then asked me, to my great astonishment, to lift up my naked foot. I thought, "What does he want to look at my foot for?" So at first I figured that we'd come to a quack. Pursuing this craziness, the doctor carefully examined the sole of my foot and then gave the same studied attention to the heel. And sure enough, he found a laceration there. A small cut had become infected and caused a gland in my groin to become inflamed. He cleansed and bandaged my heel and in a couple of days the pain disappeared. I sometimes torture myself with the thought that if I hadn't spoken up, gangrene might have set in and my leg would have had to be amputated. In my less charitable moments, I sometimes think my mother was perhaps disappointed that it didn't turn out that way rather than have her suspicion proved wrong.

Though kind-hearted, honest as the day is long, eager to help her neighbours by sewing clothes for their large broods, and extending credit to anyone in need, my mother had one great fault. She obstinately imagined herself to be an exceedingly clever woman when she wasn't that at all. Later I was to learn that many Jews, who mistake for sensitivity the sentimentality that comes with certain comforts, also suffer from a similar affliction, eager to have their prosy realism taken for profound sageness, even for brilliancy.

Several blocks from St. Elizabeth Street was an imposing church whose ringing bells frightened and delighted me with their alien din. In an area bounded east and west by St. Denis and

Bleury, north and south by Ontario and Craig, swarmed the Jews from Eastern Europe; there pullulated the Italians, Slovaks, Poles, Germans, and Hungarians. They had come to fill their pockets with the gold lying in convenient piles for them to pick up. All they had to do was to reach down for it. Naturally, the energetic would end up with more gold than the lazy. But that was only fair and no sane person would ever think to complain. Anyhow, if he did, who would stop making his pockets bulge with the precious yellow metal to listen to him?

Every Sunday morning the church bells flung their grains of music against the narrow windowpanes of my small bedroom. Their rapturous sound woke me to the sunshine that streamed in, soft and yellow on my mother's curtains, large blurs on the gleaming linoleum that my sister or Cousin Fanny scrubbed clean every Friday morning. Somehow my young brain had made the connection between the bells' joyous pealings and the priests that materialized on my street, sometimes right in front of our house. Though the linkage was vague, my childish mind was disturbed by the incongruous conjunction. What did enrapturing tonalities have to do with black soutanes and severe pallid faces, which whenever I caught sight of them made me run indoors or cross over to the other side of the street?

Many years later I discovered other churches. First, the one at St. Joseph's Oratory; later, the Church of Notre Dame. There, if the right number of coins were deposited in the machine's slot, lights appeared above the head of the worshipper's favourite saint. That inspired the following poem:

THIS MACHINE AGE

For fifteen cents
the label read,
the Virgin's halo
would light up
for three minutes.
The man dropped

the pieces of money
into the machine's slot
and looked about
the vast, empty church
empty except
for him and me.
When his gaze came back
to the halo
it was still unlit
– a dark infuriating zero.
He gave the machine
a careful kick
to bring the lights
of the circle out.
It didn't.
"Damn it!" he shouted,
"Why doesn't it light up?"
He kicked again
and muttered something
I didn't hear.
But I guess
from the way he looked
he thought divine sereneness
a poker-faced fraud
and himself taken in
by the Mother of God.

The heavy, grey-faced church also harboured in one of its small alcoves the statuettes of two Hebrew prophets. Some years later, they inspired another poem of mine, "On Seeing the Statuettes of Ezekiel and Jeremiah in the Church of Notre Dame."

Since the synagogue and my *cheder* were on the same street, hardly a day passed without finding myself on it at some hour of the afternoon or early evening. It was on that street that

I had my first glimpse of the *schadenfreude* that few human beings are free of. It related to a whorehouse raid. Cyprians emerged from the house of ill-fame laughing and giggling, the men holding their straw hats or fedoras in front of their faces. Those without head-covering looked angry or sheepish. The crowd which had gathered outside was plainly relishing the men's humiliation. Their taunts and derisive laughter still ring in my ears. Early in life I learned humans are primates who enjoy the pain and misfortune of their kind.

Every morning I woke to the smell of the coffee pot steaming on the kitchen stove. It was the first thing to hit my senses when I opened the bedroom door, to be followed by the sound of my mother's exasperated voice coming from the grocery store. As on a stage where the actors make their prescripted appearance one after the other, my mother would enter the kitchen after she had finished serving a customer, soon to be followed by Fanny and Dora.

Joshua had already left for work but Hyman remained in bed for as long as he could, hating school and its demands on his time and energies. He rebelled against having to leave high spirits and inventiveness outside the classroom while some ill-paid spinster went through the motions of teaching thirty-odd children, with aid of blackboard, Imperial reader, and pointer. The state's unimaginative bureaucrats still get away with calling this carefully regulated boredom education. I was more eager than he for the exciting sights and sounds the morning promised. I bounded out of bed to greet them.

The fragrant coffee smell mingled in my nostrils with the rich smells coming from my mother's grocery, comforting as the heat that came from the Quebec stove near which I seated myself each morning. Herring smells, sharp, marine, a crotch smell. The musty smell from potato sacks and their contained tubers, the low-key smells of flour and egg crates. Early in my childhood I learned to expect them.

Hyman was without my zeal for sniffing the insides of empty

biscuit tins, for crumpling the paper-thin onion peels to release their feeble whisper and smell. His eyes didn't devour the whiteness of beans or the modest greenness of peas with my excitement and delight. His fingers didn't ache to touch wood or glass and feel the metal hoops that ringed the herring barrels. Or did they? What do I really know about him? Imaginative, quick in repartee, big-hearted, he possessed an extraordinary sense of adventure and fun. Because he also had an excellent memory he could reel off whole chapters of the *Chumash*. My father kept hoping he might one day become a rabbi. But it takes money to send a bright boy to study at a Yeshiva and money was scarce in our home to the point of invisibility.

In this, if anywhere, the seeds of my later radicalism were sown. It began with innocent rage at poverty, a rage clear and undissembling as the face of a young boy. Afterwards it sought to cloak its honest nakedness in the mumbo-jumbo of demonized words and phrases that the massman of the twentieth century has been persuaded to accept as liberating ideologies.

Hyman was more like me than any of my other siblings. He had a gift for telling stories, and every summer he entertained the kids in our neighbourhood with them. They would line the front stairs tier by tier to hear him relate the latest episode in the life of his invented hero contriving once again to foil the villains who'd fixed yet another trap for him.

Along with his gift for storytelling, it must also be said Hyman had an equally remarkable streak of cruelty in him. Without provocation he'd twist my arm, give me a cuff on my back or shoulder. I used to fear him and made myself scarce whenever I saw him coming. I tried bribing him with marbles, and during the Passover with hazelnuts; but when, like King Saul, the evil mood was on him, nothing worked. I now see that the cuffing and arm-twisting and ear-pulling, his "sadism," sprang from the frustration both of us experienced living in a poverty-pinched home where no outlets existed for our exuberance. Fate had sourly given Hyman parents least likely to offer him the help he needed to develop his exceptional qualities of mind and heart.

An orthodox Jew, my father used to worry constantly about his children having to work on the Sabbath. So when Joshua decided he'd taken enough abuse from his sarcastic prune-dry teacher, ironically named Miss Heaven, he quit school two months before graduation. He said he wanted to work instead. The problem, however, was to find a Jewish employer who observed the Sabbath. After frantic enquiries, my father heard about an observant Jew who kept his factory closed all Saturday. Joshua started working for him as a messenger boy, bringing home each Sunday his week's wages of three dollars. Delighting my mother and father even more than the slim earnings of their son, Joshua's employer insisted on taking him every Friday to the synagogue next door for the evening service.

Without having heard of the work ethic, Joshua applied himself diligently and even put in extra hours to please his employer. From time to time, my father heard from Mr. Salomon about his son's eagerness to carry out all his orders. The factory manufactured children's clothing and there was always plenty to do. Any boy as conscientious as Joshua never waited to have that pointed out. The cutting-room floor had to be swept clean every hour, bundles had to be neatly tied, cartons filled with children's rompers or dresses.

The first day Joshua presented himself for work, Mr. Salomon took his arm and led him into the warehouse. Cartons piled one on top of the other lined the far wall from floor to ceiling. My brother wondered whether the boxes were empty or filled with merchandise. Salomon put his hand on Joshua's shoulder and said, "You see those boxes there? I don't want to ever catch you moving them. Do you understand?" The eagerness with which Joshua nodded his head seemed to satisfy his employer who nevertheless thought he detected a questioning look in the boy's eyes. He smiled, showing his nicotined teeth. "If you should strain and give yourself a rupture, your parents would hold me responsible." Asked whether he wanted this to happen to him, Joshua replied that he really had only the vaguest notion of what Salomon meant by a rupture. "Swear to me that you will never touch any of the boxes." Earnestly my brother swore he'd never touch the cartons stacked against the wall.

Since Joshua showed himself such a willing worker, after about three months his employer decided to raise his pay by fifty cents. Who could have foreseen the consequences of this insignificant increase? For when Joshua opened his pay envelope while standing in the warehouse, the unexpected coin dropped on the floor and began rolling towards the stacked cartons. He wasn't quick enough to halt its glittering progression towards the wall where it chose to disappear into one of the tiny gaps between the pillared boxes. What to do? Be true to his solemn oath or try to retrieve the fifty-cent piece still a-dazzle in his consciousness? He took a swift look around and listened for sounds. He heard none. Now Joshua drove his arm between the cartons right up to his shoulder and began probing along the floor with his fingers. Wherever it was, the coin eluded him. He pushed his hand until his fingers touched the wall where it met the floor. His fingertips felt the texture of something akin to a wire. Alerted now, my brother widened the gap, using his shoulders to nudge the cartons apart, and exposing what his fingers had touched.

Breathing heavily a moment ago, his breath now almost had stopped. The wire led into a small bore in the common wall shared by the warehouse and the synagogue next door. Mr. Salomon was stealing electricity from the synagogue! No wonder he was so keen on taking my brother every Friday for the evening service. He evidently wished to express his gratitude to the Lord of Israel for providing him with free electricity.

Flashing through my brother's mind, that thought gave him a shock from which he never recovered. At the sight of the thin wire that had been pulled through the small bore in the wall, the beliefs of his forefathers, the faith his parents and rebbes had nurtured in him since childhood, dropped between the cartons he had pushed aside, never to be retrieved. That night, Joshua announced he was never again going to put on his phylacteries, never again going to be seen with a prayer shawl around his neck and back. To the angry shouts of our parents, my mother's more shrill than my father's, Joshua shouted back that Salomon was a hypocrite, a lying fraud, and related once more with increased agitation the incident of the fifty-cent piece. All efforts to reason him out of his conviction he met with silence, stubborn defiance. My brother never again performed his morning devotions. His phylacteries stayed in their velvet sack. He never again set foot inside a synagogue. The wound had cut so deep that even many years afterwards, he could not bring himself to speak of the episode without rueful bitterness creeping into his voice.

Because he was deeply religious by nature, Joshua still yearned for the certainties his abandoned faith had once given him. Later in life, after briefly becoming interested in communism, he became a spiritualist and read the books of Sir Oliver Lodge, thumbing their pages with the same passion he had once felt reading about the early patriarchs of Israel. His greatest pleasure came from recounting his own spiritualistic adventures or those of others. He was especially eager to relate those that told of the mysterious messages he received from the other world through table-rapping. His stories were not meant to convert me to his belief in spiritualism but to convince me of his moral and intellectual superiority.

When Joshua reached seventeen, my mother paid someone to smuggle him across the American border. He made it to New York where he joined our older brother, Harry, who had been living in the Bronx for two years.

Since my two oldest brothers did not live in the house while I was growing up, I saw very little of them. The older of the two was named Avrum. Though I did not know him very well, years later his fate had an unforeseen and disastrous effect on my own.

Over six feet tall, Avrum towered above his brothers and sisters like a pine tree surrounded by scrub. His physiognomy was said to resemble my own. He and I were the only ones in the family to have blue eyes. While still a young man, Avrum had a terrible argument with our father over the time he should spend on his morning devotions. We heard loud shouting, the smashing of a cup. It ended with my gentle-natured father ordering Avrum out of the house. Soon after, Avrum became an agnostic and began reading whatever books he could buy or borrow that confirmed his unbelief.

Like Strul Goldberg, he was a customer peddlar, and he took up lodging in the home of another peddlar whose acquaintance he had made at Wiser's, the shop on St. Laurent where all the immigrant peddlars bought their merchandise wholesale to sell retail to their customers in the towns and villages that surround Montreal.

From bits of information I occasionally caught, and from our infrequent encounters, my oldest brother struck me as someone explosively impatient, but also open-handed. He had a sharp mind, critical rather than creative. Reckless, and used to perfect health, he foolishly neglected a hacking cold that laid him low and reduced his immunity to infection. At least that's the way my family explained how he'd come to be stricken with the fatal tubercle bacillus after the cold developed into pneumonia. Our boisterous upstairs neighbours having vacated the premises, my mother rented the flat upstairs. Avrum stayed there and she looked after him, until he was taken to the sanatorium at Ste. Agathe, where he eventually died.

The senseless cruelty of fate! He should not have died so young. Had he lived longer, our lives would have taken a different turn. He would have encouraged Hyman and myself to take our studies seriously and afterwards would have helped us to obtain a university education. His influence would have prevented my sisters from making their disastrous unions, taking mates that included an avaricious boor, a sadistic braggart, and a religious sot. He would have counteracted the legacy of my father's superstition and the foolish rigidities that went along with it.

I was eleven when Avrum died. I watched from the farthest end of the room as his body was being washed. After he had been shrouded in white cerements, two men lowered him into the coffin resting on the long dining-room table. The coffin was too short and his feet stuck out over the edge. The bewhiskered man wearing a *yarmulka* was straining to push the legs down into the coffin. When he succeeded, my brother's head popped up at the other end. Now the man at the head braced himself against the cadaver's shoulders and pushed downward as hard as he could, making the feet jump out again, as if about to begin a sprint up the nearest wall. The sight of the rod-like, uncovered lower legs rigid on the edge of the coffin at first horrified me, so macabre and grotesque did they appear. But after several minutes, the spectacle of my dead brother's legs pausing so long in mid-air took on a comic aspect. Why didn't they simply jump down onto the floor? That the villain Tom Mix had shot and killed should lie still on the road where he had fallen was understandable. But here was my brother, who it seemed only the other day had given me a penny to purchase the *Daily Eagle*. What I was seeing brought to mind the picture of myself and my friend Issie Cherry see-sawing in the neighbourhood playground. Finally, after crooking the cadaver's knees, they were able to shut and nail the lid closed.

No doubt the recollection of this scene, many years later, inspired my poem "The Comic Element," in which I describe a man getting shot in a cabaret and seeming to execute a piaffer before falling stone-dead to the floor. The plain truth is that the image left me unable any longer to take death seriously or to treat it other than a cosmic joke, albeit one that can start tears in a person's eyes.

FIVE

In 1925, in my final year at Alexandra School, we moved to City Hall Avenue above Duluth. The exodus of Jews from St. Elizabeth Street and those streets neighbouring it had begun. My mother had gotten some insurance money after my father's death which enabled her to buy the house where we lived while I attended Baron Byng High School.

Our new domicile consisted of three rooms and a store, this time a real store with two large plate-glass windows. Because there weren't as many people in the house, only my mother, Dora, Cousin Fanny, and myself, and because the store was spacious and bright, we did not feel cramped as we had formerly.

We had an unpaved yard which in the summer gave off the most awful smells because the sewage system didn't work properly and our neighbours opulently flung their garbage right there in the dirt lane. Our neighbours were mainly French Canadian. There were the familiar quarrels and shouts during the weekdays and the drunken revelries on Saturday nights. However, we got along very well with them because they were all my mother's customers and she was very generous in allowing them credit.

My bed, which was really a sofa, was in the kitchen. The stove at one end of the kitchen, and the painted cabinet facing it at the other, occupied much of the space and left room only for the sofa, a small, rectangular table, and a couple of chairs. But late at night it became a room of my own, and for the first time in my life I had a feeling of privacy. It was there where I later began to do my first serious reading.

That summer, instead of seeking a job as a messenger boy, I became a peddlar. My mother sent me down to an old Roumanian crony of hers, Mrs. Wiser, who had a wholesale dry-goods store. Strul had gotten his first credit there. She and her husband supplied him and most of the Jewish peddlars that came from Roumania and other East European countries. On credit, she supplied them with packets of needles, lace, overalls, linens, hosiery, and the peddlars scattered to the surrounding villages with the ambition of turning some of the inhabitants into permanent customers. Mrs. Wiser advanced me five dollars' worth of merchandise and some needed advice on how to sell the paltry assortment of goods I had packed into the small satchel my mother bought for me.

That summer I felt grown up, for my real bar mitzvah occurred when I walked into Mrs. Wiser's store. I was outfitted with knickers and what were then called golf-stockings, a pair of second-hand shoes, for I'd had it drummed into me that I had to present a very neat appearance if I was to succeed as a businessman. Yes, that was the honorific title my mother and sisters conferred on me, and I must admit it made me feel very important.

In spite of the odds, I proved a good salesman. Most of the women who answered my knock or ring were French Canadians. My schoolboy French was lamentably inadequate. What sold my threads, packets of needles, and cards of buttons, my shoelaces, children's socks, and thimbles, was not my halting French but my eagerness and the novelty of seeing a thirteen-year-old assume the role of a grown-up salesman. By the end of the summer I had two very large valises bulging with dry-goods. By refusing to let slammed doors and angry frowns deter me from knocking on door after door, I had also developed quite a large clientele. Each sale was a kind of glory, a small surprising victory. Meeting new people and going into strange homes was colourful adventure. If I can put it paradoxically, it was the poetry of business that really appealed to me. Not the moneymaking, not the satchels growing bulkier and bulkier so that their very leather seemed to be glowing with pride and satisfaction. My success gave me a kind of recognition at home I'd never been able to secure before. Hyman and Joshua, both in New York now, only knew vaguely of the triumphs I was pulling off on the battlefields of City Hall Avenue, Colonial Street, and St. Dominique.

I enjoyed going down to Mrs. Wiser's and making my order for merchandise surrounded by older, more self-confident peddlars. I drank in the respect everybody seemed to offer me. I enjoyed being treated as an equal. All this gratified me immensely, but nothing more than the admiration I now got from my mother and my sisters. In our world, admiration and money are the two most important criteria of a man's worth, and I now had them both.

With two fat valises and regular customers that bought on tick and paid me for each week, I seemed launched on the road to certain prosperity. So my words crashed like a gigantic wave on a fertile shore when I said that I wanted to register at Baron Byng High School. My mother, my sisters, and even Cousin Fanny thought I'd taken leave of my senses and loudly said so. "Why stop in the middle of such a profitable career? Why don't you just carry on and maybe Strul will give you a helping hand?" That last sentence shows how far my entrepreneurial success had disordered their wits. I was a young horse that everyone wanted to back into traces to pull forward the family's load of hopes and expectations.

Why did I yearn to go to high school? It's a genuine mystery, one that's puzzled me for many years. My experience at public school had been for the most part painful and profitless. My dismal record at Alexandra should have convinced anyone that I was no student. Bored and restless, and hating restraint of any kind, I'd been a bane to all my teachers with the exception of Miss Benjamin and Miss Franklin. My curiosity had never been awakened. Whatever penchant I may have had for beauty or excellence had been allowed to lie dormant.

It could have been in part my father's influence, turning me away from the satisfactions of monetary success, but he would not have been in favour of high school. If I had wanted to go to a Yeshiva, yes, or if I'd wanted to become a rabbi, yes. But to go to Baron Byng? Frankly, I don't think it would have meant anything to him.

It wasn't because I had friends who were going on to high school, though even if there had been someone, I doubt that it would have generated enough envy to make me want to go, because I had no clear notion of what high school was all about. I don't remember ever yearning to be an accountant or dentist, or a tradesman of any kind. I never thought about the prestige that setting broken bones or drawing up columns of figures would bring me. Equally, I never thought of myself as someone who could earn his living by being a whiz-bang electrician or plumber.

Perhaps it was simply just the novelty of studying Latin that fascinated me. By evoking in my romantic imagination names and places remote and unfamiliar, I was able to invest them with a dream-like enchantment. Algebra, about which I knew less than nothing, had the same effect. I had no idea what Algebra was all about. It was only the word that intrigued the embryonic poet. *Al-ge-bra*. I thrilled to those three syllables.

Perhaps that is the key to the mystery. What made me register at Baron Byng was the poetical evocativeness of two words, *Latin* and *Algebra*: perhaps also my feeling that learning them conferred some status on me in the minds of people as ignorant as myself of what the two subjects entailed.

My first day at school was filled with the usual trepidation.

I felt insecure and suspicious, not knowing what I'd let myself in for. Five rows of desks, six boys in each row, the teacher's larger desk at the front, the unmarked blackboards behind it, and that was it. There were no pictures on the wall except one of the reigning monarch, George V, and his queen. No adornment of any kind, no attempt at beauty. A Union Jack in the middle of the wall, to whet our patriotic appetite, sagged just above the head of the seated teacher. Nothing to stimulate the imagination, nothing to arouse or nourish a sense of wonder. Everything was spare, severe, utilitarian. A prison cell with teacher as guard or policeman.

Once settled at my desk, my first thought was who was going to be the one to try and take my crown away? Where was the challenge going to come from? Which kid would pick the first fight? I looked around to see whether there were any boys who seemed stronger than myself and, to my relief, saw none that I couldn't take on.

The thoughts that followed were more dismal. I was not as well-dressed as my classmates. They all wore suits, I didn't. And I could see that some of them were better mannered and seemed more assured, more self-confident. They came from the north of Montreal, from middle- or lower-middle-class homes, from homes more cultured than my own. Their mothers weren't forever screaming and cursing and becoming hysterical if her son helped himself to a banana or an apple. I couldn't imagine them having siblings who were constantly enraged about something or other. I couldn't see a Strul Goldberg coming into their well-furnished homes and bellowing like a bull.

Without being aware of it, I was learning the crude determining sociology of our environment. I realized, well, there are kids better favoured socially, economically, sartorially, and physically. There was a mixture of envy and resentment and sadness in my young, troubled soul, and perplexities I would later try to find the releasing words for and labour to put into poems. Sitting there in that room, my mind is a grey cloud in an empty sky, small fears and gusts of emotion are shaping into indistinct forms, into faces that keep dissolving into one another while waiting, waiting. And then the door opens and the teacher walks in.

Mr. Hoover might just as well have dropped down from Mars. He was neatly dressed in a blue serge suit and had an irritating self-confident smirk fixed on his face. His determined manner seemed to say, "I'm here to order you about for the term." In the weeks that followed, he lived up to his reputation, that of the bully who believed he made his harshness acceptable if he accompanied it with an affected smile. We began calling him "Mr. Who-re," and the name stuck. To this day it works like a Masonic sign whenever grey-haired Baron Byngers meet, generating a knowing, affectionate laugh. Because I did fairly well in the subject he taught, Latin, Hoover had some kind of respect for me but I never could warm up to him. He was too aloof and his smile never convinced me.

That first term our French teacher was Mr. Cayley. A dapper fellow with white hair. He had a pinkish face and the skin was a smooth membrane pulled tautly over the bone structure. But if I recall him now, it's not for his appearance but for the malicious way he had of dashing up and down the aisles with a little stick in his hand, a ruler or a book. For no reason, he would smack the heads of the pupils and shout out our names derisively, as if mimicking some anti-Semitic madman. The neck-slapping and ear-cuffing were psychic perks he allowed himself every day. The rumour was that he had gotten his balls shot off during the war, but I was sceptical; I refused to admit that he'd had any testicles to begin with. His sardonic inflections still ring in my ears, the taunting modulations: "Co-hen!" "La-za-ro-vitch!" "Gold-man!" At that time Jewish boys took any kind of insult that frustrated weaklings or white-haired eunuchs levelled at them.

In the second term, my teacher was Mr. Calder. He was tall, freckle-faced, red-haired, and he had wet, puffy lips that pursed grotesquely when he became angry, which was often. When he smiled, his gums showed. None of us liked him and I think I was at my worst and most destructive in his class. He was, if anything, even more sadistic than Hoover or Caley. Into what bin of rotten apples do school boards reach for teachers like these? There was no meeting on any level between Calder and his Jewish students, no possibility of him understanding where we came from and what the nature of our experiences might be. Do I have to add that he lacked the willingness or imagination to even try? A WASP, afflicted with the usual emotional anorexia, an unmelting icicle shoved up his rectum.

Imagination? One day, Calder thought up a plan to put names of all classroom offenders on the blackboard. In less than a week there were five or six names staring bleakly at us. Every time I or one of the other offenders was guilty of a misde-meanour, Mr. Freckles would put down a star next to his name. Calder's ingenious idea was this: whoever attained the first ten stars would "get the strap." I had nine, and so did Finklestein, who sat two seats behind me. Rubbing his hands, Mr. Calder pointed this out during the afternoon's history lesson. When he finished speaking I couldn't help but shout, "Sir, whoever wins, it'll be a smashing victory!" "Out!" shouted Freckles. "Go get the strap."

I went to the principal's office. The leather strap was kept in a book in which each strapping was entered. I brought it to Calder and he led me across the hall into an empty classroom. The expression on his mottled face told me plainly that he was determined to make me beg, or cry. He commanded me to put out my right hand and, raising his own that held the strap to almost level with my chin, came down as hard as he could. Then the miserable sadistic *mamzer* told me to put out my left hand and again came down on it with all his might. Though the limit was no more than three for each hand, he gave me twice that. I felt my hands becoming puffed-up cushions. But I was resolved that not a single whimper should escape my lips. What firmed up my resolve was the sight of Calder's flushed countenance growing redder and redder with disappointment and exasperation. He had no right to give me six "biffs" on each hand. Had I known that I could have reported him. It was a week before I could bend my fingers, so swollen had my hands become. Has he also joined his freckle-faced, red-haired Saxon ancestors, and are they all mouldering in the same Protestant cemetery? I'd rather imagine him still living. If he is, I hope his strapping hand is paralyzed at his side, all his fingers fat tubers, disabling him from scratching the maddening itch in his groin.

In the second term, our French teacher was Mr. Séguin. He came in each morning wearing a white boutonniere and smelling faintly of perfume. He treated the French language he taught us like a lover. Each time he pronounced a French word it was as though he were releasing it to the class with a loud kiss. Then there was Mr. Henderson. He taught us history. He had a trick of theatrically exaggerating his anger for the slightest offence, cowing not only the offender but the whole class. And Mr. Loomis or "Lummox," as we called him. Shell-shocked in the war, he was pathetic because he so obviously meant well but was too weak and gentle to enforce the needed discipline.

Between Calder and myself, after the biffing he had given me, there was constant war, and I fantasized inflicting one scurvy trick after another on him. I ended up flunking the term and again I had to ask myself what the hell I was doing in Baron Byng. I did no homework, I played hooky as often as I could, and plainly showed my contempt for the mediocrities posturing as teachers. I exhibited all the features of the bored, indifferent student – which is exactly what I was.

Then comes a teacher who prepares the way for the Messiah.

82

It is September 1926, I am repeating a grade, and I find myself in Mr. Saunders' class. He was the master who was given any boys considered difficult to handle, the rebellious ones, and I certainly fell into that category. He was short, stocky, and had a very marked burr in his speech. I took an instant liking to him. In one day during that first month he was able to influence my life more than anyone else except my father. In *one* day.

From my seat at the back of the room I watched the mellow September sunshine splashing over the desks and across the floor. Standing sturdily in front of the class, Mr. Saunders asked for silence. We all looked up expectantly. Then, instead of taking the poem we were supposed to have for the lesson, he began to read Tennyson's "Ballad of the Revenge."

He read Tennyson's poem with colour, with excitement, and conviction. He made the sea-battle come alive. Here were Grenville's ships, those small gallant boats, those dogs of Englishmen, those insignificant marauders taking on Spanish might, challenging the Spanish armada. Saunders' reading got across to us the gallantry and courage of these small English ships defiantly attacking the galleons of the armada. Small boats tacking around the tall, thick-masted ships of Philip II and taking heavy punishment but refusing to keel over, refusing to retreat. It was easy for me to identify with the underdog fighting the rich and powerful. I saw myself as Grenville, as a brave Englishman fighting for his country's honour and his own.

Yes, Tennyson was magnificent, but it was Saunders' reading that did it for me. I'd never heard the English language so beautifully read, so powerfully rendered, and I remember sitting quietly in my seat and listening enraptured as the sounds filled the room, thinking, "Holy Moses, this man takes language seriously." It was a revelation to me that someone could get so excited about words. So I lost my heart to Saunders completely and became one of his star pupils. That term I ranked second or third instead of last. From then on, I was to begin getting very good marks, not only in literature and history but in every subject Saunders taught.

I wrote one of my weekly compositions about him, and called it "Sandy." It was an affectionate portrayal of the man, which I found out he has kept to this day. (Mr. Saunders wrote me a touching letter the first time I was nominated for the Nobel Prize by Italy, several years ago. Understandably, when my *Collected Poems* was published in 1971, I dedicated the volume to the man I feel was mainly responsible for it.)

That Saturday, after Saunders' reading of Tennyson's ballads, I ran down to Diamond's Bookstore on Bleury, corner of Vitre. I'd never before been to a bookstore, and there I was at age fourteen in Diamond's, looking around and seeing the volumes by the English poets such as Shelley, Wordsworth, Sir Walter Scott, several of whose names were vaguely known to me because I'd studied some of their poems in school. Certainly Shakespeare's name was familiar.

Then my eyes lighted on a volume of Tennyson which had a rust-coloured cover that looked like stale, dried blood, gilt-edged, with the name of the poet embossed in gold on the spine and cover. I picked up the book and was carried away by the sensuous smell of age and must. Only the scent of a woman's shoulders can enchant me like one of those leather-bound, gold-embossed books. How inviting, how full of promise, was the aroma that came from the pages of *Tennyson's Poems*. It was the first volume of poetry I'd ever bought.

After that, I haunted Diamond's second-hand bookstore. Every Saturday morning I went down with whatever spending money I had been able to accumulate by doing errands for my mother or scrounging from my oldest sister Gertie. On some of these trips, my nephew and at that time my sole friend, Bill, would accompany me. He and I have remained friends for nearly six decades and our favourite recollection is that of our forays into the inviting depths of Diamond's.

Later we foraged through other second-hand bookstores. All the money I was ever able to beg, steal, earn, or borrow went into buying books. By the time I was fifteen or sixteen, I had most of the major English poets in my library.

In a lucky hour, I picked up a volume of Sir Walter Scott. Bound in soft leather, it was his *Collected Poems.* I read "Marmion," "The Lady of the Lake," and all his other stirring narrative poems. Then I found some volumes by Bulwer-Lytton who seems to have disappeared as a writer though in the last century he had a very solid reputation, rivalling that of Dickens. I also bought Victor Hugo's *Les Misérables* and a set of Dumas whose *Count of Monte Cristo* kept me up night after night, reading by candle-light. Afterwards I read his *Three Musketeers* and kept picturing myself duelling for a pair of silver candlesticks whose gleaming reflection obsessed me.

While still in high school I discovered the English essayists: Bacon, Goldsmith, Johnson, Addison, Swift, Hazlitt. I loved Goldsmith's limpidness and sentimentality. I found his prose cool and clear as the vanished rippling streams of the Eastern Townships. For one whole summer, I carried his volume with me through the hot grimy streets of Montreal. I relished the terseness of Bacon's style, like the click of two billiard balls on a pool table. Hazlitt showed me that one could combine bluffness with subtle discriminations and sensitivity.

I brought the volume of Tennyson and some of the other books to Saunders. His eyes lit up as he turned the pages and he burred his approval. For the first time in my life I had found someone who responded to my innermost self with understanding and silent applause. I could never hope for that kind of response from my family. Now I had the bit between my teeth and I was running down to bookstores and filling the shelves in the kitchen cupboard with my prized possessions. I was finding things out. One book led me to another. Before long I was plundering the shelves of every second-hand bookstore in Montreal, looking for volumes by Jane Austen,

George Eliot, or any other unfamiliar author whose name had been dropped in my hearing.

Needless to say, my new-found passion separated me even further from the directions in which my brothers were going. Whenever Larry (as Joshua now called himself) came to Montreal, there was always the same ritual. He'd give me a jacket and a shirt that he'd outgrown, then take me to a barbershop where he and I would have our hair cut. From there, we'd walk down to Horn's for a meal of French toast and coffee. After that he'd take out his pack of Camels and offer me one.

My brother Hyman, on the other hand, when he paid one of his rare visits, would take me to a whorehouse. Or at least he offered to do so on one particular visit, more to impress me with his new-found sophistication than because he thought the experience would do something for my acne. I loftily told him I was in love, which I was, and didn't want it sullied. We dropped the matter and never referred to it again.

My oldest brother, Harry, never took me to a barbershop nor offered to take me to a brothel. He had now moved from New York and was living in Cleveland, Ohio, and I hadn't seen him for many years. He had grown into a proper, reserved young man who voted Republican. He was as straight-laced as they come, without either Larry's generosity or Hyman's exuberance. I don't recall his ever bringing me a present from Cleveland or offering me a cigarette or taking me to Horn's for a meal. He didn't seem to have the slightest interest in learning what I was doing and though he had seen the small library of books I had accumulated, not the slightest interest in finding out what I was reading.

I was therefore greatly surprised when he once sent me a brief letter enclosing a crisp American dollar bill. I was touched by this unfamiliar display of affection and generosity. What better way to honour it than by purchasing a book I could deposit in my library? That Saturday afternoon I hurried down to Diamond's and scanned the shelves for an appropriate volume. This was the time of the famous Scopes' "Monkey Trial," and that year the most sensational news was the progress of the trial with the name of Scopes' defending lawyer, Clarence Darrow, being linked with monkeys as often as that of Darwin's. The big question in everybody's mind was: were men descended from angels or from apes? So when my eyes alighted on Darwin's controversial *Origin of Species*, I bought it with the dollar Harry had sent.

With the volume tucked under my arm, I think I ran all the way home, excitement mounting with every step I took. Now, I told myself, I was going to find out what all the fuss was about. I'd even seen my mother scowling and heard her Yiddishing the name of Darwin. Her tone left no doubt as to where she had consigned him. I got the distinct impression from her and my sisters that he wasn't too popular with the rabbis either. Only my brother-in-law, Bennie Cohen, the intellectual, had anything to say in Darwin's defence.

When I arrived home, my mother was taking her customary Sabbath nap. Unable to restrain my excitement at actually having Darwin's heretical volume in my possession, I bounced into the bedroom. The noise of my entry had startled her awake. When I held up the book, nearly shouting, "Ma! This man says we come from the monkeys!," she raised herself up on her elbows, opened her eyes wide, and uttered the words that have continued to ring in my ears until this day: "May your bones rot under the earth with Darwin's and the monkeys' together!"

It was in Saunders' class that I had begun to write poems seriously. My family looked on these first efforts with something like consternation. They made me feel that I was doing something terrible, that no sensible Jewish boy would ever allow himself to do. I cannot hope to communicate the panic I experienced when I found myself compulsively scribbling my poems. My mother kept telling me I was wasting my time and ruining my chances of making a living in the future. She and my sisters now looked at me as if I had contracted a hideous disease.

I wrote a long poem entitled "A Vision" after reading Shelley's "Revolt of Islam," whose language and imagery enthralled me. In my poem I describe how I climb a promontory and, looking down, see the toiling masses below doing all kinds of meaningless, absurd things in an effort to survive the wretchedness they inflict on one another. Scornful and proud, I am the visionary, hurling my anathemas at them. I ended this long poem, my first ambitious composition, with the following couplet: "O God, rather that I were dead,/Than I with daily toil should earn my daily bread." That reveals something about the conflict already beginning to rage in my adolescent soul.

In Grade Ten, Mr. Henderson was again my teacher. This time the subject he taught our class was English literature. One morning I came in with a volume by Omar Khayyam. Whenever I came in with a pile of books under my arm, instead of rushing over to see what they were, my classmates, thinking I was very odd, would back off as hastily as they could. I'd bring in Shelley, Byron, or Wordsworth, and the effect was always the same. That reaction fed my sense of superiority and bolstered my arrogance. The flavoursome taste of my imagined eminence drove me to seek out those few individuals whose simple admiration gave me sensations even the most delectable *petit four* could not equal. I considered the students and instructors ignoramuses, morons, fools. "Fools" was my favourite ascription for them, and I would fling it out at the slightest provocation. I was beginning to display all the nastiness of the frustrated intellectual snob.

Only the knowledge that a demon lived in my soul sustained me. He whispered secrets meant only for me. To this day, when I initially encounter someone, the question that pops into my head is: "Does he have a demon in his soul?" Early I concluded that far too many on this planet did not. And the world became one boundless classroom peopled with faces whose smugness rounded them to bursting like gas-filled balloons, tempting me to explode them with a pin-prick. Their comicalness made me hold my sides with laughter.

When Henderson saw my volume of Omar Khayyam he picked it up and carried it to the front of the class. Instead of praising me as Saunders would have done he began to mock me. I can still see his lips pursing derisively. In a loud mock-falsetto voice he began to read some verses. He must have enjoyed his histrionics for his performance lasted for the better part of the lesson. Affecting to skirt around the poet's sensualism as though it were a sewer, he stopped sneering at it only to assail the immortal Persian who had given it winged words. His performance done, he walked down the aisle and tossed the book on my desk. He then pulled out a volume from his desk and read "Invictus" in a clear, firm voice: "I am the master of my fate;/I am the captain of my soul." Lowering his voice dramatically to cap a performance Sir Laurence Olivier might have envied, he said in a hoarse whisper, "*This* is poetry."

So there it was, right at the start. Henley's Protestant banalities versus Omar Khayyam's luxurious sensualism. That told me everything I needed to know about my frost-bitten countrymen. (Had I owned a crystal ball I'd have discerned in it the processions of academics, of nerveless colonized English Canadians, of beer-drinking yokels and virginal spinsters, male and female, whose disapproving squeals have not ceased to astonish me ever since the publication, in 1945, of my first collection of poems, *Here and Now*.) Poetry was not for them.

Were I doing a film I'd make this episode its focal point, for nothing so clearly monitored what an erotic, foreskinless poet was up against. Henderson was a good teacher, interesting, sensitive. He was an intelligent, clean-living, Anglo-Saxon, always soft-spokenly persuasive except when he was indulging his thespian shtick. He honestly believed he liked poetry and wanted his pupils to share the pleasure he derived from reading it. Nevertheless, the above event planted the suspicion I've ever since found impossible to shake. I simply can't get myself to believe it likely that any member of the sanitized middle-class, any professional wearing a co-ordinated three-piece suit can experience the real *extasis* of poetry. Gentility and repression have destroyed whatever emotions they might at one time have had for it. Technology, the scramble for empty distinctions, the corrosive profit-motive, have blunted the dendrites of their nervous systems. Their gifts lie elsewhere. In engineering or law, in public relations or journalism. In scholarship and literary criticism which live off the sweat of the solitary genius who suffers and creates.

Later on, I learned with conflicting feelings of dismay and delight that there were at least five or six in this country who were better equipped than I to respond to the rage and wisdom of poetry. I've heard the rumour of there being more than the handful I've so far encountered. Despite false leads and many disappointments, I remain sanguine that one day I shall meet them. Sitting at a table laden with the choicest wines and graced by the presence of handsome gymnasts and goddesses with entrancing bronzed cleavages, we shall make ourselves ready for the Messiah's coming. But consider this: What if the Messiah is life itself, whose sparkling and dithyrambic inflections ask us not to wait but to see and enjoy here and now?

SIX

I am swimming underwater and catching sight of strange ferns and schools of fish silent and unconcerned about the intruder in their midst. Now and again I am startled by algae-covered boulders that suddenly rise up before me, a jettisoned suitcase, a broken oar, or a worn car tire. How long have they lain there slowly being altered? Such are the water-logged memories that lie on the lake bottom of my mind waiting for me to turn them over. What is the self but memory's secretion? Obliterate an individual's or nation's memory and you have destroyed their identity. An event is to selfhood what the grain of sand is to the pearl that forms around it. Identity is the coral reef that memory builds.

In an energetic boy, memory and cognition don't play a big part. To him, the universe is a matter of feeling and sensations, of emotion rather than thought or memory. His mind has not yet had a chance to card-index experiences. Certain thoughts remain unformed because he lacks the words for them. Death became more real for me when I was able to make a comparison between a live cockroach and the brown smudge on the wall after I had killed it. Only when I became aware there was a difference did I begin to ask myself questions about how and what and why. I was beginning to separate myself from the cosmos, to acquire an identity of my own. With the death of my father, I achieved a degree of self-consciousness, but since he was a remote figure who lived on the periphery of my life, it was not as large as that given to me by the death of my cat Ketsel.

One Friday night the family had gone to visit some friends and my mother had foolishly left the Sabbath candles burning. She must have done so because she was too pious to snuff them out and she couldn't very well ask either Dora or me to commit the sacrilege. When we came back, we found a small crowd gathered in front of our house. We saw fire trucks and thick hoses running from them or coiled like pythons outside the house. The fire had been put out and all the rooms smelled of smoke and charred wood. I was surprised that my mother was not overly distressed by the spectacle of havoc that greeted her eyes. If I'd known the word insurance, I could have imagined her rubbing her hands in joyful anticipation of the sum she was going to collect.

Ketsel must have overturned one of the candles because the greater damage in the kitchen indicated that was where the fire had started. My shod feet waded through the water that had collected on the floors. I was looking for Ketsel and found her lying inert on the windowsill. Quite plainly she had been trying to claw her way out from the suffocating smoke but the window had remained fast. That's when I first saw the tight smile that cats have for meeting death and lodged that image in my head for a poem I was to write several decades later.

I remember thinking, "Why was my precious bed-warmer given such a horrible death?" She had been a good mouser and had brought me nothing but pleasure. I had loved stroking her, feeling her warm furry body against my bare chest, and teasing her by playing with her whiskers and tail. Why would the God of Abraham, Isaac, and Jacob wish to slay her? That's when my faith in a benevolent deity received its first big jolt. Only a small cloud of doubt at the beginning, it grew bigger as I began to notice other things that didn't quite square with the notion of a caring God.

Even after the demise of my father and Ketsel, had I been asked what death was, I couldn't have answered. I was unable to connect it with anything in my experience. I saw the cat lying wet and stiff on the windowsill, but could not understand what had reduced my lively animal to this inert state.

Since a belief in immortality is not greatly stressed in Judaism, I had only a vague idea of an afterlife. I seldom thought about it. When I did, however, I found myself wondering whether I'd catch a glimpse of the God of Abraham and Isaac. I wondered also whether my father's shade would ask me to roll some cigarettes for him or the furry spirit of Ketsel jump into my lap and allow himself to be stroked. And if it did, what would be the sensation in my hand? It was the sense of nothingness that I could not accept, of an oblivion that had no bounds and seemed to expand blankly in all directions. It was the mystery of death, its unknown force, which obsessed me and made me frantically ask my mother over and over again whether I was going to die. No amount of reassurance would appease me. The thought that one day I would simply be no more pierced me with an icy chill.

A child sees the brown smear on the bedsheet that was once a bed bug, the inert cat whose warm fur he once stroked. If this child is fated to be a poet, he stares at the yellow-brown spot for a long time and at the lifeless cat, which now, for some inexplicable reason, he is loathe to touch. From that he will go on to the questions that will plague him for the rest of his days. What is the meaning of life and death? What kind of world is this? How should one comport oneself when life is so precarious and death so inexplicable and certain? What else is art but a defiance of the nothingness, this unbroken silence into which everything drops?

In Montreal where I spent my boyhood, the euphemism for death was "Paperman's." You'd hear people say, "He's been taken to Paperman's," and you'd know that they were talking about someone who had just died. Paperman's had its modest origins on St. Elizabeth Street. They were only a block or so up from where we had lived. I think I got my first trauma when I learned that the Paperman family made their livelihood from storing cadavers on the ground floor of their house. It was said that Mr. Paperman had taken on the job because he was a very pious man and no other Jew in the city wanted it. Paperman's is now a thriving funeral chapel which serves the Montreal Jewish community without discriminating between the pious and the impious. (In a funeral chapel there is no such distinction, only that between rich and poor.)

I can see myself in my knickers and knee-high stockings fastened by an elastic, walking down St. Elizabeth on some errand for my mother. I come to the last streetlamp before the dark, awesome patch that is Paperman's. Its feeble radiance gives me some comfort. I know that Paperman's is there ahead of me on the right, and with a child's perversity I challenge myself to walk past slowly, daring myself to look at the fortified windows to see whether any corpses are lying uncovered on the floor. Then the constricting fear fastens its fingers at my throat and I start running quickly, my heart beating as if it were about to jump out of my chest. Only when I reach the bright lights and safety of Ontario Street do I begin to breathe easily.

At that point in my life God held the same dread for me as death. When I tried to imagine what God's face looked like, I would see a black beard like my father's and crossed eyes like my grandfather's, which I saw in the photograph he had allowed my mother to snap before she sailed for Canada. In my childish mind, God was the "Great Forbidder." On the Sabbath, He didn't let me whistle or run or play baseball in the back lane. He demanded that I go to synagogue every morning and every evening to intone the *Kaddish* for my dead father. God was particularly distressed, I was told again and again, when a Jewish boy drank a glass of milk after he had wolfed down a chicken- or a salami-sandwich. God's archangels kept a large leather-bound tome for the sole purpose of chronicling any failure of mine to say prayers or to observe the various rituals designed to keep me in His good graces. There were so many rules by which I was supposed to regulate my young life, all of them in some way cutting into my natural playfulness. Today it astounds me how easy it is to pervert the mind of a child so that it can never straighten itself out or dislodge completely the rubbish that has been poured into it.

It is a grievous sin for an orthodox Jewish boy to eat a slice of ham, or flick the lights on during the Sabbath. The thought of my doing any of these things made me tremble, though I wasn't certain what form the expected punishment would take. For openers, God might reach out a hirsute arm and strike me dead at His jewelled feet or turn me into a pillar of salt as He had done to Lot's wife. Well, I was never tempted by ham or pork but the light-switch on the wall tantalized me like a nipple. Tiny and brown, it seemed to wink at me whenever I passed it. It tempted me because when the Sabbath came, the switch too was something that was forbidden for me to touch.

One Sabbath, when my mother was taking her afternoon rest in the bedroom, I found myself staring at the switch. By then we were affluent enough to afford electricity. Curiosity threatened to overcome my fears. Filled with apprehension by what I felt myself being driven to do, I paced back and forth, always keeping my eyes on the inviting fixture as if I were mesmerized. No timorous lover could have stared more anxiously at his beloved's white bosom. Again and again, I put out a hand to touch, and as quickly drew it back. Finally I was no longer able to restrain my impulse and with a trembling finger I flicked the switch. No sound I'd ever heard rang more loudly in my ear than the click that shattered the room's silence. God Himself had pronounced His sentence of doom and the light that came on was His lightning bolt. I fell back terror-stricken against the wall and waited for the next one to kill me. My whole body was shaking. Luckily, that afternoon God was busy with more important matters than my sinful infraction. When I had sufficiently recovered, I placed that experience alongside that of seeing Ketsel lying stiff and unmoving on the windowsill. My simple experiment had forever weakened my trust in the faith of my forefathers. Once again doubt filled my mind about the ubiquity of God. I didn't breathe a word about that to my mother and sisters. However, in the months and years that followed, my behaviour spelled it all out clearly enough for them. I refused to say *Kaddish* for my father, and later on wouldn't let any rebbe prepare me for my bar mitzvah. My mother cursed and railed, my sisters implored me not to break my mother's heart, but for me, without benefit of Nietzsche, God was now dead.

My mind keeps turning towards people and events that made me into the individual I think I am. Without doubt the three most important shaping influences were my father, Amos Saunders, and Pussela whom Kotz begat. I acquired Kotz some months after the death of Ketsel. Kotz was a big, mature cat. I do not remember just how I got possession of her. She may well have taken it into her head to follow me home. Despite my mother's loud objections, I had taken her into the house, given her a saucer of milk, and made her feel welcome.

I loved the langorous way she groomed and cleaned herself, the queenly manner with which she stretched herself out on the floor. I loved her thick fur, a patchwork of yellow and black, and her four white paws. Kotz laid the foundation for the difficulties I later had with women. Very few I've known possessed either Kotz's elegance or sensuousness. I couldn't pay a woman a higher compliment than by telling her, "You remind me of Kotz." If this woman opened her eyes wide in astonishment I'd hold forth on the fantastic nature of the cat who had rubbed her fur so often and so delightfully against my leg.

It wasn't too long before I noticed a bulge in Kotz's belly and my mother began railing that I had to take her to the SPCA. Kotz's walk lost some of its graceful elegance and she displayed a greater irritability when I pulled her tail or tried to stroke her whiskers. Seeing that I was obstinate in my resolve to keep the cat, my mother finally relented and told me to get ready for her *accouchement*. She even emptied a box, placed some old rags in it, and reminded me to keep putting Kotz into it as often as I could. After several weeks, the day arrived when she delivered her litter: five blind kittens opening their tiny pink mouths piteously. No nurse was more caring, more solicitous than I, and even my mother would sometimes be found smiling above Kotz and her brood.

No fortune-teller could have foreseen that one of the kittens would have an influence upon me as important as that of my father and in some ways even greater than that of Mr. Saunders. As the kittens grew older and began to clamber out of their box, it became evident that one of them was defective. The poor little thing could not play and frisk about like his siblings, but dragged his paralyzed hind legs along the floor while the others scampered after the ball I had thrown into their midst. It broke my heart to see him, day after day, trying to keep up with his luckier brothers and sisters. I am not using words lightly when I say the anguish was intolerable and that tears would start in my eyes each time I saw Pussela, pulling himself across the linoleum by his healthy front paws. Yet as I clutched the unfortunate creature to my chest, I experienced the intoxicating sense of power that is never separable from pity. At that moment I could just as readily have struck him a savage blow as continue to hold and caress him. Nevertheless, it was Pussela who had all my love and to whom I fed the choicest morsels of food I could find.

One day, about a year later, I came home from school and looked everywhere for Pussela since he was not to be seen on the kitchen floor. For the past several days he had appeared listless and his appetite was off. No longer did he try to compete with the others and that had perhaps saddened me more than the sight of his futile efforts. It was as though he were signalling to me that he had given up the fight and that gallantry, however heroic, was vain and useless.

I found him under the stove. And I had mixed feelings when I prodded him gently and he did not stir, feelings of relief and hurt. Both told me at the same time that Pussela was dead. I picked him up tenderly and carried him into our yard where I dug a small grave and deposited him in it after wrapping him in the cerement of a flour bag that my mother had hung up on the clothesline to dry. And the *Kaddish* that I refused to say for my father I now intoned over the small mound that held the crippled body of my kitten. Many years later, to exorcise Pussela's ghost, as well as vestigial fears and tears, I wrote the poem, "Therapy," and below are the concluding stanzas.

It was its playfulness
with a ball
broke my heart at last;
and I was glad
to see the kitten lying, one afternoon,
deadstill
when I returned from school.

Yesterday
for the first time in my life
I axed a young badger
rummaging in our garbage bin
for food.

And though he wobbled

a short distance
before he keeled over,
I am now strong enough for God and Man.

My experience with Pussela showed me something about success and failure and left me with the ineffaceable sentiment that every human being suffers from some wound, visible or invisible, and given to him at birth. The grandeur in some individuals lies in their striving to overcome that congenital blight or, failing that, to compensate for it. To this very day, I am moved by stories of men and women who meet great misfortune with as much courage and grace as is possible to summon or command.

"A quiet madman never far from tears ..." is the opening of the final stanza of "The Birth of Tragedy," a poem I wrote in 1954. If "pity" is the operative word for the English poet Wilfred Owen, for me it is "poignancy."

A joyous street sight used to be the horse-drawn vehicle. There were several that clattered up and down the street during the day before it got dark. The baker's van, the iceman's wagon, carts pulled along by small ponies. I liked to hear the clomp of the horses' hooves on the asphalt. During the summer vacation, on quiet mornings, the sound was music in my ears. After the ball-game played in the street, the red fire hydrant used for one of the bases, I'd sit on the stoop and watch the carts and vans and listen until the echoes became too faint to be heard. Horses were mysterious creatures to me and I invented my own mythology about them. An urbanized people living holed up in their ghettos, Jews had been cut off from nature for centuries, and had you asked my mother or father to identify some trees or flowers, I don't think either one could have come up with a single name.

Life is a constant oscillation between opposites. For adults it's between serious things like life and death, good and evil, love and hate. For small fries it's between the pleasurable and the painful. Their hedonistic calculus is a very simple one. One of the pleasant experiences the street afforded me was the stolen ride I'd take from time to time on the baker's van. At the back of it was a folding step or seat which the deliveryman used to reach the loaves on the higher racks inside the van. I would jump up and steal my rides when the van clattered to a stop between one delivery and the next further down the street.

One afternoon, my heart filled with July's innocent gladness, I was enjoying a stolen ride, listening to the clopping hooves and waving to some streetmates as I was being driven past them. Had I not wanted to keep my forbidden adventure from the driver, I would have sung for joy, so happy was my mood. But soon I heard sounds of a horse-drawn vehicle that was following the one on whose back-seat I was perched. I turned my head and saw a milk wagon behind us. It came close enough for me to wonder whether the milkman was going to drive his horse right into me. For a moment I thought the horse's head was about to bump against my own, but at the last moment it veered to the left and horse and wagon began to pass us. I saw the driver raise the whip aloft before he snapped it across my face. The unexpectedness of the vicious slash was as painful as the blow itself. I let myself slide down and, rubbing my sore cheek, I saw the stiff, upright backs of the two carts proceeding down the street.

My eyes filled with tears, but it was the unanticipated malice behind the slash that hurt more than the throbbing welt beginning to puff on the left side of my face. I wondered whether I would be left with a permanent scar and began to shout an abbreviated litany of my mother's favourite curses. Had I truly known about *schadenfreude* it might have reduced the pain and bewilderment. Why had he done it? I wasn't stealing a ride on his cart. I was unable to find any nobility in his motives, such as fellowship with another carter or the desire to see delinquency punished. How could I have known that this episode was fortifying the foundation for a vision of human evil that later I would find articulated with classical perfection in *King Lear* and Dante's *Inferno*?

As I walked home, thoughtfully fingering the welt on my cheek, I experienced a strange feeling of lightness. It surprised me that my mood could change so swiftly from anger to elation. At the time I could not have explained to myself or to anyone else what was happening inside me. It was the sudden awareness of new feelings, all clamouring for recognition, the onrush of new thoughts, that gave me a sense of relief amounting almost to exhilaration. My mood was both detached and cheerful, not unlike that which I had experienced when I saw my brother Avrum being forcibly shoved into his coffin and then turned into a seesaw; as though, it now seems to me, death itself was providing a humorous and grotesque commentary on human existence.

From then on, I developed an unappeasable appetite for unfamiliar sensations and feelings in my morbid search into the ambiguous nature of the human soul. I wanted to experience things for their own sake and my curiosity was like that of botanist or entomologist seeking out new flowers or insects to classify in a notebook. An entire uncharted world seemed to be looming up before me and I ran forward eagerly to meet it. My father praying in his corner of the bedroom, my mother uttering her maledictions, sister Dora's irritability as she tugged at my hair or pulled my ear, Hyman's robust cheerfulness and occasional sadism, the small tear-filled eyes of Rebbe Schecter's wife – all these things now assumed meanings they formerly had not had. The perplexing depths of experience changed suddenly from murkiness to clarity and they drew me in. I wondered, What does it feel like to betray a confidence, tell a bare-faced lie to friend or teacher, steal a fountain pen from Woolworth's, start a quarrel with a Chinese classmate? From now on, with Faust-like arrogance, I wanted to be the sole author of my emotions and not wait for events and people to thrust them upon me.

Poeta nascitur non fit. There's no way you can make a poet any more than you can train anyone who doesn't have the necessary co-ordination and body frame to become an Olympic swimmer. What are the needed genetic ingredients to make a poet? I don't think anyone will ever answer that question satisfactorily. It's probably a mixture of strains rather than any single one of them. I can toss out words like imagination, curiosity, fascination with language, sensitivity, a lust for living. These are the first things that come to mind. Add, if you wish, a visceral feeling about the world, about life and death, a morbid introspectiveness as probing as a surgeon's knife. And, of course, naïveté.

It was the Olympian Goethe who remarked that a poet stays naïve all his life. I wonder whether he meant by that the poet's sentimental impracticality about mankind, his constitutional inability to learn prudence from the scalding experiences that happen to him again and again. Were it not for this naïveté would the poet have the heart to go on writing his ineffectual verses? I think it was Mayakovsky who said that a poem is a kiss given to the world? Who else but the naïve poet is able to pucker his lips to kiss that old sourpuss, the world? Just as a woman, after she has given birth, mercifully forgets the pains that came with the delivery of her infant, so the poet blanks out from his mind the griefs human malevolence and stupidity have caused him.

However, in a blood-soaked century that has seen two murderous world wars, the deliberate extermination of millions of people, and the fire-bombings of unprotected cities, death and evil have lost whatever significance they may once have had. But the unlooked-for consequence of that is that life too has lost its meaning and significance. Only when a man's life is singular, only when death comes to him in the fullness of time, and not because of impersonal economic and social forces, can human existence be viewed as tragic or heroic. The methodical gassing and vaporization of countless individuals in the death camps, Hiroshima, Stalin's Gulags and butcheries, the death squads in El Salvador and Guatemala, and terrorism threatening to become the dominant ideology in the century ahead; these, besides making the human face a fearsome, hateful thing, have reduced mankind's struggles on this planet to the level of insects scurrying desperately for food and shelter. Several years ago I wrote the following poem to articulate thoughts which had their beginnings, I suppose, in the first cockroach I'd clubbed to death with the heel of my shoe.

THE FINAL MEMO

Sir Mortimer
why did you do it?
Both terror and beauty
lie buried in a mass grave.

After Auschwitz and Hiroshima
who believes in funerals any more,
in the dignity
of dying for Cause or Faith?

You were the singular rod
by which we measured our lives,
its meaning and worth;
in your shadow we threw off radiance.

You were the supreme Antagonist,
majestic and severe;
almost we overcame you

with tragedies and religious myths.

By your excesses
you make a mockery of everything;
show us our lives are merely
a rumble of panic and grotesqueness.

SEVEN

A mass of lovely brown curls on a white pillow. Cheeks that health had crimsoned. The child's eyes closed in sleep. The long black eyelashes. That had been my first glimpse of Suzanne. My mother had taken me, when I was little more than a child myself, to visit my sister who was then living on Drolet Street, Esther having decided to leave her sadistic husband for the fifth and, as it turned out to be, the last time. She had rented one of her rooms to Mrs. Rosenberg and her two small children, Suzanne and Sacha.

That was the first time I'd heard the word Bolshevik. From my mother's tone when she pronounced it, I sensed I was supposed to feel some kind of reciprocal horror on hearing it. I tried to imagine what crimes I was expected to associate with the hissed word, but since my experience with evil was still somewhat limited, I satisfied myself with a vague, nameless dread.

As the days passed, I began to sew together the several patches of disapproval on my mother's part. The largest patch was Mrs. Rosenberg's atheism. Shaking with anger, lips tightening with sarcasm and scorn, my mother one day exploded: "She doesn't even believe in God!" What made Mrs. Rosenberg's atheism so heinous was that in Russia she had married the son of Rabbi Rosenberg. (Many times I had brought a dropsical chicken to the revered rabbi on Duluth Street to find out whether it was kosher-edible or not. If not, my mother's two dollars had been thrown away; there would be no chicken soup, and, for me, no scrawny chicken's neck for the Friday-evening meal.) Mrs. Rosenberg was now widowed, her husband having been captured and shot during the civil war by the White Guards.

The furious snortings, gum-clackings, and lip-curlings continued for as long as Mrs. Rosenberg had her room at Esther's. My mother paid her weekly visits and each time a sour, ill-tempered argument would break out between her and Mrs. Rosenberg as the two bigots squared off to determine the existence of God, and whether a belief in His goodness was necessary for one's salvation. I was never present at one of these Homeric contests, but for many years after, Esther could never recount them without breaking into hysterical fits of laughter. My sister had my own sense of the absurd, sharpened by having lived – too long, she would afterwards snort – with a short, chicken-boned, strutting Litvak who thought he was Napoleon each time he sold a tablecloth to a French Canadian. There are victories besides those won on the battlefield. In Bennie Cohen's mind, a large successful sale was another Jena or Marengo.

Bennie Cohen thought himself an intellectual and from the height of the five or six books he had read, he looked down on the immigrant family he had married into, throwing out names like Marx, Kropotkin, Ferdinand Lassalle. Their incantation put a puzzled look on the faces of my mother and father when they heard it. Besotted as Bennie was by the importance he attached to the few paltry ideas he had rattling around in his head, there was something in my father's quiet dignity that kept his unpleasant snarling in check. Bennie's small pale-blue eyes darted with repressed indignation, his fine thin fingers drummed on the table, but he kept his voice low and respectful. Instinctively he felt my father's faith was not a matter of mere words and argument. Under the intense, meditative gaze that seemed to gather the grief and wisdom of the centuries into it, Bennie squirmed like an insect on the sharp point of a pin.

After the Rosenbergs left Esther's we lost track of them. Then, several years later, when we had moved to City Hall Avenue, my sister told us that she had run into Mrs. Rosenberg on the street. She was now living about a block away from us just below Duluth Street. The news sparked my interest and curiosity. The image of the child sleeping so peacefully that I'd caught when passing her room had not dimmed in my memory. It had been a vision of pure innocence and loveliness. Had I been older and better informed I should have likened it to Dante's first glimpse of Beatrice.

Esther gave me their address and the next day I went to see them. I had just turned fifteen and was bumping along as well as I could at Baron Byng. That was my first real encounter with Suzanne, who, two years younger than myself, had grown into an attractive girl somewhat on the plump side. She had the most dazzling white smile, the healthiest rosy cheeks I'd ever seen. Her brown eyes were humorous and candid and filled with good nature.

LYRIC

Come, my love, since life is short
and stormy as the ocean's breast
We'll anchor safely at love's port
And loudly laugh at fortune's jest.

Soon will our toiling lives be spent
And dust and ashes be our clay;
So dearest, to our heart's content
We'll live and love this very day.

This early lyric, the first *"carpe diem"* poem I'd ever penned, was written about a year before my meeting Suzanne. I don't remember which damsel inspired these lines; most likely it was the one living on Henri Julien, one block east of our street. Since Tillie also was a student at Baron Byng, I sometimes found myself walking her to school. Once she asked me to come to her house to meet her older sister who wrote verses, I was informed, and had a beautiful singing voice. The sister's name was June. I took to Tillie because she had a self-confident air and was something of a tomboy, but there was no real chemistry between us. She soon let me know she didn't share her sister's enthusiasm for poetry. Nevertheless, it was her fate to be responsible for my first obsession. It was what happened to her mouth when she pronounced the word "prunes." The lips puckered as if about to bestow a kiss, though that was not her intention at all.

Actually, I preferred her older sister who had the kind of plumpness my hands yearned to touch and feel. But being several years older than myself, and courted by swains who had coins jingling in their pockets, the hot looks I threw her from time to time only amused her. Besides, I was Tillie's property and she had heard about my obsession to hear her sister articulate the word "prunes" over and over again.

As soon as I caught sight of Tillie, I would turn into a madman, pleading to see her lips form the word. After several weeks of my steady harassment, she took to avoiding me, finally making it plain that my presence was no longer welcome by rushing into the house whenever she saw me coming. She even took to going to school by another route to make it unmistakably clear she could no longer stand the sight of me. It may sound crazy but I was terribly hurt. I thought that my yelps of admiration each time she puckered up her lips would flatter her into feeling the same delight that I did.

So yes, I think it was Tillie's kissable mouth and the never-to-be-tasted pleasure it promised that moved me to write the lyric. At that time, I had already discovered the sentimental verses of Shelley and Byron and thought myself cut from the same romantic cloth. Love and death were joined in my mind, for I had taken to spending time among the graves in the Protestant cemetery on Mt. Royal Avenue. Their evidence that all things were transitory evoked within me a pleasing melancholy that made he feel superior to the few friends I had and to the dull, insentient clods who were my classmates.

When I brought the poem to Suzanne, I told her that she was the inspiration for it. Scratch a poet and find a liar. (It's no accident that lyre and liar are homonyms.) Her large brown eyes showed her pleasure, and she asked me to read the poem.

Mrs. Rosenberg had a thin, hatchet-like face and a smile that always surprised me by its unexpected friendliness. Though a graduate with high honours in physics and mathematics, Mrs. Rosenberg had a passionate love for literature and it was from her that I first heard about Tolstoy, Dostoievsky, and Turgenev. Needless to say, she had communicated that love to Suzanne. Within a month, I was reading *Crime and Punishment* and asking for more titles. Suzanne loaned me her copy of *The Philanderer*. That was the first Shavian play I'd read. She also let me have Maxim Gorky's *Mother* and Romain Rolland's *Jean-Christophe*.

Mrs. Rosenberg belonged to a Communist cell and Suzanne was a member of the Young Communist League. They were the first Communists I'd met. Recalling my mother's strictures, it thrilled me to know that I was doing another thing that she and my conventional sisters would turn away from. In the late twenties, communism was an evil word, throwing up images of lawless men and bearded bomb-throwers. They were dangerous people that had to be watched carefully or they would destroy the state, the family, and synagogue. They stood for REVOLUTION and every right-thinking person was expected to help in their detection, and have nothing to do with them. It excited me to know that I was conversing with one of these dangerous characters; moreover, one who had herself participated in the Russian Revolution, her husband having been killed fighting for it. I felt that I was touching the lit fuse of history.

Suzanne took me to a meeting of the YCL, hoping to make a convert of me. She was a fiery advocate of communism and spoke with the infectious enthusiasm that springs from ignorance and foolishness. Mrs. Rosenberg, though no less fanatical than her daughter, always spoke coolly and objectively, a cigarette dangling from the corner of her mouth, her eyelids half-closed against the smoke that rose from it. Later I heard the rumour that Stalin himself had bounced Suzanne on his knee, so close had Mrs. Rosenberg and her husband been to the party leaders.

Suzanne introduced me to the Communist classics. She brought Marx and Lenin to my notice and as a present she gave me a paperback edition of Bogdanov's *ABC of Communist Economics*. Now, for the first time, I read about the labour theory of value, monopoly capitalism, the class struggle, and the foreordained world victory of communism. Temporarily putting aside Byron and Shelley, I devoured the *Communist Manifesto*, Engels' *Ludwig Feuerbach*, and Marx's *Class Struggles in France*. For another gift Suzanne gave me her own well-thumbed copy of Upton Sinclair's anthology *The Cry for Justice*. All of it heady stuff for a youth in his early teens and, as impressionable and idealistic as I was, my mood rapidly passed from exaltation to despair and back to exaltation again. With no ballast of experience or common sense, I spent hours declaiming before a mirror and reciting passages from *The Cry for Justice*. Nevertheless, the lyrical impulse was not entirely quenched, for one afternoon I brought another poem to Suzanne, this one had in truth been inspired by her.

> *The rains will come and pass away;*
> *The brown buds hanging from the bough*
> *Must soon adjust their twinkling fans.*
> *Will you love me now?*
>
> *Their songs are to the season sweet,*
> *And I must wait their potent prayer*
> *When grasses climb that bitten hill,*
> *I will kiss you there.*

It was Suzanne who also got me to read the thick, elephantine novels of Dreiser. In short order I ran through *The Genius*, *The Financier*, *The Titan*; all of them best-sellers at the time of their publication, now they're almost completely forgotten. *Jennie Gerhardt* and *Sister Carrie* made me one of his apostles and, by showing me what strength and veracity lay in naturalism, sent me to the novels of Emile Zola. Both writers were at war with the genteel and the puritanical who wanted to throw a blanket over the inescapable indelicacies of the human animal. I liked that very much. I also liked their compassion and sympathy for the poor, stupid, blundering creatures fighting for survival and, against all odds, for their dignity. It was Dreiser who first showed me the griefs that lay in a woman's soul.

Growing up among the self-serving hypocrisies respectability calls good sense and social truth, I was grateful to Dreiser and Zola for scraping away the varnish that family, school, and Jewish piety had shellacked on my raw encounters with the world. They gave the lonely, rebellious adolescent the courage to resist. They made him feel less lonely, less of an outcast.

Though Suzanne was eloquent, and Mrs. Rosenberg was calmly and exasperatingly logical as she screwed up her eyes into a patronizing look, they failed to convert me to their creed. One time, arguing with Suzanne, I called her great hero Lenin a murderous Tartar. Tears started in her eyes and began to roll down her cheeks which anger had enflamed. She started to sob so violently, at first I thought she was putting it on. When my apologies didn't stop her weeping, I put my arms around her and drew her towards me. This was the first time I ever held Suzanne close and I thought it was as good a chance as I'd ever get to put my hand on one of her ample breasts. She didn't push my hand away or stop sobbing so I took it as encouragement to cup and fondle her other breast. Lenin never had better allies than Suzanne's round globes, and if I wasn't won over to communism then and there, it was because I heard Mrs. Rosenberg stirring in the next room.

In my last year at Baron Byng, a classmate brought me to a meeting of the Young People's Socialist League. His name was Sol Berman. Sol was a socialist because his father was one. He'd been talking up socialism from the time we had found ourselves together in Saunders' class. But perhaps because he was a poor speaker his words never gripped me in the same way that Suzanne's rolling sentences did. He always talked earnestly and never doubted for a single moment that public ownership of the means of production would bring in the millennium of universal love and brotherhood.

Dogmatism both fascinates and repels me, my awareness of life's rich contradictions making me suspicious of formulae and moon-raking, political or literary. The burgeoning poet already sensed that words could be used as counterfeit money to fool and cheat the gullible. Like the frenzied lover, I scorned them one moment only to lavish my praise on them the next. My ambivalence towards words carried over to the people using them. The more sincere a speaker, the more perversely certain I became that he was deceiving himself or trying to deceive me. I believe that explains why Sol's earnestness, like Suzanne's vehemency, tempted and yet left me strangely detached. I listened, argued, read the books and pamphlets they put into my hands, but remained unconvinced. Suzanne took to calling me a phrasemonger and Sol, giving one of his despairing shrugs, said I was a hopeless dreamer whose brain had been softened by too much poetry.

Maybe he was right but I don't think so. If anything had been softened it was not my brain but my heart. After all, Shelley and Blake had already left their mark, so had Byron's defiance of tyranny and oppression. Lenin's iron-fisted revolutionism, like his small eyes and cruel mouth, never failed to send a chill through me.

Sol lent me his copy of Robert Owen's *New View of Society*. I fell in love with Owen's ideas for the betterment and welfare of mankind; I found myself wondering whether the Messiah, when he came, would preach a nobler gospel. Robert Owen's

112

character and ideas settled my mind. I joined the Young People's Socialist League because his humanitarianism was close to the humanism I had unconsciously absorbed from my Jewish environment. I could never imagine my mother or father, however angered, ever striking anyone. I could see Mrs. Rosenberg spilling blood for the sake of her cloud-woven New Jerusalem. Screwing up her eyes and smiling ironically, Mrs. Rosenberg would insist, "You can't get omelets without breaking eggs." She and her daughter trotted out that Leninist recipe more often than I care to remember. Each time I'd have an image of a bald-headed cigar-chomping bourgeois having his skull cracked open like an egg and the bloody yolk running down his white shirt-front.

My protests only got Suzanne angry; anger made her more attractive by deepening the flush on her cheeks and making her eyes sparkle. She never looked more gorgeous or desirable. Our disagreements usually ended with my trying to embrace her and her pushing me away . . . for the first five minutes. When I felt her resistance diminishing, I'd kiss her gently and placatingly. She always responded by putting her arms around my neck and giving me a hug. Afterwards, over cups of coffee in the small kitchen, we'd discuss her favourite novel, *Jean-Christophe*.

To make the plight of the jobless an issue in municipal politics, the Communists decided to call a demonstration. The rally was to start at Victoria Square. Of course, the city fathers forbade it, but nothing was going to stop Suzanne and other party zealots. She saw herself as another Rosa Luxemberg, as a proletarian Joan of Arc, rousing the exploited masses to storm the barricades; at least to pull some of the cops, whom she branded cossacks, from their mounts. She'd gladly have let herself be mauled under the hooves of their charging horses, so keen was she to play out her role of heroine or martyr. For the sake of the Revolution!

One Sunday, I had come early to take Suzanne for a walk to Parc La Fontaine. She hadn't said a word to me the day before about the rally that was to take place at two p.m. I could tell from Mrs. Rosenberg's nervous chain-smoking that a sharp conflict was raging in her mind. How could she forbid her daughter to follow in her own footsteps? Hadn't she stormed the Winter Palace with her husband? Hadn't she argued tactics with Trotsky and some of the other Bolshevik leaders? She had been a card-carrying Communist all her adult life, even now in a country she tried desperately to see as repressive as the czarist Russia she had helped to destroy.

But age and experience had brought her prudence, the wisdom of the philistine, bourgeois or communist. She worried Suzanne might be nabbed and put in jail, and that could have terrible consequences for her daughter who, after all, was still only a teenage girl. The authorities, servile tools of the capitalist class, might decide to expel Suzanne and then she'd have to be a factory worker and become one of the exploited. No, this was definitely not the fate Mrs. Rosenberg had in mind for her daughter. So, with increasing exasperation, mother and daughter argued back and forth, pocking the same unyielding terrain with their blasts and counter-blasts, until I proposed a solution. What if I accompanied Suzanne to make sure she didn't make herself too conspicuously revolutionary? I'd be there to keep her cat-calls and insults to a decent minimum. Shaking her head with relieved acquiescence, Mrs. Rosenberg told Suzanne she could go to the demonstration.

Suzanne hurried ahead of me, so eager was she to reach Victoria Square, and when we arrived it seemed to me cops and horses outnumbered the jobless standing uncertainly in groups of four or five as if waiting for the order that would make them coalesce. I kept a tight grip on Suzanne's arm while the demonstrators sang the "Internationale" and kept taunting the police. Several times she struggled to get free of me, but I'd given my promise and was determined to keep it. With rising anger, Suzanne called me a "capitalist lackey" and a "social fascist." Only from a safe distance did I permit her to shout "Cossacks!" and raise a clenched-fist salute aggressively at the indifferent air. When it looked as if the rally was over, I felt I could now leave Suzanne to her own devices, which turned out to be a mistake.

That evening, no sooner had I appeared in their doorway when Mrs. Rosenberg began hurling incoherent sentences at me. Surprised by her unexpected outburst, I stepped back and nearly rolled all the way down the landing below.

Only after I had sufficiently recovered did I ask meekly what the matter was.

"I trusted Suzanne to you!" she exploded. "And now she's in jail!"

I remember thinking, that's no way for a Bolshevik to talk. She's behaving like any ordinary Jewish mother. After filling my head with images of heroic self-sacrifice for the sake of the exploited working class, here she was wailing that her daughter had to spend a night in jail. To say I was disappointed would be putting it mildly. Nevertheless, looking at her drained face, I wondered what Suzanne had done, as if the answer would appear on Mrs. Rosenberg's furrowed brow. She turned her face away, as though the sight of me was intolerable, and began to roll a cigarette.

"Look," I said, trying to make the words forceful and convincing, "when I left, the demonstration was over. Suzanne must have done something afterwards, when I'd gone."

It turned out Suzanne had gotten together with several other "fire-eaters" after the demonstration broke up, and had thrown rocks at a non-offensive policeman standing quietly at one of the corners in the square. My restraining grip on her arm had prevented Suzanne from using the demonstration as an opportunity to display her revolutionary zeal. But how could the proletariat know how much she yearned to improve their lot unless she threw rocks at the police and called them "Swine" and "Cossacks"? How could they learn how much she wanted to strike the fetters from their ankles and wrists unless she gave the clenched-fist salute every five minutes?

The following afternoon Suzanne was released. Now her credentials as a Communist agitator were unassailable. She could now take her place beside her mother and fit four-square into the picture she had of herself as a defiant Elinor Marx or Emma Goldman. When I saw her later that same day, she could scarcely hold back her exuberance. Her oratory and fervour scaled heights they had never reached before.

The consequence was exactly as I'd foreseen. Suzanne was expelled from Baron Byng. No matter what I thought in self-justification, I couldn't suppress the twinges of guilt. That night when I went to see her, she hardly spoke a word and seemed strangely subdued as she cleared away the supper dishes and later helped Sacha with his homework.

Mr. Astbury was the school principal. In spite of my bad reputation at the school, I made up my mind to see him about Suzanne's expulsion. Mr. Astbury had a hectic flush in both cheeks and a patch of thin hairs on his head, but my attention was rivetted to his mouth which slanted under his long, bony nose. What dismayed me were his eyes, which never looked directly at me but darted from side to side like two pinged marbles. When he asked me what I wanted to see him about, I imagined the words dropping out sideways from his mouth.

"I'd like to speak to you, sir, about Suzanne Rosenberg who was expelled last week," I said, trying to keep the quaver out of my voice.

The principal said nothing, but gestured with his right hand for me to continue. The blood rushed to my head as I began to speak warmly on Suzanne's behalf. I said she was very young and had been misled by people older than herself. They had exploited her idealism for their own purposes. I told him she was a voracious reader and had gotten me to read many important American and Russian writers, and I rattled off the names of Tolstoy, Chekhov, Sherwood Anderson, and Theodore Dreiser. That must have impressed him though I doubt he'd ever read a single novel of theirs, or even heard of them before that afternoon.

I also thought it politic to say that Suzanne had been taught a lesson she would never forget and was now full of contrition for what she had done. That was my masterstroke. The word "contrition." It went like a bullet straight to his Methodist heart. There was no mistaking its effect, so I massaged his virtue bump for several more minutes. I could see he was beginning to be moved by the glow he felt because he was about to forgive a repentant sinner. When he told me Suzanne could return to her class the next day, the slanted smile on his face made him look like a benign shark.

After my reinstatement in Mrs. Rosenberg's affections, Suzanne and I continued to wrangle constantly about what road should be taken in order to overthrow the capitalist system. Violent revolution or Parliamentary democracy? Ballots or bullets? Peaceful reform or a bloody uprising of the working class that would wrest power from the fat-bellies who profited from the exploitative wage system? Each time I held out for gradual reform she hit me with her choicest epithets. I became a "renegade socialist." A "traitor to the working class," and a "cowardly revisionist." When I told her I had joined the Young People's Socialist League, her scorn and disgust were boundless. It still amazes me that the ties of affection and trust we had forged over the preceding months were not destroyed. We continued to meet frequently – sometimes to trade books and gossipy news, sometimes insults – either at her home or at Horn's Cafeteria, if either of us could come up with a dime for two cups of coffee.

The Yipsel membership hovered between twenty and twenty-five, but the meetings held on Sunday mornings were open to anyone who wished to attend once the weekly business was taken care of. If it got out that a well-known radical, local or out-of-town, was going to lecture, the hall was filled to bursting. Suzanne always turned up to heckle the speaker and denounce everyone present, myself included, for being "social reformists who were leading the proletariat into disaster." When she really got going, there was no stopping her flow of fantasy and invective. Neither the worst nor the best, she was "full of passionate intensity."

Political rhetoric and hyperbolical utterance were the staples of the day. Saviours were a dime a dozen, each one flogging his apocalyptic nag into the perfect society and asking the rest of us to follow. There's no drug more palatable than altruism for leaving its proponent with a good opinion of himself. At the time it seemed to me everyone I met had only one mission in life: to make me happy by showing me the one sure road to a world without poverty and conflict.

Suzanne was too young to be taken seriously as a secular messiah but the animal magnetism she possessed whenever she talked about ending exploitation and class injustice was not without its effect. If I remained unconvinced it was because, despite my excitability and naïveté, I was a mocker, as I had doubtless been even in my mother's womb. During the most solemn, the most frenzied occasions, my sense of the ridiculous kept breaking in. When Suzanne pulled out all the stops and let herself go, arraigning Ramsay MacDonald and the German Social Democrats, I'd have an image of her rising from the floor and floating over our heads like a small dirigible. Perhaps her somewhat blimpy figure lent some plausibility to the ludicrous image.

A few months after Suzanne's re-instatement, Mrs. Rosenberg took it into her head to return to the Soviet Union. Though she was doing well in Canada – her earnings as an operator in a clothing factory enabled her to provide for herself and her two children, to pay rent on a solid five-room house in one of the better neighbourhoods – she had swallowed her own propaganda about Communist Russia being the Promised Land. No Zionist could have sighed more mistily for his exile's return from the Galuth.

After the downpour of Wall Street stockbrokers from their office windows, which began in October 1929, every capitalist country went staggering into a depression. Soup kitchens were opened in the east end of Montreal, as they were in other cities, and once-prosperous merchants were seen polishing apples on street corners for sale at five cents a piece. This, and the swelling unemployment figures strengthened Mrs. Rosenberg's faith in the communist system. In church and union halls, Communist agitators told their audiences there were no jobless in Russia. In Russia, there were no rich and poor, everyone was equal, the mines and factories belonged to all, and education was free. Nobody dying from cancer or diabetes need have a day's worry since medicine was socialized.

First to take leave of their senses were the journalists. Had Walter Duranty been paid by the Kremlin to retail his syndicated omissions and distortions, he couldn't have done a more convincing propaganda job. Ditto Anna Louise Strong. Poor Mrs. Rosenberg was blitzed out of her mind. Soon the journalists were seconded by writers with world-wide reputations out to prove that intellectuals could be as stupid and gullible and naïve as anyone else. Mesmerized by their own verbiage, they signed up for passage on the Ship of Fools. It gives me an unholy glee to list their names: Bernard Shaw, Sidney and Beatrice Webb, Romain Rolland, Ernst Toller, Lion Feuchtwanger, Henri Barbusse, and Harold Laski, who became the guru of the left-wing intelligentsia.

The Rosenbergs left Montreal in the spring of 1930, and sailed directly into the whirlwind of the first Five Year Plan and Stalin's maniacal fury to collectivize Russia's agriculture. They sailed into the filth and baseness and crimes of the most tragic period in Russian history. As I was to learn, Mrs.

Rosenberg soon realized the extent of her folly, but, alas, there was no escape from the prison she had entered and into which she had dragged her two innocent children.

After an impatient wait of several months, I finally received a letter from Suzanne describing the primitive backwardness in which she was mired and from which she saw no exit. She was too proud or too ashamed to whimper, but I could read between the lines, even those she didn't write, and what it added up to was her anguished disappointment with the Workers' Paradise and the New Soviet Man. The smiling, open-shirted Stakhanovite she had seen on the covers of *Soviet Russia Today* turned out to be a vodka-swilling boor who obstinately insisted on taking his baggage of filth and primitiveness with him into the communist society dreamed of by Marx and Engels. The pamphlets and books the Rosenbergs had read and the speeches of Tim Buck and Fred Rose (later convicted as a Soviet spy) hadn't prepared them for the dictatorship's coerciveness and the incessant drumbeat of its brain-numbing propaganda.

The Rosenbergs had left their comfortable home in Montreal and their dignity as free human beings not for the Workers' Paradise but a paradise for tyrants and maniacs. Their experience was with servility, lies, corruption, and a privileged minority that kept itself in power by the frank use of terror, by the enslavement and inhuman degradation of tens of millions, by the Big Lie. Everywhere they went the rank odour of mediocrity triumphant enveloped them. Yesenin and Mayakovsky had committed suicide. Both Mandelstam and Babel were to perish in the wastes of Siberia.

Suzanne's letter was not encouraging, but since by that time I was through with school and still in love with her, I thought of following her to Russia. As a left-wing socialist, I too had swallowed some of the fables being spread about the Soviet Union. In books and numerous articles I read about the government's determination to suppress anti-Semitism and to promote culture. Completely unknown to me – presumably because I didn't want to know about them – were Stalin's atrocities and his barbarous treatment of the country's writers, composers, and painters.

I wrote to Suzanne asking her to find me a position as an English teacher in one of Moscow's high schools. She replied and, though her account of what I could expect didn't sound too inviting, I wrote back and pressed for more details. To this letter I received no reply, nor to the many frantic letters I afterwards wrote, asking her to explain her strange silence. It wasn't until many years later that the mystery was cleared up.

My mother had shown one of Suzanne's letters to Dora and they decided that something had to be done to save me, a reckless, impractical fool, from ending his life, as it might well have turned out, in one of Stalin's Gulags. So they began to intercept her letters and keep them from me until my brains had cooled and I'd stopped my frenzied chatter about going to the USSR. Ten years later, when I was cured of my illusions, my mother handed me the cardboard box which held Suzanne's yellowed letters. The anger I felt was quickly overwhelmed by a sense of gratitude and admiration for my mother's good sense.

What happened to the Rosenbergs? I learned many years later that they had lived through the murderous Five Year Plans, the show trials of 1937, the Great Terror, the Nazi invasions of 1941, and the terrible suffering of the war years. They had trembled anew when Stalin and his brutal cohorts dreamed up the "Doctor's Plot" to stoke up again the fires of Russian anti-Semitism.

After freezing and starving in one of the Siberian concentration camps, Mrs. Rosenberg died, probably without the makings to roll herself one last cigarette. Suzanne had married before the outbreak of war and her husband had been shot on a trumped-up charge. She herself spent several years in one of the camps, doubtless leaving behind some of her radiance and most of her strong white teeth which had so dazzled me when she gave me her first smile. Sacha, who, I learned, had grown into a handsome, intelligent, and fun-loving individual, took his own life. Released from the concentration camp after the death of Stalin, Suzanne remarried and afterwards gave birth to a daughter whom she named Vicky.

Recently, hearing that Vicky was living with her Canadian husband in London, Ontario, I drove up to see them and handed her the following poem, entitled, simply, "Vikki."

You bring me news
of someone
I loved a long time ago
– you, her daughter.

Achingly I retrace your lineaments
into the large brown pools
and flame-red cheeks
that once made a fool of me.

If you wipe away five decades
I was an urban pod
bursting with poems and vivas;
I was young and crazy with love.

Your mother's love
was socialism and Lenin;
she once sobbed for hours
when I called him mad and vicious.

The mean-souled Tartar
took away her youthful bloom,
her husband, her handsome dark-eyed brother:
the first shot, the other driven to suicide.

In a Stalinist camp
his minions even finished off your grandmother:

fiery, sharp-tongued Bolshevik,
a cigarette forever dangling from her lip.

In your own quivering mouth
and uncertain stare
I read contemporary history
and graph my love's lost hopes and illusions.

EIGHT

My last year at Baron Byng had been memorable for two particular reasons. I met David Lewis at the beginning of the school year and got expelled near the end of it.

Lewis was a member of the McGill Labour Club and a very ardent socialist, although there was never anything fiery either in his manner or in the weekly lectures he gave to the members of the Young People's Socialist League every Sunday morning. He became our mentor in the economics and politics of socialism. Terms like "monopoly capitalism," "class struggle," and "historical materialism," which I had heard from the lips of Suzanne and her mother now acquired substance and definition for me. Lewis had a clear, logical mind and was a convincing speaker, but he lacked the fire and disciplined passion to be an orator. There were no flashes of wit or humour. There were no imaginative assaults on mind and senses. He was too cool, too self-possessed to ever let himself go, too fearful of the unknown, too literal-minded to venture very far into that dark thicket. Listening to him, I felt he carefully planed his sentences as a carpenter might plane door jambs. Earnestness, integrity, the uplifting note of idealism coupled with a two-by-four logic that appeared to make the unattainable attainable, such were the qualities that made his audiences give him their reflective assent.

He was no Pied Piper, but an uncomplicated individual with a few simple ideas about the nature of man and society which, with the passing years, became his certainties. His unshatterable self-confidence went a long way towards compensating for the originality that he lacked. He always gave his listeners the feeling he knew where he was going, that he had the blueprints for the future safely tucked away in one of his pockets and that they would be doing the greatest service to themselves should he convince them to walk stolidly after him.

David Lewis had a large influence on me because I was young, naïve, and self-divided. My heart refused to accept what my head told me only too painly was the imperfect nature of men and the world they built. As I expressed it later in a poem, I had two legs, one metaphorically shorter than the other. What I revered one moment, I found myself mocking the next. If I was not a cynic, it was because I didn't possess the certainty that cynicism demands for its exercise and enjoyment. Not only did I have legs of unequal size but they wanted to hop in opposite directions. Adolescents are unstable psycho-chemical compounds, a hormonal riot of conflicting impulses and desires; paradoxically the most predictable thing about me was my unpredictability. What I embraced one day, I rejected the next and, no sooner had I given my admiration to a book or its author, no sooner did I embrace someone and want to have him call me his friend, when I found myself seeking reasons to undermine my admiration, to brake my feelings of amiability and trust. No doubt of it, I was split down the middle and though the two halves of me were legging it in opposite directions, I nevertheless felt they were both moving towards some kind of disaster.

Lewis was only three years older than myself but gave me the impression of being much older than that. The self-assurance that had so impressed me on our first encounter derived not only from the possession of an acute mind but also from his abbreviated stature. Perhaps because short people are closer to the ground they develop the feeling in others that they stand more securely on it. Sometimes when I looked at him, he put me in mind of a tree stump – solid, firmly rooted in the soil, immoveable. Whirlwinds might come and go or for that matter the blasts of history, of wars and revolutions, but come back and you'd find the stump exactly where you'd last seen it. Precisely because I was a young enthusiast whom impulse bent this way then that, his tree-stump solidity impressed me.

Lewis succeeded where the Rosenbergs had failed and socialism began to replace the faith of my forefathers. He convinced me one didn't have to wait for the Messiah. The Messiah was already here in the form of the proletariat and was only waiting to be recognized as such. If the meeting hall of the Yipsels on St. Laurent wasn't exactly a synagogue or temple, I could still think of my fellow Yipsels sitting on the plain, hard-backed chairs as acolytes and worshippers of the new faith, and David Lewis earnestly delivering his weekly sermon to strengthen it. The troubles and confusions that had bothered me during the week evaporated before the incantation of "the inevitable victory of the working class," "the expropriation of private property," and "the classless society." No matter how often I heard these phrases repeated, something in me thrilled to them. Political happenings became crystal clear in my mind. It saddened me that others wilfully blinded themselves to what could lift mankind out of its meaningless turmoil and suffering.

Shelley's poems in one pocket of my worn-out jacket and the *Communist Manifesto* in the other, I'd have lunch at Esther's because she lived on Clark Street only a few houses away from Baron Byng. Having to care for her two young daughters on the stingy support payments her estranged husband gave her, she always appeared worried, unhappy, and beaten down. But there was lots of spunk in her for all that, a vitality that only needed encouragement to show itself. She had a beautiful soprano voice. Had it been trained, I'm sure it would have brought her fame and riches.

Esther always prepared some tasty sandwiches. I won't say there was any great affection for me, certainly little insight at a time when what I most hungered for was someone to whom I could pour out the self-doubts that were troubling my soul. However, she did her best: when one is hungry, even a stale biscuit will do. My lunch breaks with her were of short duration. During the ten or fifteen minutes I was there, I'd bolt down my sandwich and plate of soup and then dash out to be back at Baron Byng where I could read my book in the classroom before the bell rang, and other students returned from lunch.

It was on one such occasion during my first month of classes that our new teacher, Mr. Steeves, stole quietly up to my desk where I was sitting absorbed in a novel. Since I hadn't seen or heard him approach, he startled me by putting his arm around my shoulders. It was his unfortunate face I'd taken a violent dislike to. The lips were too thin, the eyes were too pale, a light blue and sort of watery, yet they had strange yellow glints in them. There was no warmth in his manner. He was the tight-assed colonized WASP incarnate, unctuous, insincere, and dry. I still ask myself how people get to be that way. What is it that knocks the good psychic bran out of them and leaves them limp?

Steeves' subject was algebra. True to my track record, I didn't do well in it because I didn't like the instructor. He must have heard from my other teachers that I was something of a problem pupil. My reputation as a loud-mouthed maverick must have preceded me and often been a subject for conversation in the teachers' faculty room. In addition, knowledge of my almost daily visits to the Protestant cemetery increased the general mistrust and uneasiness my behaviour aroused. Indeed, my strange behaviour in and out of the classroom had already made me a legend in the school. Teachers and students were at a loss to reconcile my prowess as a scrapper with my love for literature, especially my passion for reading and writing poetry. As well, my penchant for heated political debates was generally known, as was the malicious pleasure I took in crushing my opponents with sarcasm and invective. Though I yearned to be understood and loved as only a poorly dressed, acne-spotted adolescent can, my nonconformity marked me as someone who inspired fear and dislike.

I felt myself completely alienated from my surroundings, but in the midst of my unhappiness, I would experience sudden raptures that unaccountably flooded my being like sunlight in an unswept courtyard. I was different and knew myself to be so. Though the journal I kept was desultory, there was nothing desultory about my writing verse. Subconsciously seeking to win, if not the approval, then at least the tolerance, of my classmates, I read my poems to anyone I felt had the sensitivity to respond. Repeated disappointments never cooled my foolish optimism.

This particular day there were no other students in the classroom. They were still out stuffing their craws. When Steeves put his arm around my shoulders, he leaned forward, his face almost touching my own, and said he wanted to be my friend. He said he wanted to be helpful to me in any way he could. I broke away and almost shouted, "I don't need anyone to help me, sir." My pride had been touched and I was responding to something in his voice which grated on me. His offer of help, I felt, sprang from condescension, not from concern. Had his approach been warmer, I don't think I would have greeted it with the outburst I did. Undoubtedly he meant well, if only for his own sake. This set the scene for our hostile encounters through both terms of my final year. The conflict between us began to take on a life of its own.

Steevie, as I referred to him, would raise his voice whenever he had to tell me something, be it reprimand or order. Whatever he said sounded like a sneer to me; it was laced with sarcasm. He gave me punishments – lines or detention – for the smallest infraction. Seeing me writing verses seemed to make him dislike me all the more. Purposely I made my scribbling obvious to him. The traits I hoped would bring me to his favourable

Graduation day from Alexandra School, June 1925 (Irving Layton, top left).

Brother Harry and sister Dora, c. 1958.

Brother Avrum, c. 1923, a year before his untimely death.

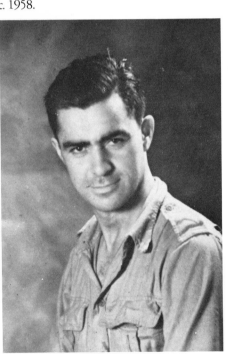

Brother Hyman in the Signal Corps, July 1944.

Brother Joshua (Larry), age 24 or 25.

Layton with his nephew and friend
Bill (Goldberg) Goodwin, c. 1931.

In Montreal, c. 1928

Suzanne (Rosenberg) with daughter
Vicky in Moscow, 1946.

In Montreal's east end, c. 1929 (right).

Montreal's Champ-de-Mars outdoor market, c. late 1920s.

David Lewis (left) and A.M. Klein, September 1926.
Courtesy Public Archives Canada

Irving Layton (left) and Louis Dudek, McGill University graduation photos, May 1939. *Courtesy Old McGill*

Layton with Faye Lynch, his first wife, in Halifax, N.S., spring 1940.

Artillery training in Petawawa, Ontario, 1943.

John Sutherland in his room on Stanley Street, Montreal, winter of 1942-3. *Courtesy Miriam Waddington/Public Archives Canada*

Louis Dudek at Irving Layton's home, Montreal, c. 1955. *Courtesy Gael Turnbull/ Public Archives Canada*

Poet and lawyer A.M. Klein,
mid- 1940s. *Courtesy Garcia Studios/*
Public Archives Canada

Frank R. Scott, undated. *Courtesy*
McGill Archives

Betty Sutherland with her brother
John on steps of Redpath Library,
Montreal, c. 1942. *Courtesy Miriam*
Waddington/Public Archives Canada

Poet Patrick Anderson, c. 1940.
Courtesy Public Archives Canada

Irving Layton teaching at the Ross Tutorial School, Montreal, early 1947.

notice – my love of poetry, my wide reading, my fervent interest in politics, my eagerness for intellectual debate – instead of winning his approval only coarsened the sneer on his thin lips. I was too young then to understand the hatred people feel for anyone who is different.

Next to literature, history was my favourite subject, the one I counted on most to pull my grades up. Unfortunately, somebody had put Wells' *Outline of History* into my hands. Increasingly, I found myself disagreeing sharply with Mr. Rexford, our history instructor. Because he was a short, dapper fellow, close-cropped and very much a martinet, we used to call him Colonel Rexford. He gave the class the usual fairytale about British imperialism being a good thing for backward countries like India, and how self-sacrificing the English were in taking up the white man's burden in faraway, dangerous places. I thought him no better than a fool; and, since Rexford was even shorter than myself, a Lilliputian fool to boot (I'd recently read *Gulliver's Travels*). Rexy held tenaciously to the few ideas his schoolmasters in one of England's public schools years ago had put into his skull. He wanted no one, least of all a Jewish boy from a semi-slum in Montreal, to destroy the comfort they had given him. Our arguments became so violent that one afternoon he told me he didn't want me in the class. When he walked in, I was supposed to walk out.

To the great hilarity of my classmates who had watched this unequal contest between "Rexy-Prexy" and myself, the following took place twice weekly: Rexford would open the door and come in, and I would stand up very noisily, making sure that everybody noticed my slow and mannered exit from the room. Once free to do as I pleased, I'd make for the library to read Shaw's pieces in *Fabian Essays* and Bellamy's *Looking Backward*. Of course, my bible was H.G. Wells' *Outline of History*. The time I spent in the library were my happiest hours at Baron Byng High School, and not only because I no longer was forced to listen to a middle-aged fogey go on about the virtuous deeds of British imperialism. In the library, I felt at home. The world's treasures of wisdom and learning were there for my taking; no one could dispossess me or push me aside. Not, that is, until the bell rang and I'd have to return to the next uninspired pedant which providence disguised as poverty had inflicted upon me.

And then catastrophe! Rexy gave an exam, and of course I was obliged to write it. Like the thoughtless fool I was, I went ahead and scored the second highest mark. Well, that was no great recommendation for Rexy-Prexy; if I could do so well without being present for the lessons, why was he drawing salary? The day the exam papers were returned, he told me that from now on he wanted me back again in the class. In the ensuing days and weeks, I didn't know whom to despise more, myself or the close-cropped martinet whose hostility towards me became more virulent each day.

Now that this sentence of doom was clearly spelled out, I again asked myself, "What in the name of all that is sane and holy am I doing in Baron Byng?" For that matter, what was I doing in a pious Jewish family? And living in a city divided between snobbish, up-tight Anglo-Canadians and anti-Semitic French Canadians more narrowly Catholic in their prejudices than even the Spanish or Portuguese?

At that time, I was questioning the myth of British imperialism, the superstitions of capitalism and Jewish orthodoxy, even the fable that had sent so many young men to their deaths – the one proclaiming the war had been fought to make the world safe for democracy. I had totally different thoughts about the war. I did not see it as a great patriotic effort at all. I saw it as the brawling of demented apes that religious and political propaganda had crazed by working on their intolerable guilts. Because civilization creates in every man the feeling that he is an unclean creature of little or no significance, only the sacrifice of life can free him of his torment forever. The Great War implanted a notion I've held onto ever since:

man is a sick animal who gets his greatest kicks when he's maiming and torturing other humans. Torture gives the twentieth-century louse a feeling of limitless powers.

About one month before matriculation, I got expelled from Baron Byng. The cold war between Steevie and me had erupted from time to time in different ways. The breaking point came in May when once again I was unable to pay my monthly tuition fee. To obtain the needed four dollars my mother never seemed to have in her till when they were demanded, she would send me off with a grocery order to Mrs. Wiser or Mrs. Schecter. Placing the bill in my hand, she'd tell me to ask for payment on delivery. If the one I was bringing the order to had money, all well and good. But it often happened that there was no ready cash in the house and I'd have to return empty handed. Perhaps the next day I would be luckier and then I'd have the money for Mr. Steeves who collected the tuition fees. By the tenth, all fees had to be in. Mr. Steeves was aware of my late payments, and the reasons for them, but this morning he almost hissed out my name.

"Lazarovitch!"

"No, sir, I don't have the money."

Steevie wasn't going to miss his chance to humiliate me. I felt my face reddening. Instead of taking my discomfort into account, Steeves said very curtly, without a trace of sympathy in his voice, "Well, go down to the office." I was stupid enough to expect sympathy.

"I'm not going down," I replied, my tone even sharper than his.

"I said, go down. You have to go down."

"I'm not!"

This argument went on for some time and it would have been amusing had I not felt my skin crawling with humiliation.

I was angry and hurt, I was butting my horns into the empty space like a tormented bull. My defiance was nothing but the reflex action of a class-conscious adolescent trying to save his pride. Any other thoughts I might have had were drowned by the rush of blood into my head. At last, seeing that the class was treating the matter as a huge joke, that his commands were only strengthening my obstinacy, he barked out: "All right, sit down!" And I, acting out of blind emotion, said, "Well, now I'll go."

So, I went down to the office and explained to Mr. Astbury what had happened. As at our first meeting, his eyes darted from side to side like pinged marbles. When I finished, he said quietly, "All right. Now go back to your class and I'll speak to Mr. Steeves." I returned to class, but at noon, when I was sitting in the library, Mr. Steeves tiptoed to where I was, bent over me, and said, "Come with me."

I followed him into the corridor. We were standing beneath a picture of King George V. I can't say that royal philatelist did anything for the queasiness in my stomach. The school clock, solid and square, with black assertive numerals on its face, unsettled me further. Steeves leaned into me and said, "What did you say to the principal?" Despite his red-faced insistence, I refused to answer him and, turning on my heels, I went back into the library.

Later in the afternoon, I was summoned to Mr. Astbury's office. When I arrived, he told me I would have to apologize to Mr. Steeves. Exactly at that moment, as if the whole thing had been rehearsed, Steeves appeared in the doorway; nervous, his face white-flour pale. Astbury repeated his instruction. Defiantly I said I was not going to apologize. So, right there, in front of Steeves, Astbury said, "You must. Do you hear me, you must!"

I guess that's the stuff of which empire-builders are made. A crushing insensitivity to someone else's feelings. The sure-fire combination for conquering other nations, for making them do your will, is self-righteousness and stupidity. Astbury completed the lessons in British imperialism that Rexy-Prexy had started. Couldn't the poor, flustered homunculus with the nervous, never-resting orbs see that I was simply acting out of injured pride? And seeing that, couldn't he have offered to talk about it a little later? Or tried to calm me with an understanding word? Instead, what he did say was, "If you don't apologize, I shall have to expel you."

And I, despite the fact that I had huffed and puffed for four long years to get through high school, found myself saying almost mechanically, though my voice had lost some of its conviction, "Well, in that case, expel me."

And that's exactly what happened. For the last time I entered the classroom and cleared the desk of all my books, note pads, and whatever other writing paraphernalia it harboured. The last book that I removed from my desk was *Shelley's Poems*.

Many years later I had the satisfaction to learn that B.B.H.S. had expunged that episode from their records. I guess neither Baron Byng nor the Protestant School Board wanted it to be known that Irving Layton, known to them as Israel Lazarovitch, was expelled from their school. However, B.B.H.S. has a sure place in history being able to number among its more distinguished graduates William Shatner, the star of "Star Trek."

I was able to keep the news of my expulsion from my family because by now I had a room of my own on De Bullion Street, a room so small that if I wanted to change my mind, I had to go outside.

My mother had remarried during the year, so it was easy to keep the news from her. Though Mr. Hershorn was several years older than my mother, walked with a stoop and used a cane, she was happy with him for he was very gentle and treated her with the chivalry of a young and ardent lover. I believe she had more things in common with him than she had with my father; or it may simply have been that he'd won her heart through the small courtesies he never neglected to pay her.

Living by myself was in no sense a liberation. After all, from what could I have been liberated? From my own oppressive thoughts and feelings? My penury? My increasing dissatisfaction with the world and the poor, frightened, hard-driven specimens of humanity I was meeting in greater numbers than before, now that I no longer had to spend my days in the restrictive environment of an institution? In my tiny room, there was a bed, a wooden chair, and a small bureau where I put my clothes and the top of which I used for a desk. Plain linoleum covered the floor. I recall neither window nor table.

Most of my writing I did in Horn's Cafeteria. My rent was four dollars per month which I paid with money earned through giving English lessons to newly arrived immigrants. Rochel Eisenberg, the librarian at the Jewish Public Library, told them I was a wonderful teacher – and cheap. Fifty cents for an hour's lesson.

The only person I told about my expulsion was David Lewis, probably over a smoked meat sandwich at Schwartz's Hebrew Deli on Main Street. Since that took place over half a century ago, my recollection of the event is somewhat dim; that is, I can't say for certain what his immediate reaction was to the news, nor what my own mood was at the time. Was I angry? Depressed? Defiant or apathetic? There's a strong streak of fatalism in my makeup, or am I dignifying indolence and passivity with a high-sounding word? What I do recall is the deli's hot spicy smells in my nose and Lewis urging me to write my junior matrics at McGill. He thought it would be a pity to let all the years of study end so fruitlessly just because of a silly clash of personalities between myself and Mr. Steeves. His concerned tone was grave and persuasive. It felt good to know that my future mattered to someone.

It was David Lewis who persuaded A.M. Klein to coach

me in Latin for my matrics exam. I had met Klein through David Lewis; they were very close friends. I never missed a debate if they were participants, as I hugely enjoyed the way they polished off their opponents. Klein with his extraordinary wit and gift for repartee and Lewis with his invincible logic that cut like a sharp knife. Once or twice, I accompanied them to Schwartz's Deli and, opening my mouth only to take a bite of my sandwich, I listened enraptured to budding politico and eloquent poet. Perhaps, I would like to believe, they welcomed my presence, realizing my own soul was a battleground where poet and politician were straining for mastery, where the socialist I had become and the Shelley I aspired to emulate made up my composite self. Perhaps both of them hoped that what they were asseverating with such magnificent valleys of spiced sound would fall on fertile ground.

Klein and I met about once weekly in Fletcher's Field just across from the YMHA on Mt. Royal Avenue, and I vividly recall the first lesson: Virgil's *Aeneid, Book II*. I can almost hear again the sonorous hexameters falling from the poet's mouth. No lover could have pursed his lips more appealingly, more sensuously than Klein as he formed the resounding vocables that fell from them. It was almost as if I were watching his own self-hypnosis, as if he were reciting out of a deep trance. Never before and certainly never since has Latin sounded so beautiful to me. It didn't matter that I scarcely understood what he was saying, what did matter was the passion and belief he put into the Virgilian lines. Here was language. Here poetry and passionate utterance completely drowned out the sound of the tram-car rattling along its tracks and the screech of a car that suddenly brakes.

I don't recall Klein ever giving me any actual instruction in Latin grammar or even asking me if I knew my lessons. He just took it for granted that I would do all that drudgery without any prodding from him. What he did was to inspire me with a love of that ancient language and make it come alive for me. A working knowledge of gerundives and the ablative case came quite naturally, was a spin-off from the excitement he left me with after each informal lesson at Fletcher's Field.

Incongruously, I thought then, he always sported a bow-tie. Even on the warmest June days he never wore his shirt open-collared, and his suit was neatly pressed at all times. I liked his wit, his ready humour and eloquence. His aliveness, his intensity even before he said anything, distinguished him from David Lewis. He was that marvellous, unique creature – a poet. He made everybody else I knew seem ordinary, their ambitions mean, their accomplishments paltry. Lewis had something solemn about him; his gravity, always impressive, made me feel that argument with him would be futile, indeed, not even to be considered. Lewis walked steadily, unswervingly ahead, but Klein soared. One had feet and the other had wings. I felt that Klein knew where I came from, that he intuited the tensions I didn't have the temerity or ability at the time to express. I never had that feeling about Lewis, though I was on more familiar terms with him than I was with his friend.

I brought Klein one of my short stories, and, even though it was not a particularly good one, he went over it very carefully. It was this genial kindness that struck me, his willingness to spend time with someone several years his junior, and to talk about poetry, writing, and politics. Later on, when I began to show him my poems, I would meet him at his office and we'd go downstairs where there was a Murray's restaurant in the building. There, over cups of coffee, I'd listen to him talk. Klein's mordant observations on his fellow poets and the events of the day, always expressed with pith and vinegar, were my food. His knowledge of Talmud and Jewish folklore was the hot meal I couldn't afford. Most of the time I couldn't even pay for the cups of coffee I consumed during the hour or two that Klein let me spend with him.

The best reason I can offer for deciding to write my matrics is the artist's imperious need to complete something he has started. It is a need as obsessive as the bee's to construct a particular hexagon in the hive. I felt I had to write the matrics in order to complete that segment of my life. If I didn't, I'd have felt that the four years at Baron Byng had been for nothing. I would have erected a house without a roof. I needed the roof. David Lewis loaned me the required ten dollars. Since he was no more flush than I was, he had borrowed the money from his girlfriend Sophie Carson, who later became his wife.

The big day finally arrived. I woke up nervous and unrefreshed. I had slept badly. My tiny room looked more cramped and inauspicious than ever. I couldn't see myself passing the exams because I didn't feel I was well-prepared for them. The matrics had to be written at McGill so I walked from De Bullion Street to the campus – very slowly, very thoughtfully, and full of dread. I had never been inside McGill and to me it was a forbidding institution. I had the ghetto Jew's feeling that this was the very bastion of Anglo-Saxondom. Despite the class-consciousness Marxism had reinforced, perhaps because of it, I was awed, really awed. I had the feeling I didn't belong there, that I was going to be exposed.

Almost as if I were a sleepwalker, I found myself going toward the room where I was told the examinations were being written. It was a large auditorium and there were hundreds of students at their seats. I was directed to take mine. When I was seated and the examination papers handed out and the sound of scratching pens kept increasing in volume, I looked about me as one dazed by a blow. There were other subjects besides Latin and I had undertaken to do them all on my own. I felt I was really headed for failure, for disaster.

To this day, I still marvel that I achieved the necessary passing marks. When I got my results I stared in disbelief at the letter informing me that I had passed my matrics. I had done very well in the subjects I liked, not so well in chemistry and physics. My highest mark was in algebra, the subject Mr. Steeves taught.

I had applied myself fanatically to its study in order to put his nose out of joint.

Nobody in my family was particularly impressed. I don't recall any of my sisters congratulating me. I think they'd given up hope on their feckless brother. They realized that I didn't want to become a customer peddlar, that I didn't want to learn a trade or acquire a profession. They couldn't make anything out of me. I was a bookworm, a queer duck headed for certain failure. My mother, out of concern for her improvident son, had the vague hope that I might become an electrician or a plumber.

With my brothers it was the same. It would not have have meant much to them even if they had known about my expulsion, passing my matrics, and the drift my life was now taking. Not that they didn't care, not that they wouldn't have loaned me the fee for the exam; it was simply that they had no idea what made me tick.

Some time after the exam, I went to New York to stay with Larry and Hyman, who were boarding with a Jewish family in the Bronx. Every morning, in the room we all shared, I would read to them from a volume of Walt Whitman which I had brought with me. I chose some sensual poems, thinking that these had a better chance of winning their approval and make them willing to forgive lines that were arranged queerly on the page. I bombarded them with Whitman's poems not only before they left for their jobs as deliverymen but also when they returned exhausted from the day's work. As soon as I saw them all cleaned up, I pounced on them to read more of his provocative verse. My poor brothers suffered these assaults on their sensibility for as long as their tolerant good natures allowed. Then one day, they decided that my virginity was to blame for the affliction I visited upon them twice daily.

Naturally, I mistook the thoughtful looks they gave me from time to time, thinking that I had made converts of them and that poetry was becoming a necessity for them as it was for me. But what other conclusion could they come to but the one they did? I was reading Whitman's erotic poems because I was still a repressed virgin and needed to get laid! They'd put their heads together and decided that only by bringing me to the mulatto girl who was servicing them off and on would the affliction end.

The young whore lived up to all the frenzied expectations my brothers' succulent description of her had created in my virginal, poetry-saturated soul. Her smile seemed to light up the small room for me. Even the torn, badly faded coverlet that was thrown over the bed appeared to be bathed in its glow. But who cared about anything else in the room but this young, lithe, dark-skinned woman whose embrace my considerate brothers had already arranged and paid for?

Alas, I was ill-prepared for the occasion. Shelley and Keats may be great poets, but are lousy romantic mentors for an apprehensive youth about to have his first sexual experience. This was no nightingale in the room, no skylark, this was a WOMAN with exposed round globes and a belly button that when she moved seemed to wink at me. She let fall her panties and, standing naked before me, she put her arms around my neck and drew me to her. A delicious spasm passed through me, alternately tightening me and making me go limp in her embrace. It was not only my mind that seemed confused but my entire nervous system. It simply didn't know how to respond, didn't know what was expected of it. My brothers must have informed her that I was less than a novice and would need lots of tenderness and patience to accomplish the deed.

Did I say Shelley and Keats were unhelpful mentors? Marx and Engels were no better. Nor was the puritanical earnestness I had unconsciously assimilated from David Lewis and the other radicals out to change the world. The young harlot did her level best, she really tried hard but nothing she did could rouse my flaccid member or make it evince the slightest interest in her ministrations. It just lay there as if drugged, infuriatingly indifferent to the ecstasy that now for the first time in its unadventurous life was there for the taking. To cover up my embarrassment, I began to ask her questions. I exhibited a sudden, touching interest in all the details of her life. I wanted to know where she was born, what her father did, what her education had been, and deciding to put my Marxism to good use, I wanted to know what her earnings were and what the Madame, who had already knocked at our door twice, took as her share. If I don't remember her answers, it's because I didn't really listen to them.

This whole business in a run-down Harlem bordello, with its noises and odours and mysterious whisperings, was a far cry from "Indian Serenade" or "'La Belle Dame Sans Merci" – I mean, of course, the feelings and thoughts those poems generated. What I felt for the girl was neither interest nor tenderness but pity for her as a member of the "exploited class." I was buying her body as the fat, cigar-smoking capitalist in a *Daily Worker* cartoon bought the labour power of the proletarian he put to work on one of his machines. Guilt and shame were the emotions I felt, and neither of them can be considered an aphrodisiac. She again tried kissing my neck and ears, kept flashing her encouraging smiles at me and gently touching my recalcitrant member but, in the end, after some more unsuccessful caresses and a final pinch to startle it awake, Shelley, Keats, Marx, and David Lewis carried the day.

Now there was a third thump on the door, louder and more insistent than the previous ones. The Madame had allowed me more time because my two brothers were good, cash-paying customers of some standing, and she hoped I would become one too. With mixed feelings, I took a last look at my somnolent member asleep on the tiny velvet cushion my ballsac made for it. It struck me – my mood was not the jolliest, you must understand – that there was something funereal about it. And indeed there was a wreath-like look about the pubic hairs on which it lay half-covered.

Does anyone really know how the human brain works, how memory ties and unties the neural filaments of experience? As I took in the sad inertness of my circumcised member, the first line of Rupert Brooke's famous sonnet sprang facetiously into my head; "If I should die, think only this of me." Though the conventional sentiments it expressed are so much blah to me, the poem had been one of my favourites in my first year at Baron Byng. And now it seemed to me that the miniaturized shades of Keats and Shelley, of Marx and Engels had come to pay their last respects and to be present for the final obsequies. I could almost imagine a funeral procession for the shrivelled prick, complete with bells tolling.

Marx talks of the transformation of quantity into quality. For him this is a dialectical law. Well, that's exactly what was happening to me now. During my early high school years, I had gone along without any visible change except for an increase in my rebelliousness, my discontent. Unbeknownst to myself, however, I had begun to forge the personality of a poet. But now I was changing into a radically different person from the one I left behind at Baron Byng. Superficially, I still appeared cheerful and gregarious, but uneasily I was living in two worlds: the humdrum world staked out by bourgeoisified tradesmen and professionals and the world of nobility and grace I had been constructing in my mind book by book. I felt myself in conflict with traditional mores, first with those of my family and now those of society. The gross materialist aims and appetites of both sickened me. I had long ago turned my back on the narrow, life-restricting superstitions of my family. My uneasiness grew as my horizons widened. The black spot which first appeared in grade eight had grown larger and larger and now covered the whole surface of an imprisoning wall.

What I didn't know, what I couldn't know because there

were no precedents to guide me, was that during those difficult years I was also fashioning the long pole that would enable me to vault over that wall with the ease and joy of an Olympian.

NINE

The area of Montreal I knew was bounded by Park Avenue on the west and St. Denis on the east, Mount Royal to the north and Craig Street to the south. That's where I saw the effects of the Crash, the 1929 bust that came after the early 1920s boom.

The Marxist wiseacres had predicted it and now here it was in full force. The factories closed down, the unemployment lines grew larger and larger. Misery and heartbreak were apparent in all the familiar streets of my neighbourhood for both were centred very largely here and in the French-Canadian areas east of St. Denis, and especially in the working-class districts of St. Henri. Westmount, the enclave of the English Bourbons, didn't feel the sharp pinch of poverty. If anything, some of the Bourbons even profitted from the Depression. What stuck out in my mind was the contrast between the sleek comfort found in one neighbourhood and the squalor in which it was set like an emerald in a base-metal ring. An early poem of mine has the line, "Westmount squats upon a slum." The slum was St. Henri.

You walk down St. Lawrence or one of the streets just east of it and you feel the terrible Depression in your bones and marrow. You feel the hopelessness and pain, the bewilderment and panic. The gilt put on during the boom years has rubbed off. From storefronts and houses, from the sidewalks and asphalted streets, the shine was peeling away. Everywhere, there was evidence of decay, plain as the bare wood from which the paint has been scaled off.

You go into a store, into a restaurant or café and you see people whose vague stares avoid your interest. These are the unfocussed stares of people who have been struck a vicious blow and are still wondering where the blow came from and Why me? Why have I been picked for this torment? Life had shafted them and shown them to be at the mercy of incomprehensible powers beyond their control. They were little people to be shoved around, ordered about, bullied, and kept all their days in a state of fear and confusion. The only significance their lives had was in the blows they took or were able to ward off. Soon, the neighbourhood became dotted with soup kitchens and columns of people lining up to receive their daily meal. There were, of course, no soup kitchens to be seen in Westmount or Hampstead.

An article of the socialist faith held that capitalism could not work in any other way but through boom and bust. At the time I was president of the Yipsels. To me and to all the other members the lesson was only too obvious: capitalism was a malfunctioning economic and social system. Dislocations were endemic. Misery, poverty, periodic gluts, and crashes were a part of the total picture of capitalism. For both socialists and communists, the basic evil of the capitalist system was the exploitation of men by other men, by those who owned the means of production, the capitalist class. The worker lived only if he could find someone to hire him. He had no value except as the possessor of labour power. He was as much a commodity as the commodities he helped to manufacture.

In winter, Montreal's cafés and restaurants became places where people dawdled over a cup of coffee just to stay out of the cold. Horn's Cafeteria took on new meaning for me. For five cents, the price of a cup of coffee, I obtained warmth and could engage in exciting discussions. Horn's became my university. I met radicals of every tinge and persuasion: socialists,

Communists, syndicalists, Trotskyites, and anarchists. Several individuals stand out in my memory for their style or personality, others for the messianic conviction with which they announced the doom of the capitalist system. "Red" Chalmers, a Glaswegian, held spellbound not only those at his table but those at the neighbouring tables to his right and left. He was a passionate orator able to invest his Marxist abstractions with the flesh and blood of human suffering. He was not a poet but I think he should have been one. His feeling for literature set him apart from the other radicals whose imagination extended no further than the bleak Utopias they constructed for themselves.

Horn's Communists embraced the gospel of socialist realism. Following Stalin blindly through various policy shifts, they also hailed him as an authority on all works of art. Stalin alone knew what made a novel or painting great. For the Communist true believer the criteria were obvious and simple. If a poem or novel heroized the proletarian, portraying him as a martyr or dedicated revolutionary, if it instilled the hope for a victorious uprising of the working class and lashed out at the evils of capitalism, then it undoubtedly possessed artistic merit. Lenin himself had given these infallible tests for assaying art. Subtleties and nuances that resisted these criteria, or ignored them, made for bad art. No class-conscious worker or Communist should waste his time on them. Anyone who praised Huysman's masterpiece, *Against the Grain*, was a "word-mongering dilettant." Innocence begets bigotry. In matters of literature and art the new faith's firebrands were intolerant evangelists. It fuelled my nasty elitism to be able to tell them so. One of my greatest delights was to come on one of these defenceless creatures and make a meal of him.

Among the comrades, male and female, who nightly held their passionate sessions at Horn's was Moe Zigler. A bushy-haired poet forever smiling, I thought, to flash his conspicuous gold-encased molar, since he yearned to be taken for the Mayakovsky of Montreal. If fervour could be equated with talent he might have realized his dream. However, since there were not too many poets about, he found it gratifyingly easy to identify the interest his personality aroused with fame. People take pleasure in satisfying a person's vanity for it makes them feel superior; his toothsome, appreciative smile was therefore considered endearing. As far as I know, he published only one collection of poems, a small booklet he brought out at his own expense which he titled *Red Song*. That was an ill-chosen title and caused him much embarrassment because there were few buyers, and it was soon tagged "Unread Song." Poor Moe lived with that all through the Depression and even when he had married, fathered children, and opened a luncheonette on McGill College Avenue, there were people cruel enough to remind him of his unfortunate authorship. He died many years ago taking his pained grimace with him into the grave.

Though I never became a member of the Communist party, I was sympathetic to the heartbeat of communism, to its idealistic vision of man and society, and to the militancy Communists were exhibiting everywhere. They were becoming prominent because they took an active part in trying to organize the unemployed. The socialists did not. Householders were evicted for non-payment of rent. Services were cut off for non-payment of utility bills.

The Communists organized groups that would immediately put the furniture back into the house from which an unemployed family had been evicted. Some of the landlords took to hiring idle men to help in the law's enforcement. There were bloody fights, and one householder, an out-of-work Ukrainian who protested his eviction, was shot and killed by the police. Of course the Communists made a big howl about that and staged a protest rally at his funeral and I remember filing past Zynchuk's bier along with hundreds of other mourners.

I made comparisons between Communists and the weak-kneed intellectualism of the socialists whose Marxism more and more struck me as emasculated and academic. Nevertheless

I still believed the capitalist system could have its carious fangs pulled by Parliamentary reform. The two or three letters of Suzanne's my mother had allowed me to see alerted me to the evils of Stalin's totalitarian rule but still left room in my mind to think she was exaggerating out of disillusionment and loneliness. It's never an easy matter, I kept telling myself, to adjust to new conditions and foolishly began to believe the silence that followed indicated such adjustment had indeed taken place, that both she and her mother were now content with their move to Russia.

For the Rosenbergs' sake and my own I had allowed myself to gobble down the Kremlin's propaganda. This propaganda had an overwhelming effect on me: on me, and many others as well. I became a persuasive left-wing socialist after reading Shaw's plays and prefaces and the simplistic novels of Upton Sinclair, the American socialist. I page-turned Michael Gold's *Jews Without Money*, Gorky's *Mother*, and Anatole France's *Penguin Island*. Whether English, French, American, or German, the outlook of these writers was solidly anti-capitalist. Anyone as impressionable as myself was bound to be affected. And now Bernard Shaw, the brainiest writer then alive, was praising Stalin and the results of the terrorism he had unleashed against the people he ruled. That clever, witty fool had visited Russia in the company of Lady Astor and returned with a mendacious account of what he thought he had seen. Even Wells had taught himself to genuflect and commend. Then there were the Webbs, who wrote a book called *Soviet Communism: A New Civilization?* In the first edition the title ended with a question mark. In the edition that followed, the Webbs boldly threw caution to the winds by eliminating the question mark. The Fabian Society's *crème de la crème* intellectuals had now convinced themselves the Soviet Union under Stalin had created a civilization superior to the one in which the West was so disastrously floundering. All this at a time of forcible collectivization when over thirty million people were deliberately starved to death. All this at a time when every shred of freedom, of liberal and humane thought was being crushed under Stalin's hobnailed boot. Is there an idea so outrageously stupid, so stale, pat, and unprofitable that some intellectual won't support it with every desiccated brain cell in his cranium? The next century, if there is one, will find it incredible that there wasn't a single Communist dictator whose ass the intellectuals of the liberal democracies weren't eager to beslobber with fervent kisses.

The triumphant march of National Socialism made communism ever more attractive. By 1932, the National Socialists had become the strongest single party in Germany, their demonic energy mesmerizing the unemployed and large sections of Germany's upper-middle and lower-middle classes. They saw Hitler as their messiah. By contrast, the leaders of the Social Democratic and Communist parties appeared stodgy and ineffectual, their noses were too beer-thickened to smell the blood and violence in the air. Their tired slogans were no match for the lightning intuitions of Hitler. In the 1933 elections to the Reichstag the Nazis polled over eleven million votes.

The Soviet Union seemed to be the only country willing to oppose Hitler. To the coffee-drinking revolutionaries at Horn's it looked as if only Stalin and the Communist parties saw the threat National Socialism posed for the world. Faced with the growing danger that menaced them, the western democracies appeared cowardly, confused, and unwilling to pick up the gauntlet Hitler had thrown down. In the League of Nations the Soviet Union kept arguing for a policy of collective security to prevent a Nazified Germany from becoming too powerful. I became convinced that the Communists had adopted the only stance that might prevent another World War from breaking out.

Only a united front of Social Democrats and Communists could have saved Germany and the world from the nightmare calamities of a war-bent Hitler. At Horn's the tactic of a united front must have been voiced more often than the orders given the waitress for coffee or flapjacks. Properly channelled, the energy expended on debating its purpose and strategy could have provided Montreal with electricity for weeks.

On Moscow's orders, the leader of the German Communist party, Ernst Thälmann, had persuaded his followers that the Social Democrats were a greater menace to Germany's working class than the Nazis. Germany's socialists were now dubbed "social fascists." Thälmann called for a united front "from below." My opinion was that this new policy was doomed to fail. The Social Democratic workers were not going to desert their leaders to make common cause with the plodding bureaucrats of the Communist party and the propaganda-blitzed followers of the party line. It must be said that the leadership of the Social Democratic party was eager and ready to form a united front "from above." Had it been achieved, the Social Democrats with their eight million votes, and the Communists with their six million votes, could have stopped Hitler dead in his tracks. Overnight, he could have been rolled into the dust-bin of history.

One evening, I voiced my suspicion to Chalmers that Stalin had deliberately foisted this no-win policy on the German Communist party. For the first time, the usually soft-spoken Glaswegian lost his civility. To his ears, my words sounded worse than heresy. I was traducing the revered leader of the international working class, and the workers' fatherland. Such was the political rhetoric of the time – delicious if you had a fancy for that sort of thing, and I must confess I did. After Chalmers had calmed down, I plunged my knife in deeper and went on to declaim that the cunning, ruthless Georgian was mortally afraid that a country as advanced as Germany, should it go socialist, would put the USSR into the shadows where it belonged. The spotlight would be taken off the Soviet Union and it would at once be seen as the backward, semi-Asiatic country it was.

However, when Litvinov argued in the League of Nations for collective security, and invited Britain and France to sign military pacts with the Soviet Union, I flung my cap into the air and cheered. My contempt for the political leaders of the democracies knew no limits. Whatever my disagreements over the tactic to be followed regarding the united front, I could not fault the Soviet Union and international communism for wanting the English and French to adopt a more aggressive policy against a Nazified Germany, whose warlike designs were becoming more and more evident each day.

Still, as one issue after another arose, the differences with my Communist sparring-mates became more violent. Temperamentally, I couldn't accept the myth of Stalin's infallibility. No further evidence, I declared, was needed to confute it than the leader's conspicuously narrow forehead. The additional fact that he was unable to express himself other than in basic Russian made complete the case against his possessing superhuman intelligence. Moreover, though I had never accepted the doctrine of Original Sin, my view of the human animal was too joyously bleak to think of this tail-less bi-ped as other than terribly flawed by vanity, egotism, greed, and the desire for power.

It didn't take long before the communist arsenal of insults was unlocked and the epithets of "phrasemonger," "social fascist," "individualist," and "Trotskyite," were again thrown at me. When the horrific purges happened and Zinoviev, Kamenev, Bukharin, Radek (Lenin's comrades-in-arms) were all sentenced to death as traitors and imperialist spies, I could scarcely keep from spitting out my disgust at those who tried to justify their executions.

Slowly it came to me that the intellectuals I was meeting every night at Horn's were trying to palm off on each other their bonelessness for idealism, their sense of failure for moral indignation. Bruised misfits, counterfeiters, actors, almost everyone of them. Of course, save for the detachment my imagination made possible, I was myself one of them. Pulled in different, often in opposite directions, I used loud declamation to conceal doubts and conflicts. The more insincere I became, the more vehement and dogmatic I also became; and the more guilt-ridden, the more sentimental. Inwardly colder, outwardly the more warm and affectionate.

Younger by several years, I was no less eager than Jack Stern (he'd shortened his name from Strujensky) to be known as an apostle of love and justice on the strength of a well-rounded phrase, especially when it moved my listener and brought an admiring look into his eyes. The best means to secure the latter was to talk freely about one's shortcomings. Here the exchange was honest because the rates were known. A confession of weakness made you appear frank to yourself and to your listener, while the latter immediately experienced the thrill of superiority and power: two coffee-drinking non-entities, nose to nose, pretending to take one another seriously! Mankind was preparing a bloodbath for itself. No less conceited, no less shallow and bombastic than the other word-intoxicated revolutionaries, I too was eager to begin the exchange of garments stinking of blood and vomit for abstractions and manifestos.

Though not one of Trotsky's followers, I admired his fiery personality. Cultured, Jewish, fluent in several European tongues, he was also an internationalist. Internationalism was the creed of the early Bolsheviks, Lenin included. Trotsky foresaw that the price for trying to build socialism in a country where the vast majority were illiterate moujiks, would be dictatorship. He thought Russia lacked the resources, material and cultural, needed for its establishment. The changes Stalin had in mind, he said, could be carried out only under the lash of terror. Trotsky might have been the greatest orator and the most important architect of the Bolshevik revolution after Lenin, but perhaps his rival had a keener sense of political realities.

As one Canuck of unusual percipience observed, "The over-sensitive write; the insensitive rule."

The only Trotskyist I knew by repute was Mike Buhay. I had never met him. I had never attended any rally that he addressed though the Trotskyist meeting hall was on St. Laurent Boulevard, a stone's throw from Horn's. Expelled from the Communist party for his heretical views, Buhay had taken a sizeable number of the faithful with him.

The great drama played out at Horn's and several other restaurants in the neighbourhood was the split between Mike Buhay and his sister Becky. Becky had staunchly elected to remain with the comrades. This being before the advent of *Dynasty* and *Dallas*, some of the gossip concerning brother and sister and their differences was flavoured according to the political leanings of the speaker. Dumpy-looking, short, Becky Buhay was, nevertheless, a surprisingly effective orator. The kvetch in her voice grabbed your insides because decades of proletarian misery seemed to have formed it. Her reputation as an orator overshadowed her brother's and even that of Tim Buck.

One May day in the early thirties, I shared the platform (though not the spotlight) with Becky Buhay in Prince Arthur Hall. After addressing an audience composed mainly of unemployed, we came out to a solid phalanx of cops, their machine-guns pointing directly at the tableau of men and women, fear-frozen, outside the hall. I almost panicked for I imagined all guns levelled at me. Luckily, some members of the audience who had reached the outside before us began to jeer and laugh. Their cat-calls and insults were music in my ears. Since the cops didn't shoot, I lost my nervousness. Evidently, the mayor and some of the aldermen wanted to have fun. Nothing like a little scare for the unemployed if you couldn't feed or find jobs for them!

Jack Stern occasionally loaned me one of Trotsky's pamphlets. Though not a Trotskyist, he expounded that revolutionist's views with great clarity. No poet or novelist I have ever met or read had Stern's exceptional gift for putting ideas and images into memorable language. When he really got started, I forgot my surroundings and circumstances, the dirty piles of snow and garbage on Montreal's streets. His words conjured up before my eyes an endless picture gallery. They strengthened my faith that words articulated with passion and style were more solid than gold coins, more enduring than the mansions on the Boulevard.

I was to learn that a poet's life gets fouled up because he wants his words and the ideas he expresses by their means to have no consequences. In a wistful, guilt-laden poem, Yeats asks himself, "Did some words of mine send a young man out to get himself killed?" It's almost as if the poet were pleading with his readers: "Don't take me seriously. I like the sound of words. I like the music their syllables make in my head." However, since words do have consequences and people do take them seriously, if only sometimes, the poet finds himself trapped by them and called to account. From being friends they become his most treacherous enemies, sending him headlong from his dreams of romantic love into the boredom of marriage, the intolerable constraints of a real event.

I think Jack Stern sensed my passion for words, my crazy need for experiences that could afterwards be put into language. All sorts of experiences, high and low, degrading or ennobling. Several times he too called me a phrasemonger, but coming from him, the word lost its sting. I felt he was no less intoxicated by the musical arrangement of syllables than myself. Who cared about their meaning? The sound was everything, the sense was only minimally important. When it came right down to it, there were just two kinds of people worth thinking about: those who were willing to die for a beautiful phrase, for a metaphor, and those eager to shed blood for a cause. Only at rare times was I confused about where I belonged. But the confusion, when I felt it, was painful, leaving me disorganized and robbed of volition.

The poems I was then writing reflected the economic and political tensions of the time. Jack said he liked them, but I thought his words lacked their usual brio. Two or three were written about a passing flame. But after Suzanne, no girl inspired me. Not old enough to know what was truly important, I was more excited by the rise in the production figures of Stalin's Russia than by the rise and fall of a girl's breasts or by her figure, however enchanting. Now when I think of what a fool I was I feel like hopping on a plane to Moscow and pissing on Stalin's grave. The nights I spent arguing Stalin versus Trotsky could have been put to much better use. Alas, youth is simply wasted on the young. Or did Shaw, in one of his less superficial moments, say that before me?

Jack Stern is probably now dead but not the feeling he inspired in an adolescent who felt himself privileged to pay for the coffee that freed Jack's tongue from its nervous stammer.

A "rootless cosmopolite," I was aware of the large world beyond Canada's borders. The seminal influences, intellectual and cultural, came not from this country but from Europe. I read the poems of Mayakovsky and Yesenin, I didn't read those of Duncan Campbell Scott or E.J. Pratt. I read the novels of Gladkov and Ehrenburg, I didn't read those of Ralph Connor, and somehow the imperishable *Journals of Susanna Moodie* escaped my notice.

What was happening in Germany and Russia, in France and fascist Italy, seemed vastly more important to me than what was going on in Canada. Though war was about to break out in Spain and elsewhere, Canada was a sleeping pygmy. In the wintertime, a big white yawn. Neither the French Canadians nor the English Canadians impressed me unduly by their cultural achievements. Their parochial aspirations left me cold or indifferent. The French Canadians, their anti-

Semitism fuelled by an ultramontanist Catholicism, seemed eternally mired in a medieval outlook. As for the Anglos, how could one expect Hitler's ominous speeches to take their apolitical minds away from the baseball playoffs at Yankee Stadium?

There were signs in the Laurentian hotels and resorts and in the province's public parks and beaches that said only too plainly: NO DOGS OR JEWS ALLOWED. I saw these signs each time I went to Shawbridge or Ste. Agathe. Later, I saw them each summer when I worked as a waiter in Laurentian hotels. Since I don't recall members of the two great founding peoples of this country bestirring themselves to mount a protest, it didn't surprise me too much when, years later, they remained unperturbed by the terror Hitler unleashed against the Jews.

The only exciting thing happening in Canada, apart from the annual rodeo show, was the creation of the Co-operative Commonwealth Federation. Its impetus was the Great Depression which lasted nearly the entire decade. Only with the outbreak of war in 1939, did the workers file back into the idle factories and the miners descend into their pits again. There's nothing wrong with capitalism, said the radical know-it-alls, that a good war can't remedy. The CCF was a political party formed to advance the interests of the desperate farmers and workers. Its first annual convention was held in Regina in 1933.

I felt myself to be a part of a world-wide movement for revolutionary change that was going to restructure society from top to bottom. The desired goal was peace, social justice, and the end of human alienation. I was conscious of a messianic purpose and experienced the liberating hubris that allows one to kill people with a clear conscience. For the first time in my life I was tasting this century's most intoxicating brew, the sense of power the conviction of infallibility gives one. Though not a Communist, I identified completely with Marx's messianic proletariat. History had chosen them in the same way that Yahweh had chosen the Hebrews. My new faith gave me an electrifying sense of unity and purpose. It integrated me. It concentrated me. It made me feel singled out for a special destiny. What kept my burgeoning fanaticism in check was my native scepticism and my love of literature. Also, I couldn't help noticing how the cafeteria's dialecticians were no less convinced of their infallible truths than I was of mine. My forefathers' orthodoxy had left in me a residual monotheism. At Horn's there were simply too many deities, each with his own congregation of devout worshippers.

It is a measure of the twilight zone I was inhabiting, of my ambivalences and the contrary political attractions working on me, that the Youth Defenders, one of the numerous front organizations of the Canadian Communist party, asked me to give a lecture. Their meeting place was also on the Main Street. The invitation came from John Slater. I was introduced to him by Joe Wallace, ex-priest and Communist, and, like myself, a Horn's regular.

Wallace was the organizer of the Canadian Defence League, the parent organization of the Youth Defenders. Having spent time in jail for his communist activities, he was the cafeteria's political hero. I liked him for two reasons, apart from the halo that his prison term had put over his balding pate. It was said he had an eye for women. It was also said by male comrades, more in anger than in sorrow, that being a Communist and a defrocked priest gave him certain advantages in the undercover sexual game played nightly at Horn's. Though Marx was on everyone's lips and Freud condemned as a bourgeois ideologue, it now seems to me the latter nightly got in more licks among the frenzied dialecticians than the revered author of *Das Kapital*. My other reason for liking Wallace: he too was bitten by the bug, and some of his verses were good enough to make Moe Zigler sweat with envy.

Joe's poems appeared in an anthology and he became known on the Main as a Communist poet. His verses were translated into Russian and published in Moscow, the Russians hailing him as Canada's greatest poet. The ex-priest was evident in his gentleness, in the soft, almost feminine way he had of speaking. One night I went to a reading he gave. Somehow, seeing him on the dais, I felt sorry for him. He seemed out of place in the large hall, reading his simple confused lyrics. There was a startling incongruity between manner and matter. What he should be writing about, I thought, was moonlight and roses, not shooting down capitalists.

It was after that reading that Slater saw Wallace and me and joined us at our table. He came to the point at once and asked me whether I'd care to lecture on a book of my choice for the Youth Defenders. I suspected he was under instructions to woo me into becoming a member of the Young Communist League. Missionaries for one party or another lurked under every table at Horn's, ready to pounce on the unwary.

The book I chose to talk about was Upton Sinclair's *The Jungle*. I didn't have a copy, but I supposed the Jewish Public Library on Esplanade Avenue would. They did, but it was out when I asked for it. I phoned John Slater and he said not to worry, that he'd find one for me. I reminded him that he'd given me short notice and that the lecture was scheduled for Friday, only four nights away. Again he told me not to worry. I unwisely put suspicion out of my mind – Slater, like Moe Zigler, was a rival versifier and a Horn's personality – and settled down to wait. He didn't show up with the book until Friday morning and when I said that didn't give me enough time to re-read it and make proper notes, he insisted I had to give the lecture anyway. The lecture had been well-publicized and there would be a huge turnout.

Foolishly, I let him persuade me. The lecture I gave was just so-so, my skill as a public speaker enabling me to cover up uncertainty and vagueness. But during the question period that followed, who do you suppose needled me and got me to look unprepared and superficial? None other than John Slater.

That taught me something about the soul's cross-hatching. There was no necessary connection between belief and conduct. The immortal bard had said it for all of us: "One could, in comradely fashion, smile and smile and smile and be a villain."

The radicals in my neighbourhood were mostly Jews. This was where Fred Rose later obtained the votes that would send him to Parliament to sit as its first Communist member. Jews had been radicalized because the Soviet Union was put forward as a haven for them. The myth was that anti-Semitism had been destroyed forever in the proletarian paradise. Divisive distinctions, nationality, race, and religion had been abolished. Most of my friends, including those of the opposite sex, considered themselves revolutionaries, militants ready to storm City Hall, if necessary. The older ones were members of the party. Those my age or younger belonged to the Young Communist League.

Nina Caiserman was a very attractive, olive-complexioned YCLer. Very troubled, very intense, a tightly coiled spring which a word might release. Her father was Chaim Caiserman. As a young man he had been known as an anarchist. In the 1920s that identification was as shameful as a Jew declaring himself a convert to Catholicism. But with the changing times he also changed and became one of the important leaders of the Canadian Jewish Congress. Since he was now a respectable member of the community, Nina's activities embarrassed and angered him. Her eyes blazed when she spoke of the plight of the unemployed Canadian worker. She fought her father like a tigress, flinging insults at him when she saw his bourgeois smugness growing with his pastrami-lined pot.

I liked her tempestuousness and wrote some feeble verses for her. We should have become lovers, instead we talked endlessly about free love. For all my advanced ideas, I was very puritanical; inexperience and romanticism allowing me to idealize any attractive young woman who had something in her head besides movie-stars and the ruthless quest for a

158

husband. It took several marriages and liaisons to give me a more realistic view of women and stop me from poetizing defects of mind and character which mysteriously enhanced their appeal.

Though something of an orator who found himself addressing workers and unemployed in St. Henri, though I looked no different from other wild-eyed revolutionaries blasting Arcand, Quebec's clerical fascism and police brutality, I knew all along my baggy trousers and sweater were a disguise. Urging my hearers to expropriate capitalists and besiege politicians for more public urinals and fewer arsenals, I knew I was an impostor. The brooding, suggestible poet was more interested in humping the fair Muses than he was in taking action. However vociferously I preached revolution, something perverse inside me laughed at the charade of rallies and demonstrations when compared to the majesty of a great poem. Had I been told to choose between writing another "Hymn to Intellectual Beauty" and bringing capitalist exploiters to justice, I would have chosen the former. But to still a starving child's whimpering for food I'd have burned down all the libraries in the world.

The demagogue haranguing an audience in Prince Arthur Hall, yes, but inside him a satirical *doppleganger* pleased he had aroused in his hearers feelings of rage and disgust. It caused me tremendous elation to know I could change them from being tolerant, amiable individuals into teeth-grinding creatures. The proletarian messiah was the risen Lazarus angrily shaking the capitalist graveworms from his locks. Any idea, however foul or absurd, that could energize them was snatched up even more desperately than a bone would be by a famished dog. I came to see that the individual able or willing to think for himself was even rarer than the true Christian. More rare than either was the cold-eyed artist who refuses to let himself be deceived by the illusions of his time and finds enjoyment in contemplating the infinite theatrical shapes life so lavishly creates.

From time to time during this period, I still saw A.M. Klein. I still brought the occasional poem and short story to his office. Though my admiration for him had not lessened, he had little intellectual influence on me. His Zionism and conventionality left me cold. I couldn't reconcile the passionate poet I knew him to be with the paterfamilias and practising lawyer he had become. I didn't see him very often since he was a busy man and I was not writing with the same conviction with which I had formerly. My creative work amounted to very little.

I never did show him my first short story, "The Chaplet." It was based on something I'd heard about my brother-in-law Strul Goldberg, who, among other things, sold religious medallions and crucifixes. The rumour went that he seduced French-Canadian girls in the outlying villages by offering a crucifix which may have cost him all of ten cents. As his fellow peddlars had the story from him, the girls would grab the crucifix while spreading their legs for him. The brutal cynicism of this story made me tremble with disgust. I never published "The Chaplet," for it was as crude as all such first efforts are and informed by a sentimentality picked up from reading too many proletarian novels. Since then, I have often wondered how Boccaccio would have told the story and whether Balzac might have found it droll enough for one of his ribald tales.

Where are the snows of yesteryear? I used to sit in Horn's on winter mornings eating my breakfast of French toast and coffee, gazing out at the dirty snow banked high on both sides of the street. The blowing wind would create spectral shapes. Warm and cozy, I would watch the billowy apparitions ambush the oncoming tram-car. It delighted me to see them re-form and dance along the street.

Where are the Marxist critics I once read with so much fervour? Where are V.F. Calverton and Granville Hicks? Where are the proletarian novelists who made the hearts of a whole generation beat faster with rage and hope? Where now are the bold messiahs who were prepared to lead us into the future? Who, today, reads their manifestos? Who, today, reads Grace Lumpkin, Michael Gold, Howard Fast? Has anyone lately seen *Waiting for Lefty*? When was the last time you read a novel by Upton Sinclair? The only Canadian left-wing poet I can recall besides the unfortunate Moe Zigler is Joe Wallace. Where is he now? Where's John Slater? Where are Becky Buhay and "Red" Chalmers, Jack Stern, and Fred Rose? And where are Roosevelt, Truman, Churchill, Mackenzie King. Gone, and only by the wind grieved.

Now that the sound and fury have died down, what were Stalin, Hitler, Mussolini, Franco? Farts in a maelstrom! Giant, reverberating farts. Five thousand years from now, when the messianic prophecies have all been fulfilled, what will their names mean? Who will recall their bloody deeds?

TEN

The ancients worshipped the god of chance. I think that makes a great deal of sense. My deciding to register at Macdonald College was entirely a matter of chance. When I'm introduced at a reading, it is sometimes mentioned that I have a Bachelor of Science Degree in Agriculture. This is usually followed by giggles. How on earth did I obtain this degree? Do I look like a farmer? So I tell my favourite story.

I'm walking along Decarie Boulevard in Montreal. Coming towards me is someone who looks vaguely familiar. I can't quite place him, not even when he's standing right in front of me, hand outstretched, smiling.

"I'm Alec Avarine," he says.

That rings a bell. Alec had been Hyman's classmate at Alexandra School. I remember Hyman telling me stories about him, that his parents were Italian and very poor. That they couldn't look after him, so he was sort of semi-adopted by a philanthropic Jewish couple. Their own son Robert, who acted like an older brother to Alec, was later killed in the Second World War. A brave officer, he was greatly loved by the men he led.

When I finally recognize Alec and settle his picture into its mental frame, he asks me what my brother is doing. I tell him Hyman is in New York, working. I'm hesitant, the dialogue sounds stilted. I'm at a loss as to what to say next. Finally, after an awkward pause, I ask Alec what he's doing. He says he's working too, but studying at the same time to become a cabinetmaker. Then it's his turn.

"So what are you doing?" he asks.

I tell him, "Nothing much, just sort of drifting."

"Well," he says, "have you thought of going to college or university?"

Imagine an explosion of laughter louder than the noise of the bus just rolling past. When I recover I say, "Where am I going to get the two hundred dollars?" McGill's tuition fee at the time. "It might just as well be two thousand."

"Why don't you register at Macdonald College? The fee's only fifty a year. What's more, the provincial government pays every Quebec student nine dollars per month each month he studies at Macdonald."

I did some rapid mental arithmetic. Seven times nine equalled sixty-three dollars. I'd be making a profit of thirteen dollars every year. How could I resist?

Located in Ste. Anne de Bellevue, on the western tip of Montreal Island, Macdonald College is a division of McGill University. At that time, the only degree it offered was a Bachelor of Science in Agriculture. I learned that room and board was only thirty dollars per month. By working during the summer, I should be able to make enough to cover that. I also told myself that, in a pinch, "Princess" Gertie would help out. Going to college had become a possibility. The thought left me dazed and happy. Something had finally happened. My days of drifting were over. Chance or providence had taken a hand. I'd study at Macdonald and become a professional of some kind. But what kind? An agronomist? A horticulturalist? I even had a vision of buying a farm and raising chickens. Why not cows or pigs? In manure-spotted clothes, over hay-stacks and barns, I was flying high. I could now say to anyone who asked what I was doing, "I'm going to college." In the weeks that followed when I wasn't flying, I was painting the most delightful pictures of my future.

The summer before entering Mac's, I found a job in one of the Laurentian hotels. I wasn't paid any wages, no one was. The waiters and busboys were Jewish students, mainly from McGill. We worked for our food and lodging, and for the tips that tanned furriers and pants-pressers, along with a paunchy manufacturer or executive of the ILGU would smilingly shove into the pocket of our white jackets. The look on their faces asking you to acclaim their remarkable generosity was calculated to make you feel they were paying for your entire college education.

At the end of the summer, since the tips I'd earned weren't enough to cover both tuition fee and room and board, and the Princess promising to send me only five dollars a month, I had to scrounge around for more money. A Montreal lawyer, Joseph Mergler, came to my aid. A lifetime socialist, he'd sometimes pinch-hit for David Lewis, lecturing on current affairs at our Yipsel meetings. I went to see him at his office. When I told him my story, without a word he wrote me a cheque for fifty dollars. Years later I offered to repay him but the good man wouldn't hear of it. With a smile he told me he wanted to be able to boast that he'd made it possible for me to start my university career.

I registered at Macdonald College in September 1934. My family was relieved that my life had finally taken a turn for the better. My drifting had come to an end and it seemed I was setting out on a course that promised some reward. Relieved? Yes. Proud? I don't think so. They would have been much happier had I gone ahead and become an enterprising peddlar. They did not know of the confusion in my mind, that I had no clear idea as to what I was doing at Macdonald or even why I wanted to be there. I kept my doubts and anxieties to myself.

The following scenario symbolizes my years at Macdonald College. On my first day there, I went into the common room where I'd been told the students assembled after supper. I could hardly keep my hands from trembling, so great was my excitement. After having had those lively no-holds-barred debates at Horn's, my expectation was that here there would be hotter and livelier debates. After all, this was a college.

There were about fifteen students in the room. Some were seated, others standing; they were all very quiet. The silence surprised me. Why weren't they already engaged in debate? In five minutes at Horn's names like "Trotskyist," "social fascist," and "revisionist" were exploding in the air like firecrackers, and here was the decorum of a cemetery. So I figured it was because there was a stranger in their midst and, out of the goodness of their hearts, they were taking it slow and easy. That they didn't want to overwhelm me with their dialectical skills, oratorical gifts. So I waited, said nothing. Felt the tears welling up – out of gratitude, you must understand, for their politeness.

Many of these students were from England. Their manner, their dress and class affectations were quite pronounced. They regarded me silently, sensing I was not one of them. They certainly looked and acted very differently from myself: for that matter, even very differently from the few English-Canadian students present. Well, I waited for the show to begin, wondering who was going to throw the first firecracker. But nothing happened. I finally decided to do them all a favour and break the ice.

At the time, there was some unrest in India and the British were confident they knew better how to govern India than the Indians themselves. I voiced my doubts: In a firm, practised voice learned at Horn's, I said that England was making a mistake in trying to rule the Indian people against their will. I dropped the word "imperialism." Suddenly, I felt everyone staring at me. Their stares unnerved me. Someone asked whether I thought England should get out of India. The actual word he used was "abandon." His voice was politely hostile. Superior and cool, as if he were talking down to a dark-skinned native of the Indian sub-continent. The voice, with its assumed authoritativeness, irritated me. I launched into a tirade against all the black misdeeds of British imperialism, completely forgetting who my audience was.

The cemetery suddenly turned into howling bedlam. I had kicked open a hornet's nest. But these hornets were wearing grey flannels and tweed jackets. Some of them were even smoking pipes. They had dropped their coolness and were now expostulating and even raising their voices. A few still held back at the fringes and continued to fix me with a supercilious stare as if to say, "How dare a mere colonial question the wisdom of His Majesty's government?"

Completely without tact or common sense, I was destined to remain an outsider for the years I was to spend at Macdonald College. I was an alien in an unfriendly environment. In the days and weeks that followed that first common-room argument, I continued my attacks on British imperialism. Later, when I mocked Chamberlain's appeasement of Hitler and warned that its outcome would be war, my troubles really began. I was at once branded a Communist.

I was a marked man on campus, an Ishmael glorying in his singularity and apartness. What did it matter that I was unsociable, an indifferent student, that I wore ill-fitting clothes and was probably the best-hated man at Mac's? I was also the most talked about. The college's single agitator, single poet, and single Jew, I was too absorbed in my messianic dreams to realize what an outlandish figure I cut among the simple-minded Canucks from Quebec's farms and middle-class homes.

That first year I lived in residence. One night when I was in the swimming pool, some fourth-year students seized me and started dunking me. They kept shoving my head under water. I spluttered. My spasms of coughing grew more violent. To no avail. I felt myself growing faint and dizzy. I was beginning to take in water and my temples were throbbing. I was scared because I thought what had probably begun as a joke was going to end with my being drowned. My lungs were bursting and I felt my last hour had come.

Fortunately, there were two English Canadians in the pool. They saw what was happening and rescued me from the hands of my tormentors. Wherever Henry Miles and Bevan Monks are, I want them to know that I think I owe my continued existence and the forty-odd books I've written to their intervention.

I moved out of residence in my second year and boarded with a local French-Canadian family. The reason was simple: I moved out because my adversaries had a very peculiar way of rebutting my arguments. One afternoon at the end of my first term, I opened the door of my room, and an amazing sight met my eyes. My books were lying scattered pell-mell on the floor, some were thrown on my cot and dresser. The biggest heap was in the centre of the room. Onto it they had emptied the floor's two garbage bins. I could guess who the ringleaders were. None other than the flannelled snobs from England, too inept in the use of their own language to engage me in honest debate. Week after week I had flayed the British government's policy of appeasing the dictators, warning that it would only whet Hitler's appetite for more concessions from the democracies, and their opposing arguments I thought more feeble than a nun's fart. On the floor, there was now not only the refuse of wet tea leaves, uneaten pieces of cake, soiled rags, empty marmalade pots, pencil shavings, and twisted toothpaste tubes, there were also the few remaining illusions I had about the Englishman's devotion to fair play.

What also got to me that first year at Mac's was the revolting arrogance these same English students displayed towards the French Canadians. They may have been in Canada no more than twenty-four hours yet, already, on encountering a French-Canadian student, they would make *him* feel *he* was the foreigner. Reinforcing native obtuseness and complacency, their snobbery was a force to be reckoned with. It never became clear to me exactly on what grounds these blazered and crested snobs from Ye Olde Slopshire gave themselves such airs of superiority. Such episodes made me understand the upsurge of nationalist feeling that later took place in Quebec. No doubt of it, they also played an important part in forming my animus against what I saw was the deadening influence of the English sensibility on Canadian poetry. Everything vital and creative in me revolted against it. My abrasive encounters with these uppity young Englishmen, and the colonized Anglo-Canadians desperately trying to ape them, reinforced my scorn. My dislike was so evident, it even discouraged them from employing the polite hypocrisy that has served the English upper class so admirably in more temperate situations.

In my second year at Mac's, on the invitation of Bevan Monks, the editor of the college newspaper, *Failte Ye Times*, I began to write a weekly column. I called it "Current History," and worked very hard at composing the pieces for it. I would start early in the morning and work up to eight or ten hours, writing no more than seven or eight hundred words, all the while smoking a pipe and drinking innumerable cups of coffee. The column had to have point and punch. I wanted it to stir up controversy among the students, even if it meant having to supply them with an Aspirin tablet for every new idea that struck them. The paper was printed in Montreal, put on a train to Ste. Anne de Bellevue, and picked up by the editors for distribution among the students having their Friday-night supper in the college's dining hall.

The Spanish Civil War had broken out. Naturally my sympathies were with the Loyalists. When the British government made a deal with Hitler and Mussolini to deny arms to the democratically elected government of Spain, and put its signature to the so-called "non-intervention pact," my polemical outbursts knew no limits. Prophetically, I said the Spanish Civil War was a dress rehearsal for the bigger war that was to come.

My satirical verses were published in the *Failte Ye Times* alongside my weekly column. Emulating Dryden and Swift, I composed a long poem entitled "Ah Rats!" It gave me an unholy pleasure to depict Neville Chamberlain as "that lanky rat from Birmingham."

Week after week I shredded the timorous, short-sighted democracies. Now the blazered and crested snobs were out for blood. It seemed to them my words were threatening the very foundations of the British Empire. I remember one of them in particular. His name was Burnell-Jones. He had frank, grey eyes and a smooth pink face, both cheeks doing their part to advertise dullness and a good digestion. We aroused each other's natural antipathy, and my sarcastic insults drove him to fury. He ended up writing his father who happened to be an eminent surgeon in London, enclosing a clipping of "Current History." His father wrote a letter to the RCMP inquiring how it was that a certain Israel Lazarovitch, using the *nom de plume* of Pero, could get away with insulting His Majesty's government week after week. Wasn't he a dangerous radical, a subversive Communist? And shouldn't the RCMP look into the matter? Because of that letter, years later, when the Communist witch-hunt was on and the RCMP had compiled their blacklist, I was denied entrance into the United States for a period of nearly fifteen years.

It soon became known to the students that the RCMP had visited the campus and made not too discreet inquiries about my activities. It must be admitted the students had cause for their worries. Since many of them hoped for appointments in the Civil Service, their future would look a whole lot less rosy should the college become stigmatized as a hotbed of subversive radicals. It didn't help me one bit to point out that I was a left-wing socialist, not a Communist, and that Winston

Churchill and members of the British Labour party were attacking the government for much the same reasons as I was.

Because of the ferment my column had generated on campus I could see the need of founding a club whose purpose would be to bring speakers of different political outlooks to address the students. I called it the Social Research Club. There had never been anything like that at Macdonald College. The first speaker invited was the president of the Royal Bank of Canada. He gave a thoughtful lecture on capitalism, pointing out the great benefits free enterprise had conferred on the unemployed, on farmers and small businessmen unable to meet their obligations to the banks.

After his lecture, with the concurrence of the other board members, I invited the well-known pacifist Lavell Smith. A Protestant minister, his congregation was in Montreal. He'd fought in the Great War, had seen its agonies at first hand. That experience made him a pacifist. His parishioners, even those who held different views, admired his courage and forthrightness. He gave a very moving speech. I remember his saying there was only one way to defeat Hitler and end the menace of Hitlerism. We should open our gates wide, invite Hitler in and show him and all his supporters in Germany that the English entertained nothing but Christian love and goodwill for them. A hard-bitten radical, I thought he was slightly soft in the head. However, the man's sincerity couldn't be doubted.

Since the Reverend Lavell Smith was by no means the only naïve idealist but had his numerous counterparts in England and in Canada, I thought it important to have their views aired and discussed. Pacifism, a strain in one form or another, will always appeal to people in the democracies unwilling to make the hard decisions or adopt the tough measures needed for their defence; we are seeing that in our own time. I don't know whether the dear man appeared as foolish to the audience as he did to me but he got a very courteous hearing. And the applause afterwards must have satisfied him.

Our next speaker was Dr. Norman Bethune. He had spent some time in the Soviet Union, returning with a great admiration for its achievements in public health and welfare. I knew something of his reputation. His innovative work in the treatment of tuberculosis, by setting him at odds with the medical bureaucracy of Montreal, had put a halo around his head as humanitarian and defiant rebel. My interest in him was that he'd been to Soviet Russia and was willing to talk about it.

My first impression of Dr. Bethune was of a very intense man, nervous to the point of irritability. He was wearing a drab grey suit, nothing that would make one look twice. I could see he was making every effort to control the jerky movements of his thin angular body. The man himself, his brittle body frame and somewhat squeaky voice, wasn't convincing. It was the urgency with which he spoke that was. Nevertheless, the more he talked the more he came across as a rather simple-minded individual, as an innocent willing to mistake confusion for complexity. The kind of person who, out of pure idealism, could embrace National Socialism, as many did in Germany, or communism, as many such did in Canada, Dr. Bethune among them.

Though gaunt, his body exuded a tremendous dynamism, surprising his audience. What impressed me most was the intentness of his gaze, the forceful conviction behind his words. Here was a man who seemed to be devoured by an idea, an obsession. He did not seem a man with whom one could be comfortable. Some people found him attractive, others, for the same reasons, were repelled.

During his lecture I was sitting in a front seat only a few feet away from the stage. Listening closely to every word, I heard him say that his guide in Moscow had been a girl from

Montreal. And he proceeded to describe her. She had healthy red cheeks, he said, and even began to praise her large brown eyes and rich brown hair. When he came to the last detail, and the most telling, that she was a bit on the heavy side, I could no longer contain my excitement. In a very loud voice I boomed out, "Was her name Suzanne?"

"Yes, as a matter of fact," he said calmly. "I remember her full name. Her name was Suzanne Rosenberg."

I can still feel the thrill that ran through me. For years I had received no news from or about Suzanne. Now, sensing I had a personal interest in the matter, Dr. Bethune went on to say he had met her because she'd been working as a guide for Intourist. He added that she had served him well during his visit to Moscow since she was fluent in English and Russian. No doubt to please me, he went on to say that he had found her not only attractive but also intelligent and vivacious. After the lecture he offered me a ride into town. In the car, he filled in the picture of what he had seen in the Soviet Union and made it quite clear that the revolutionary changes in that country had left a lasting impression on him. To my surprise, when the car stopped, he invited me into his apartment. Having lost his nervous, jerky movements, for the time it took to finish our drinks he showed himself to be a genial and considerate host.

Some weeks after his lecture at Macdonald he went to Spain to serve the Loyalist cause as a brave, self-sacrificing surgeon. After the defeat of the Spanish Republic, which the ruling classes of England, France, and the United States helped bring about, he went to China to offer his services to the Chinese Communists fighting Chiang Kai-shek and the Kuomintang.

There is a small statue of Bethune in Montreal on de Maisonneuve Boulevard, corner of Guy. It's not very impressive and indeed makes him look more frail than he actually was. Like Picasso's painting of a weak Stalin, it mocks the popular image. I've not spent too much time studying the monuments of the famous dead, but of one thing I am certain: the sculptor certainly has not captured the electrifying vitality I witnessed on meeting the unique individual that was Dr. Norman Bethune.

When it was decided to invite Tim Buck to be the next speaker at the Social Research Club, the opposition didn't lie low. One of its ringleaders, ironically named Charles Chaplin, was an English Canadian from Ottawa. Of course, everybody called him Charlie. Don't ask me why, but we actually liked each other. He and I had many vigorous arguments, mainly about politics. Very bright, he also had a wonderful sense of humour. Mac's was co-educational and Charlie was having a roaring good time. Generous and sensible, he offered me his friendly advice because he saw I was getting deeper and deeper into the mire, that my activities were arousing more and more hatred and opposition, while bringing socialism no closer. I remember him saying to me once, "Irving, why do you waste your time? Those dim-wits out there" – gesturing with his outstretched arm – "haven't a clue. Why don't you grab yourself a tit? There are lots of nice tits down here. Haven't you noticed? Why are you so stupid?" And he quoted a line of poetry: "Youth's a stuff that will not keep." I liked his joyous and ribald sensualism, the good-natured cynicism with which he viewed the world. How I wish now I'd listened to him instead of making all that froth about Russia's Five Year Plan.

When it got out that I had invited Tim Buck, my adversaries began to take up a petition. They got a large number of students to say they were against the Social Research Club inviting Tim Buck to speak. I took the matter up with Dean Brittain, who thought it was only right and proper for the college to hear all points of view. I had invited the president of the Royal Bank of Canada, Rev. Lavell Smith, Bethune, and now it was time to hear what a Communist had to say. But at the end of the interivew Dean Brittain said, "Look, I haven't got the authority to do this. You'd better go see the principal at McGill." The principal – his name was Morgan – was fresh from England

and all for freedom of speech. His final words to me were: "By all means, invite Tim Buck."

The students, however, continued their agitation. Tempers were growing ugly. Even those students who believed in freedom of speech were alarmed that Tim Buck's visit would stain the college bright red and diminish their chances of finding jobs in the Civil Service, their likely employer. So I said I would compromise and invite J.S. Woodsworth, founder of the CCF. This pleased everyone, faculty and students alike.

Woodsworth came and gave a lecture on the Depression and the socialist cure for it. A minister of the gospel before entering politics, he had come to socialism not through any economic reasoning but from a sense of justice. He thought the working class, in fact the general population, was oppressed by a small plutocratic minority using their economic leverage to enlarge their wealth. I felt that here was someone who put the life of the spirit above everything else. He made an excellent impression on everyone who had come to hear him. The audience applauded him loudly; I don't know that he won any votes but he certainly did win hearts. His success was my own, for it completely vindicated the Social Research Club, silencing many of those who'd been among its fiercest critics.

I first met F.R. Scott when I was a member of the Young People's Socialist League. He'd come to hear his friend and fellow socialist David Lewis address a mass meeting at Prince Arthur Hall. Now Scott and I were to address a mass rally at the McGill Union in support of the Spanish Loyalists. We met on the steps of the Union. The doors were padlocked and there were two policemen to make sure they stayed that way. The Padlock Law allowed Premier Duplessis and his supporters among French-Canadian Catholics to deny Quebeckers their constitutional right to free speech and peaceful assembly. Down to the last soutane and habit, Quebec's clergy were pro-Franco. If there were any dissidents among them, they were unknown to me. Scott took the fight for freedom of speech all the way up to the Supreme Court where he scored an historic victory.

I remember marvelling that somebody so tall and handsome, so elegant and so obviously English, should appear at a rally called to protest the government's mean-spirited treatment of the unemployed. Scott and Eugene Forsey lectured at McGill and both were in bad odour with its Board of Governors. Returning from their visit to the Soviet Union, their articles and speeches pointed out some of the welcome changes that had occurred in that country since the Bolshevik Revolution. The board took a poor view of their activities. Thinking themselves the university's paymasters, they held that all political wisdom was to be found only in their own narrow minds and spacious vaults. Presidents of banks, trusts, and insurance companies, well-heeled white Anglo-Saxon Protestants whose families had ruled the province for generations: it was only natural for them to believe opposing views smacked of sedition. The board even passed a resolution that Frank Scott could never be made Dean of the Faculty.

King Gordon, son of novelist Ralph Connor (a pseudonym for Rev. C.G. Gordon), had also accompanied F.R. Scott and Forsey to Russia. The McGill trio, though hardly Communists, thought the USSR had something to tell us about a planned society and what it might do to end exploitation as well as capitalism's boom and bust cycle. For expressing such opinion, they were threatened with loss of tenure. The Board of Governors huffed and puffed to get them dismissed. But to McGill's credit, their efforts failed. Eugene Forsey, who later taught me political philosophy, went on to become Senator Forsey. King Gordon continued to lecture at McGill's theological seminary until his retirement, and Scott became the F.R. Scott we all knew. But who remembers the fatuous corporation and bank presidents who tried to silence them?

For all their acquisitive instincts, McGill's Board of Governors didn't have a monopoly on stupidity. There was plenty of it at Macdonald College. One Friday night, the train bringing the *Failte Ye Times* was met by a number of students as it roared into the station at Ste. Anne de Bellevue. Burnell-Jones and Co. boarded the train and seized the issue, trashed it, and dropped the mutilated pages into the sewer, full of resolve that Mac's students should not see my column and read what new idiocy I attributed to Chamberlain's government. Nothing my enemies had done so disillusioned me as this latest act of vandalism.

Ironically, students took to calling me Hitler. Not because of my political convictions, for with the same innocence they sometimes called me Trotsky. I took it as a tribute to my oratorical powers; more truthfully, to my hysteria. In fact, I was not so much an orator as I was simply an hysterical rabble-rouser, who spoke with such frenzy that had I said the most nonsensical thing in the world, they'd have believed me. Consider how the Germans swallowed the garbage of Herr Hitler.

For whatever reason, I did have something of a reputation at Mac's through several inter-faculty debates. One day I accepted an upper-classman's invitation to debate Oxford-Cambridge. The team was touring Canada and had already defeated McGill and several other university debating teams. The resolution to be debated was: "It is better to have written Gray's 'Elegy' than to have taken Quebec." My team-mate and I had the affirmative. It seemed to me the whole college turned out that evening to hear the debate. We won handily. The event put a shine over my head that lit up the hotel's lobby for the full hour that I was present.

The reception was held in one of Ste. Anne de Bellevue's hotels, and I recall that this was the first time I had really distinguished myself. The victory surprised everyone, but the most surprised were Burnell-Jones and the other blazered

Englishmen on campus, who were shocked that a pair of colonials defeated the famed Oxford-Cambridge team! Especially when one of the victorious debaters was a Jew with an unpronounceable foreign-sounding name.

During this time, when I was making a name for myself as a campus radical and trenchant debater, I'd also begun to court, with passages from Marx and Lenin, radicalized young Jewish ladies from Westmount. I'd begun a liaison with one of them before she graduated from Mac's. I continued to see her, hitchhiking every week into Montreal for our furtive encounters, since her Jewish middle-class parents very wisely disapproved of me, sensing I was poor husband material.

On one such romantic pilgrimage it happened to be the evening of the coldest day Montreal had known in over 150 years. After twenty minutes of shivering and flicking my thumb, I saw a motorist slowing down. He stopped and beckoned me to get into the car.

My lady love and I had agreed to meet at a designated spot some distance away from her house. When I arrived she was not there, and I waited, feeling myself turning blue with the cold, for at least fifteen minutes before she appeared.

Now there was the problem of where to take her. I didn't even have a dime for a cup of coffee. So we walked and walked, my body aching with desire which, in this instance, didn't provide me with enough heat to thaw the blood I felt congealing in my veins. We ended up at a deserted building in the neighbourhood, and we went up the fire escape at the back. Our steps made a cold clatter in the darkness as we climbed higher and higher until we reached the top level, where my fingers, ten frozen parsnips, fumbled with her buttons.

There are two Mac profs, Latimer and Brunt, who stand out in my memory. Latimer taught economic theory. He was white-haired, with a squint in his left eye and a livid scar on his right cheek, as if it had been scorched. His voice and manner were both mild, yet he spoke with authority. Economic theory interested me and I seldom missed a lecture. Secretly, I was waiting to hear what he would say about Marx. Would he dismiss Marx for bourgeois reasons already well-known to me, *viz*, ignorance, superficiality, messianism, etc.? I found myself hoping that he would so that I could cross swords with him in class. Having gobbled up some indigestible chunks of *Das Kapital*, Marx's pamphlet *Wage Labour and Capital*, and the *Communist Manifesto*, I considered myself a Marxist.

Clash we did. Professor Latimer was a dyed-in-the-wool Free-Trader whose bible was Adam Smith's *The Wealth of Nations*. I had taught myself to accept the Communists' curt dismissal of Adam Smith and all he stood for. Ricardo and John Stuart Mill were Latimer's auxiliary deities. Ricardo excited me because he propounded the Labour Theory of Value and was Jewish – a successful broker at the Stock Exchange, no less. Latimer might just as well have thrown stones against a wall, so closed was my mind and so impervious to the arguments Smith via Latimer brought forward in favour of a market economy.

However, I was an eager student of economics and because the subject fascinated me, I was able to assimilate the theories of those early economists and regurgitate them in well-written essays that won an occasional admiring comment from the good professor. Back in first year, the night before final examination, my classmates gathered in my room. They had come at my invitation to hear me review the entire course for them in preparation for the following day's exam. Without opening the text or glancing at a single note, I gave sharp, concise summaries of the lives, times, and ideas of the great economic thinkers, the worldly philosophers. My passion and eloquence were reserved for the Utopian Socialists, for Marx and Thorstein Veblen. The lecture lasted four and a half hours.

Next morning I went into the examination room feeling

both virtuous and confident, eager to enjoy my brief popularity, even with those students who considered me a pain in the neck they ardently wished would go away. There was no mistaking their grateful looks and enthusiastic nods when they looked at the exam questions. Two weeks later, the results were posted. Several students who had sat at my feet, both literally and figuratively when I'd given my briefing, had scored A's and B's. I was near the bottom of the list with a C. I looked at the C and imagined the letter curling itself into a mocking sneer. I don't recall any of my classmates remarking on either the irony or injustice of the poor mark I'd received. Were they secretly happy? I can't help but think that among themselves they were gloating at my humiliation. Gratitude, after all, is a short-lived emotion and no match for the stronger emotions of envy, malice, and revenge.

When I went to see Dr. Latimer to question my unexpected low mark, he turned his innocent blue squint at me and smiled. His voice was soft with regret. "Yes," he said, "I must say I was very disappointed by your paper. I too expected you would put in a better performance than you did." And the hypocrite even added the following, "I am truly sorry." To complete the portrait it need only be added that he was a devout Presbyterian who faithfully went to church every Sunday. No doubt he too has passed on to a better world where no excitable Jewish upstart troubles him, and all the angels have a companionable squint in their eye, a flaming scar on their right cheek.

Dr. Brunt gave the survey course in English literature. Some snippets of Chaucer, some snippets of *The Faerie Queene*, and *Sir Gawain and the Green Knight*. Brunt was an effective performer. He had an excellent voice and took pleasure in using it to enthral the students, and I, for one, wouldn't have missed a single one of his weekly lectures for all the world. At times he could be very witty, though in a ponderous sort of way because of his heavy, rhetorical manner. I particularly remember the performance he gave when he read a selection from *Beowulf*, the menace and thunder he got into those syllables. No one listening to him could question the genuine delight he took in reading poetry.

Dr. Brunt was the only Mac prof I knew who made it a practice of inviting students to his home. Mrs. Brunt graciously poured tea and offered us cookies she'd baked. To someone like myself who had lived a lonely existence on De Bullion Street for several years, such decorous evenings were a revelation. I thought he was a socialist; anyhow more sympathetic to socialism than his colleagues. So I find it impossible to explain why I drew an unfair satirical portrait of him when I wrote the following poem which appeared in the *McGill Daily*.

PORTRAIT OF A PSEUDO-SOCIALIST

Dare mortal tell if Foggs is beast or man,
He's so addicted to the epigram;
And plain his reverence for all that's writ –
More famous, he, for learning than for wit.
From clever books a phrase or two he's caught,
'Tis hard to say if he is wise or not;
Human strife most eager to dilate,
Foreknowledge, Wisdom, Providence and Fate,
For then with sonorous sequence he may quote
His pilferings from all who ever wrote,
Should public dolor strike him to the core,
He mouths rhetoric phrases by the score,
And civic baseness with its aftermath
Unloosens all his adjectival wrath,
And shouting fury 'pon the system's flaws
He sits attentive to his own applause.

I suppose people enjoy writing and reading satire for the same reasons they enjoy gossip and backbiting. It satisfies the malicious streak in each of us and makes us feel superior to the one who's getting the verbal bashing. Whatever the explanation, it bothers me now that I could have written what I did with Brunt in mind. I liked the man a great deal, no doubt of it, and admired him for his humanism, for his sympathies with the poor and downtrodden. Perversely, I wanted to disqualify the idol I myself had created. But why? Because the pleasure we take in destruction is equal to that of creation since both afford the thrill that comes with power? Because we want a freedom that's untrammelled by morality, law, or obligation? Those questions, I'm sure, never came into my mind when I wrote the poem or when I saw it afterwards in its printed form. (Getting to know oneself is a long and painful business, hardly a love affair.)

I recall one of Professor Brunt's favourite sayings: "We are all much of a muchness." It was his naïve vanity that endeared the man to me. He appeared comfortable in his skin. Pleased with himself in the way that only a professor who knows he's liked and admired by his students can be. That he was willing to so openly show his pleasure, also endeared him to me.

I envied him for that ease and pleasure and wondered what it took to secure them. Age, perhaps? Would I have his flushed cheeks and soft, expressive mouth when I reached his years? Or was I forever interdicted from reaching that plateau because I was Jewish with a built-in existential discomfort? The poems I was writing at the time provide no clear answers. Several appeared in the *Failte Ye Times* and the *McGill Daily*. Though apprentice work mainly, finger exercises if you wish, poems like "Masquerade," "Thaumaturge," "Days of Wrath," and "Voltaire Jezebel" reflect my self-doubts and confusions, the beginnings of that spiritual scab-pulling that mark the poet as someone different from the rest of mankind.

MASQUERADE

That night you said the strangest things;
And somehow words were mixed with wit;

I wondered vaguely why birth brings
Such crazy lines so sprawling writ;
Such fever burning in your brain,
The mute unneeded pain.

You answered that the stars were one,
And coming from one mammoth light,
Were waiting for the April sun
To shyly lift the hem of night.
These are the syllables I caught –
The rest I forgot.

Though by the time I came to Macdonald College I had been writing verse for nearly ten years, I never thought of myself as a poet. Having studied only English poetry from public school on, having allowed myself to be captivated by the genius of Wordsworth, Shelley, and Byron, I naturally thought that in order to be a poet one had to be either English or dead, preferably both. Can you blame me? Neither at Alexandra School nor at Baron Byng had I ever been given a poem by a Canadian to study. Lampman, Bliss Carman, E.J. Pratt – whoever heard of them?

It was no different at Mac's. In all the discussions I had, even with Professor Hodgins, who taught essay writing, and Dr. Brunt, no Canadian poet was ever mentioned to me though both of them knew of my deep interest in poetry. It also seems strange to me that neither Brunt nor Hodgins ever drew my attention to free verse or made the suggestion that the writing of English poetry hadn't stopped with Matthew Arnold. Surely they must have heard of Eliot's destructive assault on the Edwardian sensibility. If they had, for all of their interest in me, and friendliness, they kept the secret under their hats.

When I think what my reading of Eliot, and Americans such as Hart Crane, E.A. Robinson, Masters, and Jeffers might have done to liberate me from conventional verse forms, it makes me want to tear out my hair. It's only because I don't want to disturb their pleasures in the Elysian fields that I won't mention the fact that neither Brunt nor Hodgins ever breathed a word about Walt Whitman. Fortunately, I'd discovered him for myself, but my teachers might have supplied the light needed for a proper understanding of Whitman's radically innovative poetry.

I try to imagine now what the effect on me would have been had one of my teachers said: "Wordsworth and the Shelley you love so much are passé. They belong to another era. Your task is to refract the world you know which is vastly different from the one that called forth their verse. They wrote about farms and peasants, you must write about factories and workers. They soared heavenward with Shelley's skylark, you must descend into the hell mankind is making for itself in our overcrowded cities whose inhabitants have been inoculated against everything except the fears and hates that turn every man against his neighbour. Since your experience of the world is different from theirs, you must use the language and idiom that contemporary poets are forging to reflect it."

Had they been less academic in their approach to poetry, and seen its liberating possibilities, perhaps I would not have later reached out so violently for the vocabulary to express my disgust with the gentility, philistinism, and cultural sterility that characterized my early environment as a poet. Intelligence and knowledge would have tempered my emotions, and placed my feet earlier on the path towards self-definition that every true poet must find.

ELEVEN

During this term, I commuted to Montreal each week. I had talked Dean Brittain into allowing students majoring in agricultural economics to get supplementary credits from McGill's Department of Economics and Political Science. I took courses in money and banking, labour problems, political theory, and even one in statistics. I am thankful McGill allowed me to audit several courses in philosophy. I sat in on seminars on the Rationalist philosophers and the phenomenology of Hegel. Though I also attended seminars on Whitehead, Dewey, and Russell, I filtered their ideas through a Marxism that need not have been so stultifying had there been anyone in the philosophy department to direct me to the early philosophical manuscripts of Marx, his *Grundrisse*. The soaring genius of Nietzsche I was left to discover on my own.

At this time, my mind was more taken up with politics than poetry. The political situation interested me mainly, I suppose, because great events were only as far away as the nearest radio. Culturally, I might as well have been on the moon. There was no literary tradition in Canada. No authors, no books that you could talk about. Imperialists in Canada had done a thorough job of attenuating whatever feelings and ideas we might have had about our own country. Our cultural cupboard had deliberately been kept bare. The Americans had Hemingway, Faulkner, Fitzgerald, and Dreiser, or Edgar Allan Poe and Whitman. We had no writers to compare with them. There was no literary scene, but there was a political one, a world situation, and it pulled me outside of this country.

Undoubtedly both factors, along with my Marxism, were largely responsible for my internationalist outlook. Canadians do not have the world outlook that comes naturally to a five-thousand-year-old Jew. Things have now changed somewhat. Canada was a cultural wasteland in the late thirties. Only in the past few decades has it acquired a literature one can talk about without wincing or having to apologize. By and large, its poets as well as its politicians were the blind leading the bland. As for Canada's novelists, what could one say about them? Goody-two-shoes all, not a single criminal mind among them.

Because I had read some of his poems which had appeared in the *McGill Daily* I became aware of Louis Dudek. He became aware of me for the same reason. It sometimes happened that his poems and my own appeared in the same issue. I'm not sure where it was we met for the first time but most likely it was at the McGill Union on Sherbrooke Street. My first impression was of somebody very intense covering up his diffidence with a kind of breeziness or abruptness that could be taken for vigour. He was about six years younger than myself and certainly lankier. I remember thinking, "Migosh, he's tall and ascetic-looking." He had an interesting face because it was sallow enough to be that of a seminarian. My imagination at once put a clerical collar around his neck.

Before our first cups of coffee were drunk, I recognized his great interest in ideas, his commitment to poetry. Already he thought of himself as a poet, and fervently wished to be taken for one. Here was someone who, although younger than myself, knew what he wanted to be, someone who felt he had it in him to be a poet. So I secretly admired him for that because it was not something I'd have thought about myself. Maybe this first meeting with Louis encouraged me to think of myself as a poet; here was somebody who actually felt there was some glory in being one. The only other real poet I had met up until then was A.M. Klein, but Klein seemed so much older than myself and more or less remote.

What Louis Dudek and I talked about on that first encounter was what he wanted to write, what I wanted to write, what our explosive, never-before-expressed ideas about poetry were. We were both excited and the excitement showed in the eagerness with which we heard each other out. I undoubtedly spouted my Marxism. He was receptive though not as intoxicated by the prospect of revolutionary change as I was. He was a mild middle-of-the-road moderate socialist.

Every time I came to Montreal, Louis and I would get together. He was living at home with his parents, so we continued to meet at the McGill Union. I don't recall ever bringing him to Horn's. By then I had pretty much exhausted what I could learn from my encounters with the characters there. That chapter in my life was finished.

The basis of Dudek's and my friendship was mainly poetry. In fact, it wasn't so much poetry as the reality that our devotion to the craft made us both loners. Keep in mind that at that time to write poetry was like having the clap; you didn't brag about it. Here, at last, was one other person who shared my suffering or joy – depending on my mood. I think Dudek felt the same way about me. Our regard for one another was to ripen with the years.

Without this common basis, I don't think we'd otherwise have gravitated towards each other, for we were really very different people. I felt he lacked my extravagance, my energy, my sensualism. He had intensity, I had passion. The thing I admired most about him was his integrity. Here, I'd say to myself after each meeting, is a man who tries to be honest about himself and in his associations with others. The dividing line between us: he was much more moralistic than I, more prone to make moral judgments about people and events. I was an agitator, he was a preacher. He had no redeeming vices.

I remember once saying to him: "Louis, a poet is more likely to be destroyed by his virtues than his vices."

I think he always felt there was something demonic about me, even diabolical. At times, the dark underside of my nature made him uneasy. Evil never held the fascination for him it did for me. I've always found sinners more exciting to be with than saints, restless curiosity if not character making me one of the former. Criminals, madmen, prostitutes, failures, and outcasts – the so-called dregs of society – are my parish. From whom else can the poet learn about the frighteningly extensive register of human emotions?

For me, evil and knowledge are twinned. A strange post-lapsarian fire burns inside my soul. This makes me yearn to understand the fascist mind, the mind of the torturer and hit-man. I believe I'd give the remainder of my life to be able to get inside for even a moment the mind of a Barbie or an Eichmann. Yahweh forgot to tell our first parents that the apple in their hand was laced with the poison of malice and egotism; perversely, I have always wanted to bite into that apple. Perhaps the greatest vice of the poet is his implacable desire to know the human soul.

Because Louis came from a poor Polish family and lived in the east end of the city, many of his concerns were similar to my own, and this instantly created a bond between us. I came from an equally poor family. His parents had been immigrants, likewise mine. He had clawed his way up, so to speak, and was now finding himself, to his astonishment, at McGill. The same could be said of me. Among other things, what we had in common was our surprise at finding ourselves where we were since both of us suffered from the same insecurities *vis-à-vis* the English-Canadian majority. We had to prove ourselves. The only way that could be done was to read more books and entertain more ideas than the dominant French and English Canadians surrounding us. Like myself, he was kicking against the pricks, suffering from the same complexes, feeling the same hungers I did. Our lively discussions ranged over poetry, philosophy, politics, current events. We became comrades-in-arms against Canadian philistinism.

What the hell, we were two very earnest intellectuals. Serious? You can bet your last dollar on that. Naïvely open-hearted? What else. Both of us were concerned about the Spanish Civil War and both sensed the coming tragedy. When we did laugh, it was the self-conscious ironic laugh intellectuals favour. The difference between Louis and myself could also be seen in our laughter. His was Voltairean, mine Rabelaisian.

Friendship between two poets is tenuous and prickly, unstable and hypocritical as it is between two attractive women. A poet will gloat over his rival's weak lines as a woman over the unsightly pimple on her friend's face.

Louis and I used to look forward to our weekly handball games at the Sir Arthur Currie Gymnasium on Pine Avenue. Since I no longer boxed or wrestled, it was the only exercise I was able to get. Louis and I were evenly matched, though his lankiness and leanness gave him a slight advantage. My strong point was my stamina. I was tireless. Week after week, we squared off on the court, the game to be neatly sandwiched by literary talk. These were unforgettable afternoons when heart, mind, and muscle were stretched to the limit, when we basked gloriously in each other's good opinion.

One day, Dudek suddenly turned to me and said: "This game will decide who's the greater poet." My mouth fell open, for whatever notion I had of my friend and comrade-in-arms, I never thought he was a humourist. True, we had played against each other week after week. Sometimes he won a game, sometimes I did. If each had won a game, we'd decide to let the next win determine who had been the champion that afternoon. This particular afternoon Louis had won the first game, I the second. Now he had raised the ante. He wanted the next game to decide not only the afternoon's handball champ, but who was the greater poet! Clearly the question had been troubling him for some time. The question had never occurred to me for I never doubted for a moment that I was the better poet, then or potentially. His verses were formally every bit as good as mine, if not better. It was purely my intuition of the man, the way I sized him up. The trim sneakers he wore on the court he also wore climbing Mount Parnassus. They were serviceable but not good enough. Looking down at my own sneakers I wondered whether they were not really seven-league boots that would carry me over mountain-tops and cliffs, which Louis would get to know only with the help of a guidebook.

There were no spectators to watch us. Driven by pride or vanity, by rivalrous folly, we bounced about on the court no less frenetically than the tantalizing black ball which seemed to be inhabited by a malicious spirit out to mock us. We made saves no one would have thought possible. We literally snatched the ball off the ceiling, off the floor, and walls. Our smacks, as glove or hand met the ball, resounded in the court like a clap of thunder, or so it seemed to me. The score mounted leadenly until it reached 20-20. A winner would not be declared until he had a two-point lead.

Now something like madness took hold of Louis and me. We played as if possessed. Already exhausted by a game that had gone on too long and too strenuously, we had to call on untested reserves. I believe I made the next point. Victory was within reach. Louis's spare frame now seemed to be everywhere, miraculously smashing the ball back and not letting me score the coveted point. Once again we were an even 21-21. And so it continued.

Finally the score was again tied at 30-30. Heaven alone knows what was passing through Louis's mind. Secretly I was thanking my mother for the great stamina with which she had endowed me. The three or four minutes we battled for the next point were gruelling, but not as gruelling as the point we strove for after I'd made the score 31-30. We were now fighting over game point. Then – O rapturous joy! – I sent the ball careening past Louis's outstretched hand, and though he turned swiftly to smash it as it bounced back from the adjoining wall it eluded him and gave me the victory.

As if at a signal, we both collapsed on the floor and lay there, our breathing laboured, both of us too exhausted to speak. Again, I kept wondering what was going on in Dudek's mind. Would he accept the verdict he himself had proposed? Or would he very sensibly decide there was no inner logic that connected athletic prowess with poetic greatness? Perhaps he felt he needed the assurance a victory might have given him, if only as a portent of things to come.

In the showers after the game, the water splashing down on our heads, Louis turned to me and asked, "Do you think you're a major poet?"

"Yes," I replied, only to goad him, "I do."

"Well, I don't think I'm one," Louis said. "I think I'm a minor poet."

"Louis, if you think you're a major poet, you might end up being a minor one. But if you start out thinking yourself a minor poet, you may not end up a poet at all."

I had spent the previous summer again working in Laurentian hotels to raise funds for room and board and other living expenses. One time I was a busboy, another a waiter. I took whatever job was offered. One place I remember well was Castle des Monts in Ste. Agathe, where I waited tables. The hotel was owned and run by a middle-aged Jewish couple and their daughter.

My job didn't last long. Working conditions were dreadful. Mrs. Greenberg and her daughter would plant themselves in the kitchen each meal time and count all the plates going out into the dining room. They suffered from a justified panic that the starved waiters might take food off the plates intended for the guests. Mrs. Greenberg reminded me of Baron Byng's principal, Mr. Astbury. Like him she had a flushed countenance and nervous eyes that darted suspiciously from side to side. We were terribly underpaid and slept in dark, ill-ventilated quarters in the basement. There was no regard for the help's comfort and dignity. Two other waiters, both Jewish medical students at McGill, thought along with me that we were entitled to more decent treatment. After all, weren't we co-religionists of the Greenbergs? Their disappointment was no less bitter than my own.

It was at Castle des Monts that I got my first live image of the exploiting Jew. It angered me greatly that the Greenbergs lived up to the stereotype of the hard-hearted, tight-fisted Jew. I was both angered and saddened, for neither my reading nor experience had prepared me for it.

When it came to exploiting their fellowmen, Jews, for all their synagogue piety, their invoking of the Law and the Prophets, their longing for the speedy appearance of the Messiah, proved as brutal as others. I learned one more important thing: the bourgeois loves his comforts, loves them – except for a few rare individuals – above everything else. The guests we served knew how ridiculously underpaid the waiters and busboys were, how we were spied on and how, with all the rich steaming food around us, we had to work our daily stint of fourteen hours on a starvation diet. Their expressions of sympathy, when none of the Greenberg trio was present, were loud and long. Their liberal middle-class hearts ached for us and their liberal middle-class minds yearned to see justice done. I know this because they let us know at every possible opportunity. Their sentiments heartened me since I was one of the ones instigating a strike. Yet, instead of rallying to our support as their expressions of sympathy had led me to expect, the guests soon began to grumble they weren't getting their cornflakes in the morning. They weren't getting their afternoon tea. Clearly this wasn't turning out to be the carefree vacation they had planned and paid for. By the end of the fourth day on strike, they turned unpleasantly against us. Gone was sympathy, gone the cry for justice. Their cry was now, "Give us our daily cornflakes."

This reminds me of another de Maupassant story, his "Boule de Suif." A coach of genteel, upper-class French ladies is stopped by the Germans during the Franco-Prussian War. Naturally they're afraid the German officers are going to rape them. However, there's a whore in the carriage with them and they egg her on with blandishments to be nice to the Germans. The kind whore, out of patriotism and an obscure fellowship with the passengers, lets herself be had by the German officers. The carriage with its occupants continues on its way. Now the genteel, upper-class women who only a short while ago had been showering all sorts of compliments on the silly whore turn away from her contemptuously as if she were a rat that had jumped from a drain onto their laps. Well, on the fifth day, I was that sewer rat and even the guests at my table had nothing to say to me. The strike was broken since we had foolishly counted on the support of the patrons. As one of the ringleaders, I was fired and the Greenbergs threatened to have me blacklisted in all the other Laurentian resorts.

Luckily I was able to land a job in Val David. This hotel was much smaller, much less prestigious than Castle des Monts. But here too it was operated by a middle-aged Jewish couple who, only recently arrived from Hungary, had also resolved to take the royal road to prosperity via exploitation. The only difference between them and the Greenbergs was that they did it more suavely. In one respect husband and wife reminded me of my parents. The husband seemed no less passive and ineffectual than my father had been and no less in tow to his wife's greater drive and energy. Having seen that Shelleyan idealism might comfort the soul like a breviary, but was not relevant in a century that men and machinery were making increasingly brutal, I pulled in my horns and lasted out the season.

That summer I was left with the abiding suspicion that culture anywhere and any time is only skin deep. Never again would Philistia fool me. Nor its flatterers and parasites. I had learned what the real priorities were in this world. It was the memory of these experiences that inspired me years later to write the following poem:

ADVICE TO A YOUNG POET

My young friend, write your immortal verse
but keep adding money to your purse;
bare words on a gold certificate
o'ersway the storm of Shakespeare's wit.

Whatever my experiences had taught me, they had not taught me tact or prudence. More ambivalent than ever, I was split down the middle. Half of me yearned to be well-liked, the other half despised that part for its cowardly surrender, and relished the solitude and freedom unpopularity gave me. My soul was a laboratory where I brewed the most nauseous compounds, in the hope I would startle awake the somnolent Canucks around me.

There was only one girl on campus who shared my political outlook. She had read my column in the *Failte Ye Times*, and wrote me a note inviting me to meet her mother and her younger sister. Her name was Mimi Cuisinier and her family had only recently arrived from France.

Right from the start I took a great liking to the two girls. Mimi was the elder, also the more intense and intellectual. Calan was the playful minx, flirtatious and bold with the knowledge of how tempting the fire in her young limbs made her. Mme. Cuisinier was a caricature of a Parisienne. It was as if someone had played a nasty joke on her by coarsening her petiteness, by thickening what once must have been very fine and delicate features. In the daytime her midriff lipped over the belt that kept her faded beige trousers from falling down. Her prim mouth was pleated with tiny wrinkles.

I was frequently asked to visit. Separated from her husband, Mme. Cuisinier had rented a house not far from the college, where Mimi was studying for a diploma in agriculture. I sometimes accompanied Mimi to the barns and sheds that were located some distance behind the cream- and rust-coloured buildings that composed Mac's neat, attractive front. She tried to teach me how to milk a cow and laughed aloud at my clumsy, inexpert fingers. But since her real interest lay in economics and political theory, we had a great deal to talk about. She was a radical by instinct, a rebel and a non-conformist, the only one I had met in my years at Mac's, and she was a breath of fresh air. Many years later Mimi returned to France with her mother and became a militant organizer for the Communist party.

One evening when the two girls were clearing away the supper dishes, Mme. Cuisinier invited me to come and stay with them that summer. I could pay, she said, for my room and board by teaching her two daughters political economy. The month of July rolled around. I took the train for La Voiselle, the name I gave to the place in the short story I based on that summer's experiences.

Each morning after breakfast I sat down with Mimi and Calan to tutor them in economics, history, and English literature. I sat between them and it took immense willpower to keep my hands from travelling up the inviting thigh on either side. At nineteen, Mimi was a physically well-developed, mature woman. I never talked with her about sex though I knew that that was prominent in her mind. She was a ripe plum waiting to be plucked or to fall into someone's waiting hand. Funk kept me from reaching out, though the invitation in Mimi's eyes was clear and frank enough. Funk? Or the quite sensible fear that I would be kicking open a snake nest? Perhaps I wasn't devoid of common sense after all.

But one night, when the two *minettes* had gone upstairs to bed and I was lying on my cot listening to the insects hurling themselves against the screen of the kitchen door, I heard Mme. Cuisinier's soft whisper from the adjoining bedroom: "*Cheri, que fais-tu?*" Only a thin, gauzy curtain separated our two rooms. Since I didn't know what to say, I said nothing. Again I heard her say, "*Que fais-tu, mon cheri?*"

Mischief, curiosity, my insane zest for experience, made me reply, "*Je pense à vous.*" Next thing I heard were heavy sighs and some stertorous breathing, real or faked I couldn't decide. By now my senses were alerted and I was beginning to shiver. I was sitting up in my cot, staring at the large windowpane in front of me. The round moon looked as if it had been pasted up for the occasion. Its smooth, polished surface had a calming effect though my mind kept imagining Mme. Cuisinier's protruding abdomen and her spindly blue-veined legs twitching with desire.

"Come to see me," she whispered hoarsely, "I burn in hell." Poor woman. God alone knew how long she had done without sex. It would be a *mitzvah*, I told myself, to restore her faith in man and God were I to pad over to her bed and lie beside her. Was I capable of such altruism? After a few seconds of agitated reflection, I remembered the crucifix just above her bed and said lamely, "The cross protects you."

I heard her say, "*La croix est tombée,*" and her words had the effect of chilling my blood and driving away whatever desire might have mounted in my loins. By now the moon had disappeared and the room was as dark and silent as a tomb. I didn't make a sound, I didn't stir. After ten minutes had gone by, I heard Mme. Cuisinier's loud rhythmic snores. I must confess that when my trembling stopped they sounded more soothing than Chopin's *études*. The next morning, Mme. Cuisinier's innocent grey-green eyes were luminous with the sin she had not committed. All the same, she hinted broadly that I'd better leave.

Although I was an indifferent student at Macdonald College, for my métier was not science, I was at the same time compelled to take courses leading to a Bachelor of Science Degree, albeit in agriculture. In retrospect, I am grateful for having had to take courses in chemistry, physics, biochemistry, and advanced mathematics, for it gave me a familiarity with science that few poets have.

My compulsory immersion in the sciences did not, however, lessen my voracious appetite for literature and politics. Whatever spare time I had I spent reading novels, plays, poetry, and political writings such as *The Handbook of Marxism* (which became my bible after a fellow student, one of my most bitter opponents, gave it to me, whether out of generosity or contempt, I could never decide), and one of the most influential books of the thirties, which I carried around as if it were a missile or a breviary, John Strachey's *The Coming Struggle for Power*.

I did not enrol for my third year at Mac's because my brother Hyman had come to visit me just when I was about to register, and he persuaded me to drop everything and return with him to New York. (The RCMP blacklist was not yet in existence, as far as anyone knew.) But what Hyman had promised would be a great adventure ended up with my working as a busboy in a hotel in Lakewood, New Jersey. After that, I spent several months in New York selling magazine subscriptions. Some adventure! I should have remembered the colloquy I always had with my brother on those rare occasions when we met:

Hyman: "What you need is experience. Be like me, go into the world and have some experience."

Me: "Hyman, you go out and get yourself all the experiences you want. Afterwards, I'll tell you what they mean."

After several more months of drifting, I decided to return to Montreal, and, in the fall, to Macdonald College to complete my last two years. I had no idea what I would do with my degree once I got it. I suppose vaguely I thought of getting a job in the Civil Service but of course I'd spiked that completely by my radical activities. Though I'd published several poems (now under the name Irving Layton) and a short story of mine won *McGill Daily*'s literary prize, I had no ambition to be a writer. Not even a journalist or copywriter. All I wanted was to hear myself speaking beautifully, to let myself be drugged by the musical syllables I managed to extract from my throat at the slightest sign of encouragement. And to count the stars each night to see if one was missing.

TWELVE

I returned from Lakewood, New Jersey, in the spring of 1937. It was then that I met the woman who was to play such a large and painful part in my life. Faye Lynch hailed from Yarmouth, Nova Scotia, and had met my sister Esther who was now into her second marriage and residing there. When Esther learned that her husband's niece, whose name I can't recall, was planning a trip to Montreal, she told her to get in touch with me. She was a young woman in her early twenties, blonde and very appealing with an open smile and frank, pale-blue eyes. I soon became very fond of her. One day, she asked me to come over for the express purpose of meeting her cousin, who had arrived in Montreal three days before.

I can't recall anything else except my surprise that Faye looked so unlike her attractive cousin. She was obese and black hairs grew on her chin and cheeks; as I found out later, she had to shave every day like a man. I wasn't aware of this condition on the day we met because her face had been freshly shaved and talcumed. I don't think the conversation amounted to very much that afternoon; at least, I wasn't inspired. The fact was, Faye did not stimulate me in that way. Very early in life I learned there was a connection between eros and creativity. Beautiful women unfailingly turn me on to speak with passion and eloquence.

Faye had a good complexion and warm brown eyes that held laughter. I liked her cheerfulness and she was witty with a fine, sharp mind. I liked her honesty; emotionally she was a very honest person. I came to admire this about her: she didn't allow her obesity and hirsuteness to destroy her sense of self. But what got to me, what struck me more than anything else, even more than her confidence and quiet defiance, was her serenity. With a physical misfortune similar to hers, I might have been crushed.

Faye had a job in downtown Montreal working for a Jew, who was a *mensch*. He had a scrapyard and sold the remains of autos, machinery, and the like to the Germans and Japanese as many Canadian patriots were doing at the time, though it looked as though war with them was close at hand. (Perhaps they believed a Canadian soldier would die more happily if he knew the bullet that hit him had been made from home-grown metal.) Faye was an excellent bookkeeper, and Mr. Seligman found her very dependable and hard-working. For all his gruffness, he unfailingly treated her with tact and concern.

Earlier I said my crippled kitten Pussela had an important influence on me, and that it always tore me apart to see him trying to run after a ball, dragging himself along the linoleum. And so it was almost preordained that when I met Faye Lynch I would be lost in admiration for her and her gallant refusal to allow her physical condition to be an obstacle. My admiration turned into a kind of affection and a feeling I was almost willing to call love, although I knew it was not. It was not love because I felt no physical attraction. Whenever we went out together, I was conscious that we made a grotesque pair; she was shorter than I and much heavier. Her generous spirit, her quick intelligence, her good humour were as bewildering to me as Pussela dragging himself across the floor to get at the tossed ball.

One evening, out of loneliness, out of not having anything to do, I phoned her. I remember this so clearly. I was on Sherbrooke. There was a restaurant, corner of Sherbrooke and Victoria, and I recalled that Faye had a room not far from where I was. I thought, Well, why not give her a call and if she's in, she might join me for a cup of coffee. So I called her.

Thomas Hardy wasn't altogether wrong in continually showing the part that coincidence plays in the lives of his characters. More than some of his vociferous critics, Hardy knew that life has its own notion of where it wants to go, that it uses chance and coincidence to upset our neat plans and calculations. And so, just as I phoned Faye, at that very exact moment, there was a man with her, a well-to-do merchant with a large store in Dartmouth, Nova Scotia, and he was proposing to her.

I didn't know that at the time, of course, I learned this later in the week when she said, "You know, Irving, when you phoned me, Hymie Jacobson was asking me to marry him." I asked her whether she had accepted and she said she hadn't. When I asked her why not, she didn't answer but left me with the strong impression that my phone call had something to do with it. And the impression didn't leave; on the contrary, it was made stronger and stronger in the ensuing weeks and months, as we continued to see each other.

It was plain she liked me. She didn't hide her feelings, buying me little gifts: a shirt, a tie, something like that. Yes, she fancied me a great deal. But why was *I* seeing her? There was no physical attraction whatsoever, and though I admired her character, intellectually we had nothing in common. She didn't read books as I did so ravenously. She certainly didn't care in the least about politics, philosophy, or literature. Yet I wanted to continue to see her.

A truly satisfying explanation for this eludes me still. Certainly the Pussela thing. And my morbid need for affection. Also, at that time, I was always railing against inequality, above all, cosmic inequality and injustice. My most engulfing thought was that life was terribly unfair. To some extent, this was sentimentality, of course, but the kind that drove Tolstoy to work side by side with his peasants and to renounce the comforts he had. Other people have also been moved by such sentimental feelings. Faye Lynch's afflictions were not those that some capitalist had imposed. Plainly, I saw the injustice as the deed of an evil deity. And I remember thinking – and it's easy here to detect the prod of vanity – I'm in a position where I can do something about this monstrous cosmic injustice. Damn it all, this woman really loves me and just because she is disfigured, why shouldn't she have the man she loves? Why shouldn't she? So vanity and sentimentality and misguided generosity and stupidity and compassion and youth's inexperience brewed a hemlock that poisoned my soul, while leaving my body sound.

Years later, I read Zweig's *Beware of Pity*. The title caught my eye one afternoon as I went past a bookstore, and as if pushed by some invisible hand, I went in and bought it. It's the story of an officer who's invited to a ball given by his commander. At the ball he meets his host's daughter. She is a cripple confined to a wheelchair. He likes her because she has spiritual qualities, and so on, but he doesn't love her. However, lacking the willpower or the brutality to extricate himself from the web his own vanity and good nature have woven, he marries her. An excellent story, and I found myself wondering whether Zweig had had a similar experience to the one he wrote about. Without that, how could he ever have described so authentically the worms and maggots that a decomposing pity can generate in an individual's consciousness?

When you know you have another person's happiness in your own hands, it gives you a great sense of power. You almost feel you have the power of life and death. And, exaggerating my own importance, I saw myself as Faye's saviour, a messiah bringing her the happiness every human being deserves.

It was somehow taken for granted that we would get married, or maybe that's the way she worked it. She just operated on the assumption that after a while, since I was seeing her, I was going to marry her. And every now and then she kept bringing up the fact that if I hadn't come along and phoned her that night, she'd have married Hyman Jacobson. So I began to feel very guilty. I saw myself as her last chance and because of her disfigurement, nobody else would want to marry her. But, I now see, that it went beyond that. My weaknesses alone were responsible for my not having halted the forward march towards the wedding canopy.

Though we had never been formally engaged, Faye told all her friends, her relatives, and her parents that we were. She was tightening the noose and making certain that every wriggle of mine to free myself only tightened it more. Finally, my self-contempt moved me to tell her bluntly that I did not love her. Seeing the tears beginning to form in her eyes perversely made me say in a taunting tone, "Did you ever hear me say that I did? Did you?" Alas, the more sincere, the more honest I tried to be, the more loud her sobs became. The tears rolled down her cheeks.

There was another thing rattling about in my poor confused head. My brother Avrum had been engaged to somebody and had broken off the engagement. The girl's parents wrote to the rabbi in Roumania (she and her parents had also emigrated from that country), telling him what had happened. The rabbi cursed Avrum and said he would never live to marry anyone else. It was soon after this that Avrum contracted tuberculosis and died. I was not religious, yet the rabbi's curse haunted me, and because it had always been remarked that I resembled Avrum, the association I felt with him was always in my mind. This operated strongly to weaken my will. I had no wish to share his fate.

I understood the nature of my dilemma but not my paralysis. I could feel the forces pushing or pulling me, but understanding did not stop me from being dragged in the direction I did not wish to go. I saw myself being pulled towards the falls, but the current was too strong to resist. What I should have done – all I had to do – was to stop seeing her. But because of guilts, fears, superstitions, and need, I continued to see her even while all my best instincts were telling me to run.

I began to see more clearly to what extent egotism forms the basis for human conduct. The brutal outbursts my self-contempt initiated could leave no doubt in Faye's mind about my true feelings. My great unhappiness, my turmoil, must have been quite evident to her, as was my weight loss, which made us look even more grotesque as a couple. Out of pride or blindness she did not acknowledge the pain and anguish clearly etched in the hollows of my cheeks. She was determined to run over me like a steamroller, if necessary to plough me into the ground, as long as she got me to the altar.

I can only assume her parents thought and felt as she did, because there could be little doubt in their minds I was a reluctant bridegroom-to-be. I could almost imagine this giving their knives a keener edge for the sacrifice. Though I was literally fighting for my life and happiness, I was unarmed. My own family were, as usual, uninterested in my doings. My mother had met Faye, and liked her, but she did not concern herself in the least with the progress of the relationship.

The whole thing began to become an interesting event to witness, as though it were all happening to somebody else. I was actually starting to enjoy the theatre, the drama of it. The emotions, the comedy, the tears – life's nourishing sludge. For the first time, I was beginning to see that art is the distillation of life's sewage. You have to pay a terrible price for a really good poem, I told myself, by way of excusing my fecklessness and to moderate my self-disgust. The true alchemist is the poet, transmuting the dross of daily life into insight and ecstasy.

One afternoon, Faye and I were in a greasy spoon on Prince Arthur, right near McGill. We were supposed to leave the next week for Saint John, New Brunswick, where our wedding was to take place. And once again I was telling her I couldn't go through with it. I thought that this time, definitely, I would make her understand the union was absolutely impossible. Again I was stupid. If you want to break off an engagement, you just break it off. But the unconscious guilts and fears were operating in full force. My lips were moving but my body wasn't. Nothing I said would change her mind. So I asked her to excuse me, telling her I had a doctor's appointment on Milton Street. The doctor's name was Ruben. He was one of the medical students who had worked with me as a waiter in Castle des Monts. We had gotten on very well. He was a beautiful, life-loving guy, and when I told him my problem he just laughed and said, "If you don't want to marry the girl, nothing is forcing you. Tell her that you can't go through with it."

"Yes, I know," I said, "I keep telling her that."

So he said, "Well, stop telling her and just go away."

And then I thought: What if I went back and told Faye I had some horrible disease? What if I told her I had tuberculosis and that the doctor forbade me to marry? Have you ever seen a trapped animal that doesn't know which way to turn, a tormented cockroach? Its movements are totally irrational. That's exactly the state I had reached.

I was exultant as I walked back to the restaurant. At last I had a real plan to extricate myself (the irony of which escaped me at the time). I kept saying to myself: "Faye, I've got TB. The doctor says I have to go to the san in Ste. Agathe." In the restaurant, I said those sentences aloud to Faye. I had been losing weight, anybody looking at me could see I was not well. Though the causes were entirely psychological, my haggard appearance lent colour to the story. I repeated that Dr. Ruben, after examining me carefully, had pronounced me ill with TB. The sooner I put myself into a sanatorium the better. Faye started to cry and her loud sobs were audible in the restaurant. Accepting the fact that we couldn't get married, she continued to sob in complete sympathy with me. Here, I felt, was genuine love, genuine grief. She wasn't crying because the marriage was off, I told myself, but because I'd been stricken with this awful, perhaps fatal, disease. The thought undid me and I began to weep. The more she tried to console me over my fabricated disease, the more I wept.

We were a comic duet replete with tears instead of laughter. No performance could have had a more attentive audience. The other people in the restaurant kept staring at us as the tears continued to flow into our cups. It was ridiculous, it was magnificent, we both should have been on stage. I was crying out of self-pity and out of pity for Faye. I was crying over the human condition that brings an individual trying to follow the dictates of his heart to this absurd pass. And the more she wept, the more I sobbed over the thought that I was playing out such a shabby, ignominious role. To this day the idea still haunts me that perhaps she too was playing a part. I felt this display of emotion on both our parts had created a communion, an authenticity between us that had been missing all along. Overcome and deceived by a relief that was so intense I mistook it for rapture, I blurted out that Dr. Ruben was not entirely sure and had to make another test. Her eyes brightened. I had thrown away my best card.

The wedding was performed in Saint John, on September 13, 1938. My brother Larry, having left New York several years earlier and bought himself a farm in Ste. Sophie, had come to see me off at the train station. Had he been more sensitive or concerned, he'd have put a hundred dollars in my pocket and sent me far away. All it would have taken was for him to say, "What the hell are you doing? Here's some cash. Go to the Adirondacks for a few weeks." But, alas, this didn't happen.

From my family, only Esther turned up at the wedding. Maybe a couple of other relatives, I can't remember. By then I had lost contact with reality. A scrap of paper caught in an autumn wind would have had more volition than I. I was suffering from alienation which, out of conceit and inexperience, I mistook for artistic detachment. A fragment of myself was playing out my role in the wedding and another fragment was watching the performance. I saw myself going under the canopy to hear the rabbi drone out the binding formula. In a trance, I saw all the people as if they had been projected onto a screen. The whole thing felt completely remote and unreal. That experience gave me a key insight into the nature of the twentieth-century malady. It enabled me to understand that people doing things to which they do not bring their whole selves – a job, a marriage, an affair, even a friendship – provides the real meaning of inauthenticity.

After the wedding, we returned to Montreal and got an apartment on Drummond Street. I was entering my final year at Macdonald's, Faye still had her job with Seligman.

It did not take long before the hideousness of my plight became clear to me and provided me with a new definition for marriage: two strangers using the same toilet bowl. Faye and I had not one thing in common. She was practical, literal-minded, and, without really understanding my needs at all, she tried hard to be a devoted and loving wife. My own soul was filled with dark chaos and an overwhelming compassion.

One morning something happened that jolted me out of my somnambulist condition. I began to write a poem and just couldn't leave it. Oblivious to everything going on around me, I wrote and wrote and wrote. It was a Saturday and Faye wasn't working. She asked me to come eat lunch. I neither heard nor saw her. So she left a sandwich and a glass of milk on my table and went out. When she returned around three or four o'clock in the afternoon, the sandwich was untouched and I was still writing with the same intensity. The poor woman had never before seen a poet feverishly intent on writing down lines and images that are seething in his brain and she thought

I'd flipped my lid. She hurried out to fetch our dentist who lived on St. Catherine right around the corner, and brought him her anxiety. I remember how she and the dentist came tiptoeing in. They didn't want to disturb the madman, fearing he might do heaven alone knew what. I saw Faye's anxious face peeping around the corner of the passageway. I said nothing and just went on writing. She and the dentist shuffled away quietly, no doubt to engage in further discussion about my mental state. By the time evening came I was, of course, perfectly calm. Nevertheless, she kept on looking at me with doubt and scepticism, as if asking herself what kind of person she had married? The feeling was mutual.

I titled the poem, one of the longest I'd ever written, "Medley for Our Times," and the *McGill Daily* published it. Only young martinets and Ontario farmboys could have deemed my *cri-de-coeur*, which the menacing times we were living through had called forth, an anti-war poem. Faye was alone in the apartment one day soon after it was published, when members of the Officers Training Corps came down to rough me up and adminster a salutary lesson in patriotism.

My last year at Mac's came to an end in May 1939. I graduated with respectable marks. I could now write B.Sc. (Agr.) after my name – whatever that would mean. As far as I was concerned, my degree in agriculture was just a piece of paper I could wipe a cow's ass with. Mind and pockets were both empty. I was not thinking of going on and getting an M.A. War was in the air. I was twenty-seven years old, married, and I hadn't the faintest idea where I was headed or what I wanted to do with the rest of my life.

The following autumn, we moved to Halifax where I thought there would be better job opportunities. My first job was selling insurance for Confederation Life. The war had broken out, and in Montreal I'd tried to enlist in the Medical Corps. However, at the interview, the pink-cheeked, clean-shaven major eyed me suspiciously when I said in all innocence that I wished to join the Medical Corps because I wanted to be with the men. Over and over I kept urging, "I want to be with the men, I want to be with the men!" I shall never forget the perplexed look faintly tinged with disgust in the major's eyes. My request to join the Medical Corps was turned down, for reasons that totally escaped me at the time.

I lacked the needed ingredients to make a good insurance salesman. My confident know-it-all air had fooled the manager, just as it had fooled Mac's students and the characters with whom I'd verbally jousted at Horn's. But it was not really aggressiveness at all, it was insecurity that made me eager to give battle, to contradict, and argue. After all, if someone disputed with me, it obviously meant I was being taken seriously. It did not take the manager of the company long to see that I was ill-suited for the job since I barely averaged the sale of one small policy per week.

I then became a Fuller Brush salesman. I was now like any other married man with responsibilities and a wife. I even found myself a part of the Jewish community, and because Halifax was both smaller and less diversified than Montreal, it was also more philistine, more narrow-minded, more conventional. Not a single Heinrich Heine among them. Spinoza? Not even his wan ghost. The main things the Jews of Halifax had on their minds were money-making and bar mitzvahs, and the rabbi's orotund platitudes that asked to be taken for profundities. The picture I had of myself was that of a trussed-up eagle on a poultry farm, moreover an eagle that was expected to take seriously the pecking order paraded before his eyes.

For several months we lived on what I earned as a Fuller Brush salesman. My territory was Dartmouth and the only interesting person I met during that whole time was a mad theosophist who claimed she had powers of divination. Her husband had died some time ago but he still remembered her fondly, bringing her affectionate messages from the beyond that, since he had had a scatological mind, were written on pink bum paper.

The end of my stay in Halifax was brought about when I was summoned by Sam Jacobson, brother of the same Hyman Jacobson who had proposed to Faye. He asked me to meet him at their warehouse in Dartmouth and said he wanted to talk to me on a matter of grave importance. But apparently the warehouse wasn't private enough for the discussion he had in mind, for, when I got there, he had to find a particular place, one that was isolated and seemingly sealed off. Wondering what he'd got on his mind, I followed him dutifully from storeroom to storeroom. He strode ahead of me with the stolid assurance that money, good digestion, and a total disinterest in ideas confer upon the middle-class Jew.

Reaching the centre of the room, and thinking it private and secure enough, he suddenly wheeled around to wag a thick forefinger at me and he said, "You know you're disgracing the Jewish community here." When I asked him why, he told me: "I've got a report that you're a member of the Communist party and we can't tolerate this. We're a good Jewish community. We've never been in trouble with the law. We want to keep our good name. We don't want the likes of you coming from Montreal and spoiling it."

I said: "Look, I'm not a Communist. I never have been. In Halifax I did go to one meeting of a Communist cell and when I heard the organizer say there was no difference between British imperialism and German fascism, I told him to get lost, that he was talking bull." All my contempt for mediocrity was in the articulation of that expletive, for the Sam Jacobsons of this world and the Communist organizers with their packet of lies and dogmas.

However, Sam wouldn't listen. He just stood there indignant, self-righteous, and I saw before me an irate turkey shaking his red wattles. Well, this was the best thing that could have happened. I needed the nudge. God had indeed moved in a mysterious way.

One afternoon, about a week later, I was on the Dalhousie campus. I was lying on the grass looking up at the trees and the blue sky, my Fuller Brush valise beside me. Suddenly I thought, What the hell am I doing here, selling Fuller Brushes, and truckling to fat, sly, middle-class Pharisees, even trying to interest them in poetry? I laughed aloud at the comedy of my efforts. I could see students enjoying the mild April day, walking gaily arm in arm across the campus. And there I was in my double-breasted suit, with a valise of Fuller Brushes to sell to dull, shapeless housewives. Seized by an acute feeling of nausea, and without any further thought, I picked myself up, grabbed my thick black valise, and made for the house.

It was my good fortune that Faye's mother had come to take her to shop for a stationery store for me to purchase and run. I could sell notepads and pencils and pens and erasers, New Year's and bar mitzvah cards for the rest of my life while taking care of Faye. I had less than three dollars in my pocket, but I dropped off the valise and ran all the way down to the train station as if ten devils were pursuing me. I asked the ticket agent how far two dollars would take me. It was something like fifteen or twenty miles, but at least it was out of Halifax. From there, I would hitch rides all the way back to Montreal.

My first lift was to Saint John. By this point I had no money at all. I hadn't eaten all day. There was a slight drizzle which made the city appear even more dismal than I remembered it, and I needed to find a place to sleep. I ended up going back to the hotel where Faye and I had spent our first nuptial night. And there, cold, wet, and hidden behind a huge potted plant stationed right outside the room where Faye and I had stayed, I slept.

I got up early the next morning. At the gas station near the hotel I saw a car with a suit hung up inside the rear window.

210

Its owner, when I approached him, said he was headed west and would be pleased to take me along since the trip was going to be a long one. He was a nice chap, friendly and chatty. Talk about the long arm of coincidence; he was running away from his wife. When I told him I was doing the same thing, he laughed, and from then on paid for my meals, and for the night's lodging en route. He brought me to within twenty-five miles of Montreal. My next lift took me straight into the city. I was back home.

It did not take long before Faye heard where I was and came hot-footing it to Montreal, where she ended up staying. Week after week she waylaid me, there's no other word for it, outside the Jewish Public Library where I was again teaching English to newcomers. She out-generaled me till I gave in and went to stay with her in her room. There were times when I imagined she had an X-ray of all my inner compulsions and, more skilfully than any surgeon, knew which one to probe. Yet some part of me, not the least admirable either, applauded her iron-willed determination even though I knew myself to be the victim of it.

The old heartbreak returned, the old Pussela complex. I finally knew I was headed for a breakdown when I found myself staring at – no, watching for – the black bristles. Faye would emerge from the bathroom after her morning shave, her skin soft and glowing with health. Her eyes were bright, she had a beautiful skin, an appealing face. But in the late afternoon, when she came home from work, I knew there would be these black bristles pushing through the white powder. I couldn't avert my gaze from her unshaven cheeks, from the raw blueness of her chin. It was as if I were watching tiny little insects pushing up from her powdered skin. And then she'd go to the bathroom to shave and she would come out and her face was again smooth and lovely, and smelling fragrantly of talc. I knew I had to do something, because if I didn't, I'd end up in a lunatic asylum. One day, standing at the corner of

Drummond and St. Catherine, I couldn't get myself to cross the street. I just stood there frozen with anxiety.

My inner conflicts were literally tearing me apart. The real, life-loving, sensuous man I knew myself to be was at war with the ideal, self-sacrificing man that a sentimental humanitarianism persuaded me I should aspire to be. I now find it incredible that anyone as tough-minded and clear-sighted as I am could have allowed himself to be led down the garden path towards self-betrayal. However, some part of me must have wanted the experience of self-humiliation, to know the ache of spiritual desolation, my own and that of the culture that seemed bent on exacting it from its naïve victims.

One night, lying in bed beside Faye, I rolled over on my side to put a space between us. Faye reached out her hand to touch me on the shoulder. As if I'd been seared by a red-hot poker, I threw the coverlet off me and bounded out of bed. This unexpected response to her tender advance startled her. I was no less bewildered and alarmed than she was, for I had no idea what I was doing. Some dike in my mind had broken and the flooding emotions of revulsion, anger, and self-hate were bearing me before them as if I were an empty canister in their turbulent path. They pushed me towards the door that opened onto the balcony, and I found myself standing on the railing looking down at the asphalted lane below. I embraced the post connecting our balcony with the one above it. I saw Faye coming towards me and I shouted, "If you come one step closer, I'll jump!" Fortunately, she sensed the madness or desperation in my voice and did not take the step that might have rendered me a helpless cripple, for out of pride or stubbornness, I would have made good my threat.

Hitler came to my rescue, having been encouraged by Stalin's perfidy and the signing of the German-Soviet nonaggression pact to unleash the war by bombing Warsaw. The Minister of Defence, Ralston, was acquainted with Faye's father and, in 1942, I was given second lieutenancy and signed up for command training in Brockville, Ontario. In less than two weeks, I had put on weight and was back to my robust, vigorous self.

I was in Brockville for six months or so; there I got my second pip and became a first lieutenant. Then I went to Petawawa for intelligence training. However, they looked up my record and found that I held radical ideas and had been involved with movements alarming to the Canuck's native conservatism. It didn't take long before I was pulled from the course.

The major had called me in and said, "Well, we can't let you go on with this course, but if you wish, you can take artillery training." I hoped my contempt didn't show. A Jewish anti-fascist, I couldn't be trusted to fight the Nazis, but I was good enough to be blown up by a cannonball! So I studied artillery, fired off cannons, and read in what spare time I had. There wasn't a single soul to talk to in the officers' mess. Healthy, untroubled Canucks, every one of them. Their normalcy was overwhelming, reminding me of the trim vegetables, the fresh turnips and carrots my mother had bargained for in the Champ-de-Mars market.

One day I was in the officers' mess and saw my name posted on the bulletin sheet: Lt. Irving Layton, Brigade Commander. This meant that that day I had to lead out the entire brigade for the day's manoeuvres. I hadn't observed what my fellow officers had done day after day. Had I watched, I'd have known what to do because the exercise never varied in the slightest. But at that time, I'd discovered Santayana and used to slide down the hill to read while the exercise was being carried out. I would turn the pages and hear the guns booming, booming, booming. Only when the last boom had sounded did I climb back up.

So, feeling that the situation called for a dramatic gesture, I waved my swagger-stick and boldly said, "One platoon over there, one platoon over here. You over here, you over there." With the swagger-stick giving me authority, no one would have guessed that I hadn't the foggiest idea what I was doing or saying.

It turned out I had so deployed the troops that the platoons were facing each other. All I had to do was shout – as I had been about to – "Fire!" and two hundred Canucks would have been dead. They were using live ammunition and were waiting for the order to be given. Fortunately, someone's guardian angel was on the alert, for the major happened to be present. I can still see him running and shouting, "Stop! Stop! Stop!" and wildly waving his swagger-stick and free arm.

Everyone was nice about it. The major called me in and said, with a twinkle in his eye, "I don't think you've got the makings of an artillery officer. What you can do to help our cause is to enlist in the German army." They gave me an honourable discharge, which was very decent of them, really. Perhaps the military mind is not as obtuse as it's often said to be.

Some years ago I wrote a poem titled, "Fortuna et Cupidas." What I said in that poem is that if you take a moment in any person's life, two intersecting forces will be found determining why he is where he is doing what he's doing. These forces are *cupidas* and *fortuna*; appetite and chance. Looking over the events of my own life, I find a great deal of evidence confirming the truth of my observation. This is nowhere more clear to me than when I consider my first encounter with Betty Sutherland.

I was in Brockville at the time, getting my second pip. One day in early March I had gone to Montreal on furlough. My sister-in-law Eckie was supporting herself as a waitress while Hyman, who had come back from New York to enlist in the Signal Corps, slogged his way up the Italian boot with other Canadian soldiers. Eckie was working at the Diana Grill, a restaurant on St. Catherine, just opposite Eaton's. She occupied a room at my mother's house. I went to see her and, after a few minutes' chatter, she said, "You know there's somebody who works at the Diana as a hat-check girl who's just as kooky as you are. Crazy as a loon." To Eckie, anybody who was at all interested in the arts was crackers. I immediately pricked up my ears and said, "In what way is she crazy?"

"She thinks she's an artist. She's forever drawing and doodling and making sketches and talking wildly. And she has a brother, John, who thinks he's a poet."

My curiosity was sparked even more. I asked if she was beautiful too, and Eckie said: "Oh yes, she's very attractive. She looks very much like Ingrid Bergman, really a cross between Ingrid Bergman and Greer Garson." I think she also mentioned Barbara Stanwyck. So my interest grew sharper and sharper with every detail.

"Where can I meet this paragon of beauty? How do I get to see her?"

"All you have to do, Irving, is phone. Give her a call at the Grill and say you want to meet her. You're both crackers."

I phoned and made a date with Betty for that same day. I was to meet her at her room on Stanley Street after she got off work. The afternoon dragged but finally the time came when I stood outside her place and pressed the doorbell. She had not got back from work yet but her landlady allowed me in to wait. She led me to Betty's room, which I found in glorious disorder. I was later delighted to learn that this was one of Betty's signatures. I waited and waited and waited and I was getting a little bit irked because almost a half-hour later there was still no sign of her. I began to think she wasn't going to turn up. Curiosity alone kept me from putting on my coat and leaving. I was eager to see what she would turn out to be like, how well she would measure up to my sister-in-law's glowing description.

I must have been there a full hour when I heard the front

door open. A moment later, in walked this very, very beautiful woman. I couldn't believe my eyes or my good luck. She was even more lovely than I had imagined her. Her white teeth, red cheeks, windblown hair, and the outgoing warmth with which she greeted me, were all part of an exquisite dream from which I didn't want to awaken. I just stood gazing at her, wondering at the providence that had made this exceedingly attractive woman also an artist; better yet, a "crazy" artist, by my sister-in-law's account.

I was attracted to Betty, but not only physically. There was something about her personality that I knew with certainty fated me to know her beyond this brief moment. She was wearing a raccoon coat, the kind students used to wear at football games. Undoubtedly she had picked it up at a second-hand store, probably the Salvation Army. (I later learned that most of her skirts and velveteen jackets came from the Sally Ann.) Anyway, there she was, engulfed in an oversized raccoon coat, her face suspended above the fur, her light brown hair blown wildly in all directions. Now a strange thing impelled me. I stepped over to her and took her in my arms as if we were going to start to dance. We did in fact do a few steps, then I embraced her more closely. "Betty," I said softly, "you and I are going to have beautiful children."

When she showed me some of her drawings and sketches, remarkable as those of Käthe Kollwitz for their compassion and humanity, I was absolutely sure that from that day on our destinies were linked. I had more or less separated myself mentally from Faye, loosened her tenacious grip on me. The nightmare I had lived through was beginning to come to an end. Once I'd enlisted in the army to get away from her, I had quickly lost my anxiety neurosis. I was myself again. My health and self-confidence restored, I was back in full swing.

In the restaurant I took Betty to that night, we danced and ate and drank wine and talked non-stop till closing time. I hadn't had a night like that in years. Before we parted I knew nothing would ever come between my dream and the realization of those beautiful children I had promised her and myself. In mind, if not in body, Betty and I had become one.

Back in her room, before leaving to return to Brockville, I withdrew two poems from among a number I had recently written, and I handed them to her to give to her brother John Sutherland. He was the editor of *First Statement*; for me, the best little mag in the country at that time. These were the poems:

LADY ENFIELD

Lie down beside her, soldier,
And do but use her well,
And she can ease your passion
With cries and powder smell.

Be reckless in your loving,
Her grace makes no one poor
For only bullets issue
From such an iron whore.

DRILL SHED

The passive motion of sand
Is fluid geometry. Fir needles
Are the cool, select thoughts
Of madmen; and
Like a beggar the wind wheedles
Pine cones from the pines.
Inside there's no violence,
Only the silence
Of an empty church;
Drilled zygotes shift
From foot to foot or lurch
With half-closed eyes against the guns
While the ackeye shows

With delphic joy
The deeper things a dial-sight knows.

Curious now,
I marvel how
Lord Euclid's dream
Can stiffen a boy.

THIRTEEN

I left Petawawa behind me forever, for even my memories of army life quickly evaporated, and I returned to Montreal in late 1943 with a new feeling of confidence and a greater faith in my destiny as poet. I was most eager to meet John Sutherland from whom I had received an encouraging note accepting my poems. I was pleased as an antlered stag to think these early efforts were good enough to be accepted by a magazine. I sensed that there was a new literary scene shaping up in Montreal and I wanted to become part of it and, if possible, give it some direction.

I didn't exaggerate to myself *First Statement*'s prestige or influence. It was, after all, only a mimeographed affair brought out by John and his girlfriend Audrey Aikman, who later became his wife. Betty helped out whenever she could. The three of them toiled heroically at mimeographing and stapling the sheets and then sending out copies. There were few subscribers, less than seventy-five, I'd say. John held down some menial job to pay for the whole thing and even Betty contributed something from her meagre earnings as a hat-check girl to help keep the magazine afloat.

Sutherland had started the magazine when some of his submissions of his own work to *Preview* were promptly returned to him. Smarting under what he took to be a deliberate insult, John decided to publish his own magazine. Now he would no longer need to pull at his moustache, waiting for an answer from *Preview*'s editors, consisting of such poets as F.R. Scott, P.K. Page, and Patrick Anderson, the magazine's editor-in-chief. Scott had already acquired a considerable reputation as a poet; it wasn't long before A.M. Klein, who was almost as well-known, joined the editorial board.

Betty and John had grown up in Nova Scotia, and had both suffered from TB as well as from a stepmother whom they didn't particularly like. These two shared childhood calamities had created a very strong bond between brother and sister. They also had a father who didn't care very much for art, being one of Canada's many hustling Babbitts who would have poked his forefinger up the devil's arse if he thought he'd loosen down on himself a shower of black pearls. John dreamed of becoming a famous poet and Betty wanted to be a painter. Life is a supreme ironist. A crass philistine with not even a minimal interest in poetry or painting, in ideas or books, produced a son who became one of this country's most influential editors, a daughter who became a very fine painter, as well as a writer of poems and short stories, and another son, Betty's half-brother Donald Sutherland, who became an actor with an international reputation.

The day after my return, I went to call on Betty, who took me to see her brother, also living on Stanley Street only a few houses north, just below Sherbrooke.

I took to John right away for the same reasons I had taken to Betty at our first meeting. In him also there was something warm and outgoing. I liked his boyish grin. He had a sharp, decisive way of speaking. He had no hesitation in letting me know what he thought about a book or an article, about an author, or anything under the sun. He was full of opinions, and they exploded all over the place like firecrackers. He had an attractive face, smooth-shaven except for a poorly trimmed moustache. Almost at once he asked me to become one of *First Statement*'s editors.

After that meeting, I phoned Louis Dudek and asked him

to come with me to see Sutherland. When he did, John extended the same invitation to him. Now *First Statement* had five editors: John Sutherland, Louis Dudek, myself, Audrey Aikman, and Betty.

Louis's ideas about poetry were similar to my own. We were both fed up with the gentility that had crept into Canadian poetry, and believed that only a strong dose of realism could eliminate it. Louis concerned himself with the quality of civilization. He thought capitalism was creating a moral and intellectual swamp into which everything precious that man had created, and man himself, were sinking. His outlook was more Poundian than mine, even then, though I don't think he had read too much of Pound at this point. Dudek's attack was on a civilization which capitalism had spawned. So his concern was with culture, mine with the individual's place in it, and with economics, which I considered the most significant factor in defining a culture. But Louis and I loathed the capitalist system with equal intensity and wished to see it replaced by co-operative socialism.

Dudek impressed me as more wordly – perhaps I should say urbane – than Sutherland. As much as I had a spontaneous affection for John, he struck me as being parochial. He was, after all, from the Maritimes, the Canadian backwaters, as far as I was concerned. He was not particularly concerned with current politics. Nor was he terribly interested in economics, science, or philosophy. He was interested in Nietzsche, though largely for personal and literary reasons rather than philosophical ones.

As a discerning editor, Sutherland was not eclectic by choice but by necessity. Prior to Louis's and my joining the board, he'd published most of what was sent to him because there were so few contributors. At the same time, John was always looking for something fresh, something that was novel and as critical of Canadian gentility and materialism as he was. I think this is what appealed to John in my poetry and in

Louis's. Dudek and I were both unhappy about the war, though we both supported it. Naziism had to be stopped. But had the democracies not been so cowardly, there would have been no war in the first place. Hitler had been given the go-ahead by the capitalist states, so Louis and I could only share our bitterness at the foreseen result. At first John did not accept our views since he hadn't given much thought to capitalism's inequities or malfunctioning. The discussions we had on that subject were many and always heated, though never without some good-natured bantering.

John came round eventually to accepting the Marxist critique of capitalist society. So now the three of us found ourselves very much of one mind. Whatever our minor differences, we were united in our critical view of Canadians and the society they had created. We were in full agreement in our attacks on its gentility, anti-eroticism, its materialism and profit-seeking, its complacent indifference to the needs of the spirit.

I got several things from my encounters with Sutherland. Perhaps the most important was an introduction to modern British poetry. My readings of the English poets had stopped with Rupert Brooke and Wilfred Owen. Now I was getting to know Eliot and Yeats, to sample Auden, Spender, and Louis MacNeice. However, these poets didn't change our conviction that the American poets were more vital and we continued to read them with growing appreciation.

Modern English poetry struck me as being literary, composed strictly for the classroom. The poems of Eliot and Auden unfailingly reminded me of the snobs at Macdonald College – flannelled, affected, and prudish. When they didn't smell of incense, they smelled of the lamp. Their poetry was cerebral and bloodless when compared to American poetry, which was grounded in life and possessed an earthiness that made it anti-academic. The Americans were more direct and more straight-from-the-shoulder. They were not writing poems that required an array of exegetical footnotes to explain or elucidate. The three of us felt that one of the most attractive aspects of American poetry was its criticism of a civilization which democracy and the machine had created. Like the poets we read and admired, we felt that civilization was more than manners and good taste. It also meant the way people lived, the way they thought and felt about the larger moral, political, and social issues of the day. We wanted to emulate the poets south of the border, and go them one better if we could.

I had come upon Nietzsche long before I met Sutherland, but I knew almost nothing about Lawrence. It was John and Audrey who made D.H.L. a reality for me. I began to read his poetry and fiction, his criticism, and indeed everything he wrote, with increasing astonishment and reverence. Lawrence despised English gentility and puritanism as much as I did. No writer, I felt, had his ear closer to the febrile heartbeat of our sick civilization than did Lawrence. He confirmed my outlook to such a degree that many times, when reading him, I felt spooked. I was completely at one with him in his philosophy of sex and views of Christianity. Lawrence's criticism of Christianity, particularly of its romanticism and sexual repressiveness, is every bit as forceful as Nietzsche's. For this reason, Lawrence, for me, became the archetypal anti-Canuck. And whenever I wished to give myself huge belly laughs, I imagined him walking the streets of Toronto or Calgary. As for the priest-ridden Québecois, it never occurred to me for a single moment that Lawrence could ever have a place in their thoughts or affections.

It wasn't only Sutherland's views and ideas that won my admiration but his wonderful zest for life. That's why John had cottoned on to Lawrence and Nietzsche, why it made him a maverick among the pale academic literary critics of this country. He was as hungry for experience as I was, eager to get hold of large, earthy gobs of it. We both held our noses whenever Bloomsbury was mentioned. That's where John and I differed from Dudek. Louis was less keen on experience than he was on culture: chewed up and digested experience. John and I liked our meat raw, the more raw, the better we liked it.

John Sutherland was an unforgettable character; he was a refreshing wind that blew over the stagnant bogs of Canadian political and cultural life.

We had our printing press on Craig Street, the one I bought with my army discharge money. On it we ran off copies of *First Statement*, and, in 1945, we also ran off my first collection of poems, *Here and Now*, followed soon after by Patrick Anderson's *A Tent for April*.

The weekly editorial meetings were quite informal. We were very democratic, allowing any other poet who turned up to vote on submissions. I recall A.M. Klein dropping in to many of our meetings. His opinions were listened to with respect. He was far more conventional; a practising lawyer by this time. We doubtless struck him as wild-eyed juniors sowing our literary oats. I'd say it was we who influenced his style of writing rather than the other way around. Only after he had met all of us and had become a member of *Preview* did his style of poetry undergo a very marked change. We didn't regard his decision to join *Preview* as a betrayal. It was an appropriate move. He was older, and a poet with an established reputation. He belonged with people like Frank Scott and A.J.M. Smith. We had a long way to go before any of us would surface. What I relished about Klein was the fact that he could dance at two weddings. He had one dancing foot in *First Statement* and the other in *Preview*. Stimulating him to try for new rhythms, new images, his "ambipedrousness" had a beneficial effect on his poetry.

In order to pay the rent for our Craig Street office, and buy paper and ink to feed the press, John and I worked part time, at fifty cents an hour, for a firm which demolished houses and then sold the rough material after it was cleaned. In addition to cleaning the mortar off the bricks, we also had to shovel coal to keep the furnaces going in a huge pit three-quarters filled with coal.

Four hours steadily shovelling coal, or two hours of cleaning bricks, required a great deal of stamina. Having just come out of the army, I was in good physical condition, but John had neither my robustness nor my endurance, not at all, yet he never once complained. Truly, if any man made a sacrifice for Canadian literature, it was John Sutherland.

In the pit, both of us sweating and grimy with coal dust, we invented a game. We called it "Stumping." It was the Bible vs. Nietzsche's *Thus Spake Zarathustra*. For example, John would bring out a quotation from the Bible, and I had to find one from Nietzsche equally incisive. So while we flung the coal into the furance, I would say something like "Lo, the Superman cometh," and John, bent over his shovel, would answer, "And lo, the maidens must keep their lamps trimmed." This would go on until one of us failed to come up with a quotation. For some time, this was one of our favourite games, and we even got Audrey and Betty to play it with us – though not, of course, in the coal pit.

Now the point to remember is: with a printing press, we could have made a lot of money. John and I could have banked thousands of dollars with the greatest of ease. There were very few printers available; most were abroad with the armed forces. People would come to our office pleading with us to print their invitations to weddings and the like. I remember one fellow begging us to print a bar mitzvah card. There were actually tears in his eyes. But John and I self-righteously declared, "No, no, no, we do not use our press for anything commercial."

How stupid could we have been! Here was a poor, desperate man ready to pay John and me – a pair of schmucks working for fifty cents an hour shovelling coal – seventy-five dollars, and we wouldn't do it. We didn't want to sully the good name of *First Statement*. The press was a virgin whose chastity was not for sale, and no one, but no one, was going to violate her. It was really Sutherland's Presbyterianism that kept our faces dirty and our hearts pure and clean. If it had been left up to me alone, I probably would have printed the bar mitzvah cards for the poor Jewish father. My heart went out to him. Besides, moral purity has never been one of my hang-ups. I leave that to cardinals, chief rabbis, and young nuns. During the Renaissance I would have been one of the corrupt, art-loving cardinals (though I'd certainly have stopped short of pederasty and sodomy).

Louis also had a very strong moralistic streak in him. Whenever he'd start criticizing anyone, it would always be from a very lofty moral position. I envy people who can do that. They obviously have a self-assurance and a moral purity I have never been able to acquire. John fascinated me because his moralism, his unpredictable spasms of Presbyterianism, went hand in hand with his criticisms of Canadian gentility and anti-eroticism. The same could be said of Dudek. Yet both John and Louis were on the side of life, even though they both could exhibit at times the squeamishness of a Mrs. Grundy.

For instance, John wrote an essay in *First Statement* on Patrick Anderson's homosexuality as he thought it was revealed in his poetry. Patrick threatened to sue him, and John had to back down. But why Sutherland would be moved to write about something like that seemed to me strange. But John could get on his moral high horse and Louis could ride double with him, the two of them bravely trotting along on the same nag towards the offending windmill. They were always sur-prising me, for I never knew when or where they would display their moral fastidiousness. After a while, I began to see there was some kind of pattern, something to do with confusing convention with morality. A.M. Klein also suffered from the same confusion, it seemed to me, and, like Dudek and Sutherland, could adopt a high moral tone, especially when voicing his distaste for the delinquencies of a rival poet.

When you look back, it is usually the social occasions that are recalled with the greatest fondness. We were the Three Musketeers – John, Louis, and I – and each had his lady love. John's was Audrey, Louis had Stephanie, and mine was Betty. The six of us would go to the Kit Kat together, and we had some wonderful nights drinking beer, the only intoxicant we could afford, and arguing about poetry and politics or anything else that, along with the beer, could loosen our tongues. On Saturday nights, John could drink us all under the table when we'd go to the Kit Kat after our weekly editorial meeting. We would fortify with food and drink the arguments we had started earlier. Then John would make one roaring speech after another, and his blissful smile after each sally is one of the things about him I remember most fondly. We would also meet at the Hofbrau where we'd have a sumptuous meal – sauerkraut and fat German sausages, a thick soup and beer – all for under a dollar. Those nights were truly magical, and then the circle widened and we got to know better the *Preview* editors, Anderson, Smith, and Scott.

One of the joys of these evenings was Audrey's humour and bell-like voice. I remember her as an astonishingly beautiful woman. I had met her years earlier when I attended a seminar at McGill on the Rationalist philosophers. I recall her coming into the seminar. She was dressed in white and she was absolutely gorgeous; she quite literally took my breath away. Now imagine my surprise when this vision of loveliness began to talk about Spinoza, and so very lucidly, so very logically, and incisively. I did not venture to talk to her because she struck me at the time as being ineffably remote as an angel.

The realization, after all my false starts and confusions, that

I was a poet took a long time coming. Though I'd written many poems before, after I'd written "The Swimmer," there was no doubt in my mind. That happened in 1944, when my friendship with John and Louis had become closer and we regarded one another as comrades-in-arms and met as often as we could.

At that time Betty and I had been living on University Street on the top floor of what was really a factory building. The bottom floor was rented to somebody who manufactured cardboard cartons. Betty painted in her studio and I worked in my room across the hall giving private lessons. Since the building was poorly ventilated, the smell of glue emanating from the carton factory was everywhere. Even if we kept the door closed there was no escaping it. Betty and I decided that was sufficient reason to spend some of our food money on an outing in Caughnawaga, the decaying Indian Reservation on the other side of the St. Lawrence. John and Audrey came too. I remember the great time we had, unpacking our picnic lunch, swimming, talking, arguing until the sun began to go down and we decided to return to the city.

Back in Betty's studio, I said I wanted to go out for a walk. I felt restless and out of sorts, as if the day had somehow been misspent. Betty picked up her paint brush and began to work on the portrait of the only other occupant in the building besides ourselves, a French Canadian who made costume jewellery.

I headed up University towards St. Catherine then turned right and continued walking. I passed Child's restaurant (which is no longer there today), right near the Princess Theatre, which is still there but under another name. On a sudden impulse, I turned back and went into the restaurant, sat down, and ordered a cup of coffee. The waitress brought it to me and left it on my table without even glancing at me. I looked like a poor tipper. All of a sudden, a dazzling tumult of images came into my head and with them a tremendous excitement. I rose from my chair and signalled frantically to the waitress. When she was standing beside me, I grabbed the pencil out of her hand and was about to also grab her order pad when I seized a napkin instead, and, quite lost to everything going on around me, began writing furiously on it. Within five minutes an entire poem had written itself. I looked at it incredulously, as if it were a missive which the waitress, who had not moved away, had just handed to me.

It was "The Swimmer." That's just the way the poem happened. The premonitory excitement, the pell-mell rush of images, the inspired language, of which I didn't have to change more than a word or two. I looked at it and knew I had written my first major poem. I also knew with the same certainty I'd had an experience only a poet can have. Never before had I known such ecstasy, such release and joy, or felt my whole being concentrated with such intensity. That event convinced me that I was a poet. It was like hearing the voice of God. I had heard it as plainly as Moses had, as Abraham when the Lord bid him to light out for Canaan.

After that, there was no turning back. Nothing, after that experience, could shake my belief that someone up there had blessed or cursed me with the poet's vocation.

THE SWIMMER

The afternoon foreclosing, see
The swimmer plunges from his raft,
Opening the spray corollas by his act of war –
The snake heads strike
Quickly and are silent.

Emerging see how for a moment,
A brown weed with marvellous bulbs,
He lies imminent upon the water
While light and sound come with a sharp passion
From the gonad sea around the poles

And break in bright cockle-shells about his ears.

He dives, floats, goes under like a thief
Where his blood sings to the tiger shadows
In the scentless greenery that leads him home,
A male salmon down fretted stairways
Through underwater slums...

Stunned by the memory of lost gills
He frames gestures of self-absorption
Upon the skull-like beach;
Observes with instigated eyes
The sun that empties itself upon the water,
And the last wave romping in
To throw its boyhood on the marble sand.

Altogether this was a very wonderful period of my life, filled with excitement and colour, filled with affection and poetry.

The one sad note, the one fly in the ointment, was that Faye, whom I saw from time to time out of lingering guilt and compassion, still hoped for a reconciliation, though she knew I was now living with Betty.

Betty handled the Faye situation very well. She was confident that in time the tiny clouds that still remained would be cleared away.

Eventually, I was to break the news to Faye that Betty was pregnant. Only then did she realize that the tragi-comedy of our union was over. From that day on, she made no effort to waylay me at the Jewish Public Library, where I had resumed giving courses, at McGill, or anywhere else she thought I could be found. Only then did she agree the sensible thing to do was to get a divorce.

I married Betty in Montreal one week after the divorce came through; and, as though to outrage the gods, or to defy them, the wedding took place on September 13, the same day of the month I'd married Faye, seven years earlier. Our son Max would be born the following spring.

FOURTEEN

The Montreal I knew in my early days was, and will always remain in my memory, a city of churches, brothels, and writers. These, or the presence of these around me, were the stepping stones of my spiritual evolution. The order in which I encountered them corresponded to my increasing awareness of the city's troubling charm, the varied confusions it offered for contemplation.

To be found in almost every part of the city, Montreal's churches muted somewhat the harsher, more strident sounds of commerce and industry. They were the very architecture of the withdrawn, contemplative life. They produced in me an indescribable feeling compounded of the conflicting emotions of anger, fear, and regret which came with the knowledge that I was an outsider and would always remain one. It seemed that the city's brothels were as numerous as its churches. Located on both sides of De Bullion, they had been no less mysterious and awe-inspiring than the churches or the remembered synagogue of my childhood. Here again was evidence that life's singular compass needle pointed at one and the same time to the sacred and the profane.

I have always thought of a writer as a peculiar blend of holy man and whore in the sense alone that he desires to give pleasure while feeling himself engaged in a spiritual quest. It was therefore fitting that Montreal should harbour so many literary talents.

The importance of Montreal to me as a poet cannot be overstressed. The city gave me the confidence, the tools, the stimulating friendships and rivalries. It gave me a literary milieu comparable to what Paris had given the American expatriates, Hemingway and Fitzgerald. In the early forties, it was in Montreal where Canada's first sounds of poetry were heard. There, a cluster of gifted poets seemed to be fashioning new images and rhythms, new techniques to capture the staccato vibrations of a world shaking itself free from Victorian repressiveness and conspiracy. These poets had a sharp eye for hypocrisy, for conformity, and timidity striving to palm itself off as good taste, and for the vapid outpourings of colonized fossils mouldering in newspaper offices and university faculty lounges. They satirized old pretensions and pomposities, gleefully exposing the social cysts which long-fingered profiteers and their retainers were determined to keep hidden from public scrutiny.

In the midst of all the creative excitement that punctuated these years, I was barely making a living. John and I were working for fifty cents an hour proofreading for the new defunct *Montreal Star*. Audrey and Betty worked alongside us. Picture the four of us straining our eyes for four hours so that we could earn two lousy dollars apiece! I also continued to give private lessons to newcomers, and I lectured at the Jewish Public Library two hours each week at four dollars per hour. My total income was less than twenty dollars per week.

In the early *First Statement* days I got to know Arthur J.M. Smith. I'd first met him at a downtown tavern, most likely the Prince of Wales located on University near St. Catherine, and dubbed the Pig and Whistle. It had become a place where local and out-of-town writers met to discuss their hot-off-the-griddle masterpieces and to learn from their peers where they stood in the literary pecking order. At that first meeting, he gave me an inscribed copy of *New Provinces*. Though Smith was professoring at the University of Michigan, he often came to Montreal to see relatives and friends and to learn from the latter what his reputation was – had it risen or fallen? – among the literati.

Was it then or many years later that he expressed his distaste for Whitman and Hemingway? It doesn't matter. What did matter, if only to myself, was that he slipped several notches in my estimation. Whitman, he told me flatly, was a barbarian. What excited me, what held me spellbound page after page – Whitman's innovative vigour and feeling for life – was to Smith a nauseating, formless brew. For a long time, Smith's own polished verses reminded me of the barbered lawns of Westmount, each blade of grass cut to the same uniform, unobtrusive size. Each with its dot of pale green to indicate that it was really grass and not straw. They were poems that a YMCA secretary, parsonical hair parted in the middle, might have written. Not that Smith was without passion or exuberance. Not that he didn't flay gentility or thumb his nose at the old maids of the Canadian Authors Association, the literary establishment at the time, whose members praised one another's sophomoric offerings in reviews and articles. His bark, however, was much sharper than his bite. For instead of the "barbaric yawp" he praised in his criticism, his own verses were delicately shaded whisperings on themes of no surpassing urgency. To me it seemed Smith was trying to squeeze the brutal experiences of the twentieth century into the forms and molds of the eighteenth; and, since John Donne's influence was evident in the style and content of some of his poems, of the century before.

His equally denigrating observations on Hemingway, when they came, didn't surprise me. What did was their lack of originality. I had heard it all before from many prune-dry pedants: Hemingway's basic English, the absence of complex ideas, the boorishness and well-publicized machismo, and other similar blah blahs from tight-assed academics who envied Hemingway's masculinity and success with women, his enormous appetite for sensations, his resolve to live dangerously. Never a word from them about the poet in Hemingway; about his almost feminine sensitivity to pain and death; and Nietzsche's paramount influence on him. It did not therefore surprise me that Smith remained similarly ignorant of Nietzsche's influence on W.B. Yeats, a poet whom Smith greatly admired and fondly believed he understood. But Nietzsche, as far as Canada was concerned, was a remote star, which was still many light-years away. Nietzsche was not for this country's literary parsons and Boy Scouts.

In my more malicious moments I used to imagine a meeting of A.J.M. Smith and my two spiritual heroes, Whitman and Hemingway. I imagined the Canadian expatriate professor handing each of them a copy of his book, *A Sort of Ecstasy*. The fantasy was a wonderful pick-me-up, better than an espresso for terminating an afternoon's *Weltschmerz*.

There was a kind of coolness to Smith, a sort of imperturbability that brought out the sadist in me. I always felt like ragging him whenever we met. He knew it all, at any rate gave the impression he did. He knew what poetry was all about, knew it inside out. He was proud of his "good taste." My own feeling was that, because he was so far removed from the nitty-gritty of human experience, he couldn't really understand literature in any true sense. I felt he knew words, he knew language. But I, who among other things had been brought up on the earthy Russian novelists and poets, felt he was like a eunuch imagining passions he knew only from hearsay. For all the noises he made, his outlook was basically genteel, and his approach to literature that of an English gentleman. To me, a rebellious street-fighter and a born muck-raker, the English-Canadian writers, without exception, seemed like discreet interlopers, innocents more at home with words than with a world that was beginning to stink of Hitler's death camps and Stalin's Gulags. A.M. Klein, on the other hand, struck me as being the real article. I felt that in his poetry he was trying to say something about the contemporary situation, and since the Jew is always in the middle of whatever the contemporary distress happens to be, Klein was addressing himself fully to the abominations and obscenities of our time.

F.R. Scott, Smith, E.J. Pratt, John Glassco, and P.K. Page, for all their devotion to fine writing, were as remote from what was painful and nightmarishly real in the brutal twentieth century as the planet Earth is from Saturn. I thought Smith was trying to shelter himself from the tempests rising all around us, from the sickening fumes of human depravity and viciousness that were spreading to every patch of the globe. His breed was blind, fatally incapacitated by the culture in which they'd been nurtured, to comprehend the moral cataclysms making their swift death-bringing way towards us.

So, whenever Smith and I got together, our meetings would begin or end in a donnybrook. But I liked him. I liked Smith – parson and Boy Scout though he was – a great deal and, paradoxically, for the same reaons I liked ragging him. Fortunately for myself, his upbringing had been that of the polite Anglo-Saxon gentleman. Anyone else would have punched me in the jaw.

My early encounters with the Montreal literati inspired several ill-tempered poems. P.K. Page and Smith both put an itch in some part of my body that I was unable to scratch. They were a constant irritation. It was precisely because I felt they were poets that I expected from them so much more rage and wisdom. They were visible targets for my *chutzpahnic* barbs as well as criteria against which I measured myself with some relief and satisfaction. But there was also something more basic. I knew we worshipped different gods. Their man of sorrows, though a Jew, had died centuries ago, and his suffering and death were now only good for a literary frisson. The despair and ecstasy of the Jew in their midst were forever out of their reach or comprehension, as were his faith and scepticism.

Above I called Smith a Boy Scout. That epithet more rightly belongs to F.R. Scott, who was the older of the two. Smith was a Wolf Cub. Boy Scout and Wolf Cub, that is how I saw the pair. Smith's *A Sort of Ecstasy* was followed by Scott's *Events and Signals*. Out of a conversation that was reported to me as having taken place between F.R. Scott and Art Smith, I composed the following:

IMAGINARY CONVERSATION

Art said to Frank:
'Layton's verse is mostly
fart for fart's sake.'

Someone who overheard him
said with a twinkle:
'What's wrong with fart, Art?

It's a sort of ecstasy
and most emphatically
both an event and a signal.'

One of the most intriguing characters in the Montreal literary scene was Patrick Anderson, the editor-in-chief of *Preview*. I believe we first met at the Kit Kat or at some small gathering. As he lived in the neighbourhood, after that we got together with some regularity. He was tall and rather gangly with poor posture. His hair was worn plastered down and looked almost as if it was a wig. There were freckles and thin blond hairs on his chin and cheeks. For me, there was something rather charming about Anderson. He was animated when he talked, but when he wasn't talking, he was the languid, diffident Englishman, bored with the natives.

Someone, probably his wife Peggy, had converted Patrick to the secular religion of Marxism. The two of them were certainly very dogmatic Communists when I met them. Patrick's dogmatism didn't repel me because I never took his Marxism seriously, though perhaps I should have. I always thought it was a get-up he had donned, a kind of uniform, a dress-suit for the occasion. Still, when he talked, it was with great conviction. He was capable of making very funny satirical jibes, which he would deliver with the cool effectiveness of an Oxford don. He intrigued me because he was so different from anyone I had known. Dudek could be professional, yet he could never quite make it as a don. Sutherland could be pontifical, but there was an earnestness to him that Anderson escaped.

Louis and I differed in our opinions of Anderson. I always admired his poetry, and still do. However, Louis considered him shallow and, I think, something of a phony. He couldn't bear to hear me say a good word spoken about Patrick. He thought he was an English snob and that his style was very foreign. Anderson's "Englishness" repelled him, on paper and off. I must say I can understand somebody at the time taking a dislike to Anderson. A.M. Klein cared neither for the man nor his work, though they didn't add up to the *bête noire* they became for Dudek.

I remember the effect Anderson's poem "The Drinker" had on me. It was fresh, original, and very different from the home-spun quality of Canadian poetry at the time. There was a daring imaginativeness in his verse I didn't find in the poets around me, including A.M. Klein. Indeed, despite the fact that he cared neither for Anderson the man nor for Anderson the poet, Klein learned more from Patrick than perhaps any of us with the exception of Frank Scott or P.K. Page. Even Dudek learned a great deal from him, however much he may be loath to acknowledge his debt.

I recall the first time I read Anderson's "Summer's Joe." It immediately convinced me that here was a talented poet. Marxism had given him something to talk about and he talked well, with eloquent conviction and passion. I envied the man

238

who could write "Summer's Joe" and "The Drinker." I envied anyone who could write as fluently and imaginatively as he did. He tended to look down on colonials, an old English habit. But since I'd been to Macdonald College, this was nothing unfamiliar to me, and I could forgive him that. Alongside my admiration for the originality and razzle-dazzle of his verse, I intuited that Patrick didn't have all that much to say; that if you took away the clothes-horse of Marxism, the uniform or dress-suit would fall into a heap on the floor. And indeed that is precisely what happened after Patrick returned to England and his poetry lost the underpinning of Marxism.

Anderson's name has been almost expunged from the literary records of this country. Nobody dipping into some of the current anthologies of Canadian poetry will find an adequate selection of his poems or any reference to his contribution. In his anthology *The Penguin Book of Canadian Verse*, Ralph Gustafson allows him a selection from his "Poem on Canada," but in their *Anthology of Canadian Literature in English* (Vol.1), Bennett and Brown make no allusion to Patrick Anderson as one of the important shapers of modern Canadian poetry. The anthology *Canadian Poetry* by Jack David and Robert Lecker, with an introduction by George Woodcock, though alluding to the long poems of Birney, Ondaatje, and b.p. nichol, makes no mention of Anderson's "Summer Joe" or his "Poem on Canada." However, there are favourable references to him in Doug Jones's *Butterfly on Rock* as well as sensitive interpretations of several of his poems. *The Oxford Book of Canadian Poetry*, edited by Margaret Atwood, prints only two poems, one of which is the already anthologized "Cold Colloquy."

During this time, because of his association with *Preview*, I became better acquainted with F.R. Scott. Although I didn't know him very well, one of the things that struck me about him was the sense that he was holding back, or being held back, from achieving self-definition, and with it the larger significance he might have had. He could be clever. He could be brilliant. But so often brilliancy is paid for by shallowness. Whenever I was with Scott, I felt there were levels of experience of which he was unaware; or, if aware, wished to get away from as swiftly as a quip or an epigram could take him. There were abysses he would never allow himself to plunge into because it would make him uncomfortable; it might shatter his raw play-the-game optimism, muffle the upbeat note of the bracing faith in which he'd been reared.

Frank always wanted to have his finger in whatever literary pie was being baked at the time. He was always aware when something new was stirring. He wanted to be *au courant*, on top of things, which I thought was admirable and very much to his credit. One day, Scott, the Westmount socialist patrician, invited Sutherland, Dudek, myself, and our women to his home. This was our first visit with him and his wife Marian, and we were tongue-tied. Perhaps we were made dumb by the thought that in his eyes we were the uncouth, barbarous *First Statement*ers. He didn't have the gift for drawing people out, for putting them at ease, at least not then. My view of him might be altogether wrong, but I didn't think there was much easiness in him, or that he knew how to deal with anyone who wasn't a student or an intimate friend. So John and Louis and I just exchanged looks. We felt we were there for careful inspection by General F.R. Scott, and we wondered how we were shaping up. What does one say to a patrician socialist who reminds you of Sir Stafford Cripps?

Well, Scott saw we weren't performing as brightly as he had expected; and he was not insensitive to our plight – or his own. Finally he hit on a marvellous device to loosen us up. He went into the kitchen and returned with a clay pipe and a bowl of soapy water. Imagine this neatly dressed patrician blowing soap bubbles. The bubbles began to float all over the room, ironically winking at us as they burst. This one hits a wall. That one lands on the piano. Another decides it's a different kind of bubble and floats its blue and gold reflections up towards the ceiling against which it bursts, all its fragile beauty becoming mere wetness. And here's this tall, angular aristocratic-looking WASP, uproariously slapping his thigh and reaching out to grab one of the bubbles.

It was undignified and crazy and totally unexpected, but it broke the ice. After that we all became much easier with one another. That is something I shall always remember about Scott, that he could risk looking ridiculous to make us feel at home. We ended up having a lovely time, and I fondly remember the good humour and bonhomie we felt at the end of the visit. I also remember how taken we were by Marian Scott's intelligence, sensitivity, and forthrightness.

Perhaps unjustly, I thought Scott's socialism was luke-warm and entailed no great risk. He was simply playing the game of the bourgeois well-heeled intellectual who likes to flaunt his radicalism to the dismay of his elderly great-aunts. My view stemmed from the fact that, again perhaps unfairly, I considered him emotionally shallow, and his socialism a matter of head rather than heart. Scott's humanism, his Boy Scout human-itarianism, like Smith's, Patrick Anderson's, Louis Dudek's, P.K. Page's, and Dorothy Livesay's were as crisp and irrelevant as the freshly incised lettering on a tombstone.

I have the feeling that my Jewishness made Scott uneasy. As with so many upper-class gentiles, perhaps the reason for his discomfort derived from the awareness he had of the tragic history of the Jew. Perhaps it was the distemper of the man who knows he's out of his depth, and wants someone to blame for his predicament. With that consciousness went a certain resentment at being put off balance by something he had neither the insight nor the appetite to apprehend.

Just as A.J.M. Smith went down in my esteem when he disparaged Whitman and Hemingway, and later compounded his sin by disparaging D.H. Lawrence, so did Scott lose points when, years later, he expressed his ideas about Israel and Zionism. They should not have astonished me, for by then

I was acquainted with left-wing anti-Semitism and the murky pools from which it bubbles up. My brother Jesus and the dreadful legacy he unwittingly left behind have so warped the gentile's mind it's unlikely this psychic Zuyder Zee will ever be drained. Anyhow, not for many more centuries to come.

The Bible warns us that men's hearts are base and corrupt, forever deceitful. So it did not astonish me that the Holocaust had changed nothing. The proof it offered that the Christianized world had eagerly embraced every vile depravity imaginable was as harrowing as it was incontrovertible. But what was also incontrovertible was that the event had stirred few Canadians to examine their consciences or beliefs. Tomorrow the hate merchants would be back again in full force. Despite all this, I was unprepared for what I felt was Frank Scott's curt dismissal of Israel, the Jews' one hope for survival, and the half-smile with which he told me Zionism was a lost cause. To his mind, it was only a matter of time before Israel would be no more.

I liked Scott's poems and thought some of them very good indeed, but ultimately I did not consider them anything more than minor poetry. A troubled individual, he managed to conceal that aspect of himself so well that nobody suspected. His mind was more analytical than creative. I felt he was best in his satires, but he kept astonishing and delighting me by writing some fine lyrics, mainly about nature, but several that women had inspired. Only after I had kicked open that door, and made it respectable to write frankly about Eros, was Scott emboldened to submit for publication some of the love poems he had hitherto kept safely hidden in his drawer. I provided the same brevet for Arthur J.M. Smith. For me, Scott was a perplexity, a man whose character held many contradictions. In an effort to articulate some of my own thoughts about him, I wrote the following poem:

F.R. SCOTT

Drops his arm
on your shoulder
  like heavy plastic;
drives a witticism
into your thick, dull skull;
waits for the smiles
     to start
in your eyes, roll down
your cheeks;
   espies
another: undubbed, virginal,
and leaves you gasping
  your delight.

For all that,
weary of his too clear sight,
his icy brain,
would rather be
  an ignorant Italian
grinding his hurdy-gurdy
for coppers
  under a lady's balcony.

Even if, friskily,
he lifts high
   his long, tailored legs,
and higher… so … so …
making one wonder
what tormenting ghost
has got him by the ankle
  and won't let go.

I met P.K. Page only two or three times, and I believe it was always at Scott's place. She was tall, gracious, and very attractive. Page and John Sutherland had known each other back in Nova Scotia when he was sick and there had been a kind of platonic love, at least on John's side. I didn't see much of her. It was her extreme graciousness that put me off. She was altogether too ladylike for my taste. Since I was unused to such graciousness, perhaps it came across as condescension, even though I'm certain it was not that at all. But I did think her perfect manners and charm were a means to ward off any attempt to forge a closer bond. Her poems, exhibiting Anderson's influence, impressed me by their imagery and well-crafted rhythms. Page counselled me to study Buddhism – she didn't specify which school – for she thought it might do something for my Jewish angst. Doug Jones, on the other hand, several years later recommended I plant a flower every time I thought of the Holocaust. I envied their *goyische* innocence. Their juvenility endeared them to me for more reasons that I can ever hope to articulate.

For the Jewish-Canadian writer, Canada is not a melting pot, nor is it a mosaic. Since he's a five-thousand-year-old Canadian whose history begins with the only successful slave revolt ever recorded, he possesses a distinctive personality and outlook that keeps him at a distance from a culture he finds, to his amused surprise, to be both parvenu and moribund at one and the same time. Fortunately for him, there are two Canadas, French and English. It is this wonderful fact that has allowed him to escape the stagnation of the one and the low blood pressure of the other. The opposition between Jewish realism and anglophone gentility, Jewish cosmopolitanism and WASP nationalism (the latter, in essence, a cowardly flight from reality) will continue and even grow more intense with the decades.

This was to become the root cause of the friction between

myself and some of this country's best-known critics and poets. But can these Canadian intellectuals understand me any better than they do Mandelstam, Babel, or Paul Celan? I doubt it. Having the sensibilities of a Jew, I was not able to cover my nakedness with a maple leaf nor find refuge from this century's infamies in one of Canada's pine forests or by crawling into an igloo, or between the covers of Northrop Frye's *Anatomy of Criticism*.

After "The Swimmer," in quick succession I wrote "Newsboy," "De Bullion Street," and "The Death of Moishe Lazarovitch." I knew these were paramount poems, and I sent them to *Poetry Chicago*, at the time the most prestigious poetry magazine in North America, where they were accepted with gratifying promptness. Now I was more certain than ever of my vocation. Dudek was very nice about the whole matter, and thoughtfully discharged his role as friend by pooh-poohing the acceptance so that I shouldn't get an inflated notion concerning my talent. I have often mused on his thoughtfulness and vainly hoped that one day he would give me the occasion to repay the favour.

By early 1945, *Preview* had pretty well exhausted its run. It had become increasingly noticeable the magazine wasn't going anywhere. It was still being brought out as a mimeographed handout compared to *First Statement*'s attractively printed format. And its editors envied us, despite their understandable complacency. They had F.R. Scott, A.M. Klein, and A.J.M. Smith, this country's foremost anthologist, as well as a poet and critic. *Preview*'s regional editors were Dorothy Livesay and Ralph Gustafson. Bruce Ruddick was also on the editorial board. He was exceedingly witty and always in good spirits. I didn't have very much faith in his talent, believing him to be too clever to make a good poet, and indeed after a while he just gave up the effort and became a psychiatrist. His talent, he had discovered, lay not in poetry but in puns. Alas, though many are called, few are chosen!

Now, since *Preview* had the more widely known writers and *First Statement* had the press, there were voices heard in both camps that said our interests would be best served by a union. The marriage took place in 1945. It was a marriage of convenience and the offspring it produced was named *Northern Review*. It was an uneasy union right from the start.

I recall the first night we got together; I believe it was at Sutherland's apartment. All the editors were present, including Neufville Shaw who, though he was not a poet, liked good writing. His admiration for it, when it came his way, was very pronounced and clear. Though we never became very close, I liked him and we got on well. I remember somebody making the remark – was it Bruce Ruddick or A.M. Klein? – that if a bomb dropped on John's apartment that night it would be the end of Canadian poetry for the next one hundred years.

I was continuing to study at McGill, where I had registered in its Department of Economics and Political Science to do an M.A. on Harold Laski. His attempt to bridge, to somehow reconcile liberalism with Marxism I found unconvincing. At the Jewish Public Library I was now teaching English to Holocaust survivors of Hitler's death camps. My view of human nature and of my gentile compatriots, whose indifference or hostility had made them in my eyes accomplices in the Nazi attempt at genocide, grew darker with every tale of horror and atrocity I heard from my students.

My conviction was beginning to grow that the most plausible, and indeed the most satisfactory explanation for the Holocaust lies in the awareness of an historical sequence: the imprisoning and torturing of heretics, the burning of witches, and the gassing of Jews. These events each had a common factor in the religious mythology that posited an eternal struggle between God and his powerful antagonist, Satan, and demanded an overspiritualization from the individual that took too little account of his animal origin. With the insights that Freudian psychology provides, it is not too difficult to understand why the animus of the "sick Christian" against the heretics, witches, and Jews exhibits several features in common. All three groups have been depicted as lascivious, unclean, immoral, and resolutely engaged, at Satan's urging, in a conspiracy against everything decent and honourable. Indeed, in Nazi Germany – but other European countries readily accepted the stereotype – the Jew was often pictured as the devil himself, or, at any rate, as bearing a close resemblance to him.

This philosophical perspective, however, did little at the time to abate my disillusionment and rage. Though I wrote several poems and stories, the floodgate of invective was not to be fully opened until several years later. But then, even as I gave literary expression to these feelings, I began to doubt the effectiveness of literature to deflect mankind's rush towards self-destruction. There were indeed times when I found myself hoping for it to happen as eagerly as the believing Jew waits and hopes for the Messiah. Anything other than a curse or a scream seemed a deliberate lie, a decorous evasion of the brutal truth, polite drawing-room chatter. A glittering trinket in the nose of the cannibal.

When Louis Dudek went to New York, to study at Columbia University, John and I heard from him every so often; he let us know of his burgeoning love affair with the poetry of Ezra Pound. Every now and then he submitted a poem or a short essay. John had become *Northern Review*'s managing editor. Right from the start he knew he was a fish out of water and felt used. He felt the *Preview*-ites were not treating him with the respect he deserved and his grievance continued to grow with every editorial meeting. Scott and Anderson, in particular, took a dim view of the poems and articles he regularly submitted for publication in *Northern Review*. John's resentment grew with every rejection. Finally, when the *Preview*-ites cavilled at a review John had written on Robert Finch's *Selected Poems*, it came to the breaking point. Robert Finch belonged to the same generation as Scott, Smith, and Klein, and Sutherland scornfully regarded them as the Old Guard. His bitterness at the treatment they had been meting out to him prompted him to make his review mercilessly severe. The enraged *Preview*-ites threatened to resign from the editorial board en masse unless Sutherland withdrew it. He refused, and they did. The break would have come sooner or later. I took John's side and helped to edit the next few issues until John wrote what I thought an unnecessarily splenetic review of A.M. Klein. After that, I also resigned. In truth, this review was the straw that broke the camel's back. John's militant Catholicisim, after his conversion, caused him to abandon his early literary ideals and idols. This made it increasingly difficult for me to continue to work with him.

In addition to Scott, Klein, Smith, and Dudek, there was Dorothy Livesay, who appeared from time to time. Even John Glassco was a presence, though only a ghostly one. He was our link to the Paris of the twenties. I didn't know any of his own work at the time, but someone told me he had known Gertrude Stein and Hemingway, Fitzgerald, and Picasso. I wanted to know the man who had known them. Later, I did get to meet him, to read his poems, and to play a part in getting him to finish and publish his masterpiece *Memoirs of Montparnasse*. In his Prefatory Note, Glassco states, "I did not look at the manuscript again for thirty-five years." It was during one of my visits with him that I got him to take the mildewed notebooks out from the drawer where they'd been kept for over three decades, and read large sections to me. My exclamations of surprise and delight visibly moved him. He told me he hadn't looked at those pages for so long he'd almost forgotten he had ever written them. I like to think it was my frank enthusiasm that encouraged him to complete the work by the addition of several more chapters.

Betty and I moved from our University Street dwelling to a

room in my mother's house on City Hall Avenue, my mother having decided after the death of Mr. Hershorn to take possession of the empty flat she owned above what used to be her grocery store. Though my mother, an orthodox Jewess, was not too happy about my marrying a gentile, she was very understanding about the matter. It turned out that she and Betty got along very well, perhaps not surprisingly since both were good-hearted people. Betty painted a portrait of my mother having her noon-day meal. That was forty years ago and vividly brings her back to my mind whenever I look at it.

Life was difficult but Betty never grumbled or reproached me for spending most of my time reading and writing. I wasn't aware just how pinched our circumstances were because my head was in the clouds. I was writing poetry and breathing poetry and talking poetry and nothing else had any reality for me. I was totally insensible to the grim bleakness of our situation except for the endless cockroaches and the unpaved backyard that forced themselves into my notice. Something had gone wrong with the sewage system, and the smells were just abominable. They seemed to come up from hell, not from any broken sewer drain. At night we couldn't sleep and our son would wake up crying. I am astonished that the three of us didn't fall sick from the foul odours that wafted up from the yard. If this wasn't bad enough, every Friday and Saturday, when night fell and the stars came out, our quarrelsome neighbours would get drunk and then there'd be wild fights and much shouting and smashing of plates and furniture.

This was our situation at the time, with no prospects for the future. None whatsoever. At no time did the thought enter my head that I should bestir myself to change our circumstances, or make some effort to improve them. My sole aim was to write poems, to compose those miraculous interlacings of sound and sense that endure forever. My imagination was still on fire. Now, however, I could no longer show a new poem to John or Louis to get their reactions. Before Louis lit out for New York, I would exultantly read a new poem to him over the phone and he'd respond by reading one of his, and then we'd jabber on for hours. Yet now, more than ever, I was sure God was neither love nor goodness. Nor was he justice or truth. He was creativity. And we had all been made in God's image. The divine and the creative were one.

I knew myself to be impractical but also that what for me was life itself meant less to the dulled millions than yesterday's newspaper ads. Their god was money. Nor was I taken in by the self-flattering plaudits of culture philistines. Living among them, I was vulnerable and defenceless. How long would it take me to learn how to arm myself against them? An uneasiness, bordering on an anxiety neurosis, took possession of me and became the unsettled condition of my mind. Though I'd heard no one pronounce it, I felt that a sentence of doom had been laid on me. Henceforth, my only loyalty would be to the Muse whose visitations were becoming more insistent and numerous. Like Shaw's Dudebat, I knew myself capable of sacrificing others, as well as my own comfort, even self-esteem, provided I could feel the excitement and snare the insight that eventuated into the poem under my hand. At best I was a lotus-eater, at worst a junkie. I also felt myself to be spy and traitor, a messenger from the dark gods.

My improvidence, moreover, was reinforced by an outlook that saw people and events as illusion or fog, as Maya from which they could separate themselves and acquire realness and significance only if I put them into a poem. Later, this trait was to be construed as arrogance and unsociableness. But in the grip of forces more powerful than myself, I could do nothing to prevent this misunderstanding though in considerable measure it added to my woes by threatening my chances of being able to earn a living.

One morning in the summer of 1946, Betty and I were sitting in the kitchen having a cup of coffee when the telephone rang. It was Burton Kierstead, Chairman of McGill's Department of Economics and Political Science. By now I'd finished my thesis on Harold Laski and gotten my M.A.

"Irving," he said, "would you be interested in a job? There's an opening out west."

A small theological college in Winnipeg was looking for somebody to give a course in political theory. Two years earlier I'd had a teaching fellowship at McGill, and I'd more than proved my competency as an instructor in that field.

My heart did a somersault. A job! I was speechless and stayed that way for a couple of seconds. Then I managed to blurt out, "Please give me ten minutes to think about it." I told Betty, and continued to sit there, dazed. My swimming eyes focussed on a small cluster of cockroaches on the wall. Seven or eight of them were holding a town meeting and no doubt passing resolutions. Suddenly, for no apparent reason, one of them, looking somewhat more spare than the others, detached itself and began to crawl towards the window-pane and the light coming through it. I kept shaking my head. I felt as if I'd been clubbed by this unforeseen job offer that would take me out of this misery, but also out of Montreal and the stimulation which was now as necessary as the air I breathed – foul though it might be when a breeze lifted the stench from the dirt yard below. I felt the decision should rest with Betty. My life and future were in her hands. If she told me to take the job, I would accept the offer. So I looked at her and told her very quietly that it was up to her.

"No, Irving," she said, "it's up to you. Whatever you say is fine with me." And that was all she said.

I called Kierstead ten minutes later to thank him for the offer and to turn it down. That was perhaps the most momentous decision I've ever made, for certainly had I taken the job and gone out to Winnipeg, I would not have become a poet. Had I cut myself off from the nurturing milieu I found in Montreal, I'd have become a political scientist, another professor in political theory.

Betty and I went back to our coffee and I remember the silence. Neither one of us spoke a single word. We just looked at each other, feeling unsure of what we'd let ourselves in for and what the future held in store. This must have convinced Betty, whatever else was going on in her mind at the time, of just how completely improvident I was.

I had turned down an available job, and from now on I could see the danger of my using each successive poem I wrote as an alibi for my unwillingness or incapacity to meet the world on its own very practical terms. Given my conviction that the worship of chance was the only choice open to a free man in a nihilistic, money-oriented society; given my increasing alienation from that society, failure might spur me on to write better and better poems and to improve my craft. But even that wouldn't put food on the table. I now found myself asking whether I really wished to forge such a tie-up between wordly failure and artistic achievement. Could my happy wayward temperament support that connection, that self-destructive dialectic, and, if so, for how long before everything came crashing down around me? Psychically I was skating on very thin ice. Kierstead's phone call had jarred me awake to the harsh reality of my situation. Betty's quiet resignation, the look on her face when she told me the decision to accept or reject the offer was wholly mine to make, was only more ice-water thrown on the mental traveller asleep on the hill.

And so, about one week later, I was walking down Park Avenue and on a sudden impulse decided to ask whether there was a job for me at the Ross Tutorial School, whose name-plate I'd seen on one of the buildings I'd just passed. That was a school for the "not-so-bright," or lazy students who had failed their matrics, or for those vets wishing to use their grants to get into university. I went up the three flights of stairs with decreasing hope. I reached the top floor and turned to the right, went down a long, narrow passageway that led to an office, where I found myself looking at Harry Ross. I still had something of a reputation from my radical and debating days, and I knew my left-wing activism would be familiar to him. And, since his brother was Fred Rose (Harry had changed his name), I thought he might be sympathetic to me.

Without any preliminaries, I said evenly, "Do you have a job for me as a teacher?"

I can still see the queer look he gave me. He smiled and said, "This is very strange. My history teacher just quit on me today. Can you teach history?"

"Yes," I said, "I can teach history."

Again he smiled. He looked at me questioningly, hopefully. "Do you think you can teach poetry?"

I met his eyes with a fixed gaze, my heart singing with elation and knocking furiously inside my chest.

"Yes, Mr. Ross," I said. "There's no subject I'd like to teach more."

On the way home, I kept imagining the look on Betty's face when I told her the good news. How could I have known I had just taken the step that would launch me on a teaching career which would enable me to feed my family and myself, and to pay for the wear and tear on my typewriter for the next forty years.

ACKNOWLEDGMENTS

I wish to thank the Social Sciences and Humanities Research Council of Canada for the generous grant that gave me the time and leisure to work on this memoir. And Jack McClelland who, years ago, first put the notion of writing it into my head.

I also wish to thank David O'Rourke for helping me to begin these memoirs, and for his assistance in the assembling of early drafts of the manuscript. His sensitive probing of my brainfolds helped me recall long-forgotten episodes in my life and to observe experiential connections that might otherwise have gone unnoticed.

Thanks are also owing to friends and acquaintances for sharing with me their recollections, and for allowing me to see letters that I had written to them over the years.

Without the patience, good humour, and insights of Anna Pottier, who typed and retyped the manuscript, this memoir would never had reached completion.

I am greatly indebted to the good sense, intuitiveness, and devotion of Ellen Seligman, a truly superb editor. No praise of mine can do justice to the valuable suggestions she made for the book's improvement.

Irving Layton
Montreal
July 1985

INDEX

"Voltaire Jezebel," 181